The Convent of Pleasure

AND OTHER PLAYS

Here on this Figure Cast a Glance,
But so as if it were by Chance,
Your eyes not fixt, they must not Stay,
Since this like Shadowes to the Day
It only represent's; for Still
Her Beuty's found beyond the Skill
Of the best Paynter, to Imbrace
These lovely Lines within her face,
View her Soul's Picture, Judgment. witt,
Then read those Lines which Shee hath writt,
By Phancy's Pencill drawne alone
Which Peece but Shee, Can justly owne.

The Convent of Pleasure

AND OTHER PLAYS

Margaret Cavendish

DUCHESS OF NEWCASTLE

Edited by Anne Shaver

The Johns Hopkins University Press

BALTIMORE AND LONDON

© 1999   The Johns Hopkins University Press
All rights reserved. Published 1999
Printed in the United States of America

2   4   6   8   9   7   5   3   1

The Johns Hopkins University Press
2715 North Charles Street
Baltimore, Maryland 21218-4363
www.press.jhu.edu

FRONTISPIECE:
Margaret Cavendish, duchess of Newcastle. This engraving from the
original by Abraham van Diepenbeke (1596–1675) is the frontispiece
for both *Playes,* 1662, and *Plays, Never Before Printed,* 1668.
Reproduced by permission of the Huntington Library,
San Marino, California.

Library of Congress Cataloging-in-Publication Data will be found
at the end of this book.
A catalog record for this book is available from the British Library.

ISBN 0-8018-6099-7
ISBN 0-8018-6100-4 (pbk.)

Contents

Acknowledgments

The work that led to this edition was begun in 1985 in a Huntington Library conversation between Susanne Woods, Margaret J. M. Ezell, and Stuart Curran about the lack of attention to early women writers in the then burgeoning publications on women. That conversation engendered the Brown University Women Writers Project, founded by Susanne Woods. Without the support of the project, publication of this book and many other editions, anthologies, critical books, and essays would not have been possible. Dissertations on early women writers themselves and on their place in the culture they helped to produce proliferate, making this field one of the most exciting in the academy.

I was enabled in part by a Robert C. Good Fellowship from Denison University to spend two years at Brown as the Women Writers Project was getting under way. In 1989 I taught an experimental section of Brown's early British survey, inserting nine women writers, including Cavendish, into the already crowded syllabus, using xeroxed printouts from the project computers. I thank the Brown English department for the opportunity to teach exciting texts to exciting students.

For continuing the conversation about early women writers in many different ways over the years I thank Carol Barash, Anna Battigelli, Stuart Curran, Carol Deboer-Langworthy, Jane Donawerth, James Fitzmaurice, Juana Green, Elizabeth Hageman, Judith Hallett, Margaret Hannay, Elaine Hobby, Barbara Lewalski, Jeff Masten, Barbara McManus, Nancy W. Miller, Naomi J. Miller, Fred Porcheddu, Anne Prescott, Josephine Roberts, Jay Stevenson, Julia Walker, Gary Waller, and most constantly Susanne Woods.

I am grateful to the National Endowment for the Humanities for funding a University of Maryland symposium on Sappho and Lady Mary Wroth, which I attended in 1994, and to the Center for Renaissance and Baroque Studies at the University of Maryland for its assiduous Attention to Early Modern Women. Three conferences by that name, in 1990, 1993, and 1997, have done much to further our research and recovery of early women writing in English.

Thanks to the Newberry Library for providing the copytexts for this edition and to the Newberry, Huntington, and Folger Libraries, the Bodleian, the British Library, and libraries at Harvard and Princeton for the use of their fine research facilities. At my home institution, I thank the many librarians and computer experts who have helped in time of need.

Heartfelt thanks to the ten women who learned editing procedures along with me in an honors seminar at Denison in the spring of 1996. Erin Deas, Kelly Gautier, Lindsay Greer, Anne Heath, Jen Lawton, Deb Margolis, Elena Rudy, Jigisha Thakor, Jessica Turk, and Kristel VanBuskirk: your intellectual companionship and practical help in my project has made the finished book much more than it could possibly have become without you.

In 1997 the international Margaret Cavendish Society was formed and held its first official meeting in Oxford, England. Only considerations of space prevent my thanking each member by name for her or his contribution to the study of the duchess of Newcastle, but I am especially grateful to the group's founder and current president, Nancy W. Miller.

Most of all I thank Susanne Woods, whose vision is matched only by her skill and power to make that vision real. Because of her, scholars already working on their own have been brought together, and much teaching and research on early women writers continues in joyous connection and frequent collaboration. Partner in life, travels, and happy labor, she inspires all I do.

Chronology

1623   Margaret Lucas is born at St. John's, Colchester.

1625   Margaret's father, Thomas Lucas, dies. Charles I accedes to the throne, marries Henrietta Maria.

1642   The Civil War begins; the theaters are closed.

1643   Margaret Lucas becomes a maid of honor to Henrietta Maria at the court in exile, Oxford.

1644   The queen and her attendants escape to Paris. The battle of Marsden Moor is won by Parliament; William Cavendish (1593–1676), marquis of Newcastle and commander of the king's forces in the north, goes into exile.

1645   William Cavendish and Margaret Lucas marry in Paris.

1646   Civil War fighting ends.

1647   Cavendish's mother, Elizabeth Leighton Lucas, and her sister die; her brother Charles is executed by order of Lord Fairfax; the family tomb is desecrated.

1648   Civil War fighting renewed. The Newcastles move to Antwerp.

1649   Charles I is executed; the Commonwealth is declared. Newcastle is banished and his estates confiscated.

1651   Cavendish and her brother-in-law Charles Cavendish go to London, where they attempt with some success to compound for confiscated estates; Charles saves Welbeck and Bolsover.

1653   Cavendish returns to Antwerp and publishes *Poems and Fancies* and *Philosophical Fancies*.

1654   Charles Cavendish dies in England.

1655   Cavendish publishes *The World's Olio*.

1656   Cavendish publishes *Natures Pictures*, which includes her memoir.

1660   The Restoration; the Newcastles return to England and begin residence at Welbeck, repairs to Bolsover.

1661   Charles II is crowned.

1662   Cavendish publishes *Playes* and *Orations of Divers Sorts.*

1663   Cavendish publishes *Philosophical and Physical Opinions,* a revised and expanded version of *Philosophical Fancies.*

1664   Cavendish publishes *CCXI Sociable Letters* and *Philosophical Letters.*

1665   Charles II makes William Cavendish duke of Newcastle.

1666   The Great Fire of London. Cavendish publishes *Observations Upon Experimental Philosophy, To which is added, The Description of a New Blazing World.*

1667   Cavendish publishes her *Life of William Cavendish;* visits the Royal Society.

1668   Cavendish publishes *Plays, Never Before Printed;* reissues *Observations Upon Experimental Philosophy* and *Blazing World* separately; reissues *Poems and Fancies, Orations,* and *Philosophical and Physical Opinions,* revised as *Grounds of Natural Philosophy.*

1671   Cavendish reissues *The World's Olio* and *Natures Pictures.*

1673   Cavendish dies. She is buried in Westminster Abbey on 7 January 1674.

1675   Cavendish's *Life of William Cavendish* is reissued.

1676   Newcastle publishes *Letters and Poems in honour of the Incomparable Princess Margaret, Duchess of Newcastle;* dies and is buried with his wife.

Source: Margaret Cavendish, *The Blazing World and Other Writings,* ed. Kate Lilley (London: Penguin, 1994), 35–36.

Note on Editorial Method

The copytexts for this edition are the Newberry Library copies: *Loves Adventures* and *Bell in Campo* from *Playes,* 1662; *The Bridals* and *The Convent of Pleasure* from *Plays, Never Before Printed,* 1668. Neither collection was ever reissued, and extensive comparisons with other examples both by other Cavendish scholars and by me have so far unearthed no printed variants. I have noted the few changes made by a seventeenth-century hand in the Newberry texts as they occur. I have also included, as appendix E, the list of errata appended to the 1662 volume as it applies to this edition, and I have inserted the changes in the edited text in curly brackets.

With a few noted exceptions, I have retained Cavendish's eccentric spelling, grammar, and punctuation because these are aspects of her works that have occasioned comment from the moment they appeared (see Kate Lilley's introduction to *The Blazing World and Other Writings,* xxxiii–xxxiv). Even so, it is not always possible to know which variants were her choice and which are a result of contingencies at the press. For example, are question marks used in place of exclamation points as indicators of intonation, as deliberate eccentricities, or because the press ran out of exclamation points? Occasionally I have silently added periods at the obvious end of sentences left unpunctuated, and I have consistently used a standard dash to indicate interrupted speech where Cavendish used a variable number of dashes.

For clarity, and in deference to modern dramatic conventions, I have standardized the typeface of act numbers and scene numbers and changed the few stage directions not printed in italics to agree with the italicized majority, continuing also their contrast with proper names by printing these in plain text within the italic text. I have regularized the position and typeface of the speakers' names both in the text and in the list of characters preceding each play. In the copytexts each new scene begins with the name of the first speaker centered above his or her speech; I have changed these instances to conform to the rest.

In the appendixes, for ease of reading, I have changed letters to the readers and other preliminary matter that were originally printed in italics or larger boldface to plain text of standard size, again retaining the contrast with proper names by printing them in italics.

The Convent of Pleasure

AND OTHER PLAYS

Introduction: Margaret Cavendish's Life as a Writer

Margaret Lucas Cavendish (1623–73) was a writer all her life, producing copious pages even as a child.[1] Her short but unsettled time as a lady-in-waiting in Queen Henrietta Maria's exiled court (1643–45) may have stilled her pen, but after her marriage in 1645 to William Cavendish, then marquis of Newcastle, she soon began to write again. Her first two publications, *Poems and Fancies* and *Philosophical Fancies*, which appeared in 1653, were written when she lived briefly in London (1652–53); but *The World's Olio* (1655), her third book, is made up of earlier writing, done during their European exile. *Philosophical and Physical Opinions*, a retitled, augmented, and revised version of *Philosophical Fancies*, also appeared in 1655. *Natures Pictures*, a collection of fiction, essays, and verse that concludes with her autobiography—"a true Story at the latter end, wherein there is no Feignings"—followed in 1656. After this there was a hiatus until the first volume of plays in 1662, in part because the manuscript of plays intended for an earlier printing was lost at sea and had to be re-edited from original copies.[2] Also, her husband's lavishly illustrated oversized folio on the training of horses was produced in Antwerp in 1657–58 at the cost of more than £1,300, a fortune by the standards of the time;[3] it is possible that this outlay as well as the expense and effort of the permanent move back to England stopped Margaret Cavendish's printing, if not her pen, for some time.

The Cavendishes, along with most other exiled royalists, returned to England with the restored Stuart court in 1660. Beginning in 1662, Margaret Cavendish brought out a torrent of publications, many on science or natural philosophy, at the rate of one or more volumes each year except 1665, culminating in 1668 with seven new or reissued folios.[4] After that, ill health must have slowed her: 1671 saw the second editions of *Natures Pictures* and *The Worlds Olio;* at the age of fifty, in 1673, this prolific author died. Why did she write and publish so much? And why, having done so, has she been so little studied as a writer?

Cavendish's stated motive for writing and publishing was a passionate desire to be known. She wrote her autobiography at the age of thirty-two because, she says, she did not want to be confused with William Cavendish's first wife or with any subsequent wife he might have should she die.[5] Almost everything she published contains prefatory matter in which she reiterates her desire to be recognized and remembered as long as possible: being remembered seems to be even more important to her than what she is remembered for, as long as her honesty is not questioned. Honesty, for Cavendish, comprises not only the usual female concern for chastity (though this is a continuing point of anxiety) but also a reputation free from charges of imitation. She admits that her handwriting, her spelling, her rhetoric, her knowledge of the classics, and her patience to revise leave a great deal to be desired, but she insists over and over that her work, imperfect as it may be, is always and only her own.[6]

Her insistence on originality is evident in her self-presentation as well as in her publications. A much loved youngest child, she was allowed by her strong but indulgent widowed mother to dress up in clothes of her own design, and she continued this practice as an adult, especially after the 1660s brought the restoration of much of her royalist husband's wealth. The Duchess of Newcastle in the science-fiction romance *Blazing World* declares, "I endeavor . . . to be as singular as I can; for it argues but a mean nature to imitate others . . . for my nature is such that I had rather appear worse in singularity, then better in mode."[7] This declaration and others like it are born out by the way the duchess presented herself during her 1667–68 sojourn in London, as reported by a good many fascinated and a few appalled observers.[8] Still, she wanted to be remembered for her "wit," her creative intelligence, far more than for any other attribute. "I should weep myself into water if I could have no other fame than rich coaches, lackeys, and what state and ceremony could produce, for my ambition flies higher, to worth and merit, not state and vanity; I would be known to the world by my wit, not by my folly, and I would have my actions be wise and just, as I might neither be ashamed nor afraid to hear of myself."[9]

Although her writing is now beginning to receive some of the serious attention it deserves, most of her previous fame has indeed been based on her "folly," or to put it another way, on her character as perceived by various male or male-influenced sensibilities—including that of Virginia Woolf. Cavendish garnered attention in her lifetime in part because she was the wife of William Cavendish, duke of Newcastle. Commander of the king's forces in the north until the fatal loss on Marsden Moor in 1644, Newcastle was made duke in 1665. This honor was given by the king, who found conferring the title more expedient than making a place at court for the old cavalier who had been his governor when he was a boy. Thus Cavendish found herself flattered as a duchess but not always taken seriously as a person of wit or fashion.

On the other hand, the marriage enabled her to become a serious writer. Her husband encouraged her to write and apparently underwrote the cost of her publications.[10] William Cavendish, then marquis of Newcastle, had been for many years an amateur and a patron of the arts when, at the age of fifty-two, he met, courted, and married twenty-two-year-old Margaret Lucas at the court in exile in Paris in 1645. He encouraged the daughters of his first marriage to write; two of them produced but did not publish a play dedicated to him.[11] Gerard Langbaine, a near contemporary, calls Newcastle "our English Maecenas," honoring him with the name of the poet Virgil's patron.[12] Ben Jonson had written masques for the marquis's entertainments of the king and queen at his seats at Welbeck Abbey and Bolsover Castle in 1633 and 1634. Newcastle himself wrote at least one play before the Interregnum, *The Country Captain*, in collaboration with James Shirley, whose patron he was. The marquis's first wife, Elizabeth Bassett, the wealthy widow of Henry Howard, younger son of the earl of Suffolk, had died in 1643; now exiled by Parliament, no longer able to fight in the king's lost cause, the famous general pursued the serious, shy but "comely" young lady-in-waiting, courting her with a river of verses, to which she replied in cautious prose.[13] The general had a reputation as one who loved women as much as they would allow; for all her bashfulness, Margaret managed his ardor well and brought him to the altar, in fact to the private chapel of the English ambassador, in December of 1645.

The marriage and the ensuing long exile, mostly in Antwerp, where the couple leased the painter Rubens's magnificent house, gave Cavendish time not only with an encouraging and indulgent husband who respected the arts and who wrote himself but also with William's younger brother Charles, a much more serious intellectual than his brother. If William, when he was not busy training horses, was an amateur of the arts, Charles was a virtuoso of natural philosophy, interested in the Baconian arguments for experimentation under discussion in the informal meetings of like-minded men that would result in the Royal Academy of Science, chartered in 1662. Meanwhile, in Paris and in Antwerp, philosophers such as Hobbes and Descartes came to dinner. Cavendish says that she took no part in their conversations: indeed, since she did not speak French, she could not have conversed with Descartes; still, these men and their ideas were part of her life in exile, feeding Cavendish's already considerable interest in speculation about the natural world, both the seen and the unseen. The various interests of all these men, none of them theologians by training or temperament, possibly helped to keep her writing secular.

The marriage produced no children. Because William Cavendish had fathered ten children by his first wife (five still living in 1645), Cavendish accepted blame for the barrenness, when in fact the marquis's age and reputation as a womanizer suggest that he himself may have become sterile. Further, her insistence that she never loved him inordinately has caused some scholars to speculate about whether the marriage was sexual often or at all, though the warmth and physicality of William's love poems written during their courtship and the abiding affection shown in the epitaph he created for her tomb are witnesses to an enduring close connection. Although she insists that her love for her husband "was not amorous love," Cavendish too gives many evidences of an affectionate closeness.[14] She admits to regretting their childlessness for her husband's sake but shows no sign of sorrow for herself; in fact, *The Convent of Pleasure* provides typical examples of the negative view of pregnancy, childbirth, and raising children that is evident throughout her writings. None of her fictional married "heroickesses" has children.

Motivated by a desire for fame, supported and inspired by her husband and her brother-in-law and their many intellectual and artistic connections, undistracted by children or other domestic responsibilities, Margaret Cavendish became a prolific and original writer in many different genres. Why, then, are we just now beginning to pay her work respectful attention?

She suffered some scorn simply because she was a woman. In her own day, even after the Restoration and even in the case of a socially well-placed and generally reclusive middle-aged wife, any public self-display by that half of the human race relegated to the private sphere was regarded with deep suspicion. The earliest recorded response to her work is not really to the work itself but to the fact of it. Not surprisingly, this response comes from a woman corresponding with her future husband. Dorothy Osborne, writing in April 1653 to William Temple, asks if he has seen "a book of Poems newly come out, made by my Lady New Castle." This, of course, is Cavendish's first publication, *Poems and Fancies.* Not having read it, Osborne is not judging its literary worth when she declares, "Sure the poore woman is a litle distracted, she could never bee soe rediculous else as to venture at writeing book's and in verse too, If I should not sleep this fortnight I should not come to that." Three weeks later, Osborne writes to tell Temple that he need not send the book for she has "seen" it (but had she read it?) "and am sattisfyed that there are many soberer People in Bedlam, i'le swear her friends are much to blame to let her goe abroade."[15] Although Osborne does not articulate her gender theory in so many words, it is clear that she sees herself, a writer only of private letters, as being a much more acceptable woman, wife, and "friend" or kinswoman than the "Lady New

Castle." That Cavendish herself had internalized the general prohibition equating women's publishing not just with insanity but with unchastity is made clear in her many protestations of chaste devotion to her husband and in her twice paraphrasing the damning satire circulated by Edward, Lord Denny, against Lady Mary Wroth for publishing the first part of her *Urania* in 1621 in order to insist that the criticism did not apply to her.[16]

Then there is the matter of her personal self-display. As early as 1653, Dorothy Osborne had heard that the duchess's book "is ten times more Extravagant than her dresse." Samuel Pepys has left us a description of the way thrill-seekers, including himself, would follow her equipage when she took the air in London in the spring of 1667, hoping for a glimpse of her extraordinary clothes. John Evelyn, that same spring, describes her "fanciful habit, garb, and discourse" with amused approval, but his usually liberal wife, Mary, writes to her son's tutor that she had been offended by the duchess's dress and theatrical demeanor, both of which she describes in unflattering detail.[17] Sir Charles Lyttelton recalls meeting the duke and duchess in York in 1665: "Hard by his house mett us on the way my Lord of Newcastle and my Lady, whose behavior was very pleasant, but rather to be seen then told. She was dressed in a vest, and, instead of courtesies, made leggs and bows to the ground with her hand at head."[18]

Some have found such behavior at odds with the self-described bashfulness of the young lady-in-waiting and the reclusive preferences the duchess never stops claiming, but of course it is not. Pepys's description of her visit to the Royal Society on 30 May 1667 again focuses on her extravagant dress and her pretty attendants, but Pepys also reports that she was almost speechless in response to the experiments performed for her, that all she could say was that she was "full of admiration, all admiration."[19] For a shy woman who nonetheless desired fame and who had a strong sense of the honor due her rank, her recourse to theatrics, to playing herself-as-character in order to protect her true and vulnerable self, makes sense. More than at court, or out in her carriage, or in the relative safety of receiving the Evelyns in her own drawing room, she would have been abashed in the laboratories of the Royal Society, to which as a woman she could not belong, though as a duchess she could command an invitation and a display. Legitimate members of the society feared lampoons on the subject of the visit; some even wrote their own.[20]

"The whole story of this lady is a romance, and all she doth is romantic," wrote Pepys in his diary entry for 11 April 1667, sometime before her famous visit to the all-male science club. Until very recently the romance of the duchess of Newcastle has colored and distorted appreciation of her work even by those critics who purport to make the work their focus, and it is the primary source of fascination for many of her fans. Charles Lamb, who called her "the thrice-noble, chaste and virtuous—but again, somewhat fantastical and original-brained, generous Margaret Newcastle," wanted to have her to dinner.[21] Virginia Woolf, famously searching for foremothers in *A Room of One's Own*, finds Cavendish's writing an embarrassment: "What a vision of loneliness and riot the thought of Margaret Cavendish brings to mind! as if some giant cucumber had spread itself over all the roses and carnations in the garden and choked them to death. What a waste that the woman . . . should have frittered her time away scribbling nonsense and plunging ever deeper into obscurity and folly."[22] The biographer Douglas Grant, whose *Margaret the First* (1957) is a fine research tool, exacerbates the problem by beginning his book not with Margaret Lucas the precocious child or Margaret Cavendish the passionate writer but with the dramatic caricature produced by the likes of Pepys and Mary Evelyn. The legend has proved almost irresistible.

Another impediment to her fame as a writer is her own continual and not always accurate self-description. In her *Memoir*, in the *CCXI Sociable Letters*, in the *Orations*, and in her many prefaces she tells the reader over and over how she judges herself. For some, even when they are annoyed by her apparent contradictions, her statements become the only reality. Although Cavendish says she is too impatient to revise her work, she does revise and republish much of it. She says her work is all her own, uninfluenced by the artists and intellectuals who were guests in her home and whose work permeated the age she lived in, and too many of her critics and admirers seem to think this is both possible and a reason to scorn her. In truth, she had no formal education; if we believe her, she lacked even the usual education of a young gentlewoman. But she had her own questing intellect in a time of great upheaval; she had Charles and William Cavendish as mentors, and she did read, if not always systematically, in a deliberate effort to strengthen her dialogue with other seventeenth-century philosophers of science.[23] Her writing deserves our serious attention.

And so does she. Contemporary readers, of course, do not share Dorothy Osborne's prejudice against women writing for publication, and most are not trapped by Virginia Woolf's rage for formalism or her definition of wit as irony. Nonetheless, many who believe in the intellectual equality of men and women have not found it easy to claim the duchess, who, while she creates astonishingly resilient and capable heroines, can say such things as "It cannot be expected that I should write so wisely or wittily as Men, being of the Effeminate Sex, whose Brains Nature hath mix't with the coldest and softest Elements."[24] Catherine Gallagher points to this passage as typical, and there are others like it;

however, it occurs in one of Cavendish's earliest publications and is one of very few such statements not in a context of arguing that women would benefit from a rigorous education.[25] Claiming the duchess as a foremother demands that modern readers take a diachronic perspective on her work because although she was successful in achieving the singularity she desired so much, she was also of her gender in her time. What to a contemporary reader may seem to be vacillation about women's worth comes not just from a modesty topos but also from a sincere effort to claim for her sex access to the virtues of men without having to give up the special virtues of women. This effort, though it can lead to apparent incoherence, also produces a powerful challenge to clichés about gender.

Plays

Cavendish wrote and published nineteen plays in two folio volumes, *Playes* (1662) and *Plays, Never Before Printed* (1668). Seven of the plays are in two five-act parts; another, *The Presence*, is followed by a long series of scenes edited out of it. Yet another, appropriately titled "A Piece of a Play," is unfinished.[26] Two of her plays are tragedies; most of the rest could be called comedies, though her work often challenges traditional categories. The four plays collected here, a representative sample of this prolific writer's dramatic output, could be described as two heroic romances in which women are the heroes (*Loves Adventures*, parts 1 and 2, and *Bell in Campo*, parts 1 and 2), one fairly typical comedy of manners focused on what makes a marriage good or bad *(The Bridals)*, and one highly original blending of pastoral and masque that challenges even the possibility of a good marriage *(The Convent of Pleasure)*. All end in ways usually termed happy; all suggest ways to question that happiness.

In spite of their complexity and innovation, Cavendish's plays are among the least read of her works. Until recently, when critics did praise her writing they usually chose her *Life* of the duke as the one work deserving attention and republication, and most seemed to be more impressed with the worthiness of its subject than with the execution of the biography. Although it is not surprising that in an academy of specialists her scientific work has until recently stymied most professors of the humanities, it is remarkable that almost all of her biographers or editors, if they mention her plays at all, dismiss them in strong terms, many giving no evidence of having read them.

There is the phenomenon of scholarly men dealing with a handsome woman who is also a wealthy duchess. A collection of letters and poems published by the duke as a memorial to his late wife contains a good deal of the sort of flattery—especially from Cantabridgians[27]—that we would expect a modern development office to direct at a potential donor. The collection includes a letter from Thomas Hobbes, who declares that he has perused most of the duchess's 1662 *Playes* and that the volume "is filled throughout with more and truer Idea's of Virtue and Honour than any Book of morality I have read." Since the duchess's seventh prefatory epistle affirms that this is her main intention, Hobbes's words must have been welcome praise. On the other hand, the tone of his next words is closer to that of commentators for nearly the next three hundred years: "And if some Comique Writers, by conversation with ill People, have been able to present Vices upon the Stage more ridiculously and immodestly by which they take their rabble, I reckon that among your Praises."[28]

Conflating the woman and her work, critics are charmed by her writing's "feminine" qualities, by which they mean that it is modest, fanciful, and charming, while those who are most disgusted call her work ridiculous and coarse. On the first page of his introduction to *These Select Poems of Margaret Cavendish, Duchess of Newcastle*, with which he inaugurated the Lee Priory Press in 1813, Sir Egerton Brydges regrets that "we are too frequently shocked by expressions and images of extraordinary coarseness; and more extraordinary as flowing from a female of high rank, brought up in courts." In the initial book-length study of the Cavendishes, *The First Duke and Duchess of Newcastle-upon-Tyne* (1910), Thomas Longueville writes that "her plays were of such a character that, as they stand, the most lenient official censor of our generation would certainly refuse to allow them to be acted. . . . they combine indecency and obscenity with the stagnate dullness so usually the accompaniment of literary dishwater."[29] In 1918, Henry Ten Eyck Perry turned his Harvard dissertation into *The First Duchess of Newcastle and her Husband as Figures in Literary History*, the first book to deal more than superficially with Cavendish's work. A more disinterested critic than Longueville, Perry still designates act 4, scene 5, of *The Bridals* as "unspeakably low," saying, "No commentary on Restoration indelicacy could be more striking than such work from the pen of the noble and virtuous Margaret Cavendish."[30]

Even when indelicacy is not the focus, her plays are dismissed over and over by critics who often seem to be using previous opinions as a substitute for reading. Even some of the most recent attention to her has been affected by the centuries of dismissal accorded her plays and the assumption that they are not meant for the theater.[31] They are not closet drama, a term for plays deliberately written to be read in one's "closet" or private room; it is not a term appropriately applied to plays that simply were not produced. Yet here, as always, Cavendish blurs the customary boundaries. She tells the reader in "The Epistle Dedicatory" preceding the 1662 collection that she has decided to publish her plays even though she knows that will spoil their chances of being staged, since a society that values novelty will not go to see a play it has already read. Her reasons are various. She declares that she was inspired to write plays because her husband had already done so; but she chooses not to imitate his holding them in hopes of production because hers lack the "quick spirit" of his, being instead "like dull dead statues" likely to be "hissed off from the stage." Comments like this one, by the way, have been leading critics astray since Cavendish made them; modesty topoi, instantly recognized when used by male authors, have been taken as women's honest, appropriately modest evaluation of their own inadequacy.

In her second epistle to the readers Cavendish gives other reasons for not seeking production. She points out that because of the long hiatus imposed by Parliament there are few trained actors available, and it will take time to train new ones. Although she admits that some of her plays are so long they might bore the audience, she says their variety necessitates it and adds, "I believe none of my Plays are so long as Ben. Johnson's *Fox* [*Volpone*], or *Alchymist.*"[32] In the third epistle she both admits and defends the absence of classical unities in her drama. Her tone in these epistles suggests that she may have been discouraged by friends whose opinion she contested but finally followed. There is no doubt, despite her declarations to the contrary, that she was apprehensive about how her works would be received, and of course staging plays depends on many more interpretations than that of a single reader. In the tenth prefatory epistle, Cavendish provides detailed instruction on how her plays should be read aloud, and again in *CCXI Sociable Letters* she worries that she, the writer, might be blamed for a bad performance.[33]

Cavendish makes clear, however, that she would like to live in a place or time in which her plays could be produced and appreciated. In her novella *Blazing World,* after the Empress and the Duchess have returned victorious from the war in the Empress's native land, the Duchess is pleased and flattered when the Emperor asks her to stay a while longer for the express purpose of producing some of her own plays that have been declared "incapable of being represented or acted" by the wits of her world. Although the Emperor supports the same critical principles the real duchess published in her front matter to the 1662 *Playes,* her homesick fictional counterpart will not stay. She does promise to return, however, presumably to take advantage of an eager audience.[34] In the single epistle to the readers from the 1668 collection Cavendish declares that she does not write for the ingrates of the present mode but for the wiser audiences of a future time.

Because we now inhabit the duchess's future, the four plays in this collection can challenge our appreciation. All sorts of gender issues are more interesting to today's theatergoers and readers than they were to the gentleman scholars of earlier times, and many twentieth-century playwrights have created theatrical magic without benefit of classical rules. Audiences have spent entire days spellbound by long, two-part plays like *Nicholas Nickleby* and *Angels in America*, and we are used to the instantaneous travels in time and space made possible by the movies.[35] It is hard for a reader used to the fast cuts of cinema to imagine that Shakespeare's *Antony and Cleopatra* was ever condemned for its rapid juxtapositions of Egypt and Rome.[36] The duchess's plays are structurally closer to some of Shakespeare's than to the neoclassical ideal espoused but not often happily achieved by Ben Jonson and most Restoration playwrights.[37] Her works cohere not through the unities of time, place, or affect but through an underlying question or idea that may be treated fantastically, realistically, comically, and pathetically all in the same work.

On the other hand, we may be impatient with long speeches like Lady Happy's elaborate description of the epicurean joys of the convent in *The Convent of Pleasure.* The plays as well as their author demand to be understood from a diachronic perspective because they are of their own time even as they are just now becoming accessible: for example, their seventeenth-century language constructs and typical Restoration character names may seem strange today. More profoundly, they exhibit seventeenth-century royalist attitudes toward class hierarchy and war that may cause discomfort in a more egalitarian and pacifist time. Still, they are always also about those old perennials, love and war between the sexes.

Loves Adventures will be the most superficially familiar to those accustomed to Shakespeare. In the main plot, a courageous girl, Lady Orphant, puts on boys' clothes and outperforms grown men in ways that conflate the virtues of Shakespeare's cross-dressing heroines Rosamund, Viola, and Portia. She does this to win the love of a man who, never having seen her, has rejected an arranged marriage with her, and of course she succeeds, though her methods are not limited to those of her precursors. The two subplots, which to Cavendish's genre-bound contemporaries may have seemed to belong in another play entirely, are at first glance more like comedies of manners than like heroic fantasies. In one, a bored and restless wife, Lady Ignorance, persuades her husband to become more sociable; he does, but with comically dire results. In the other, a young heiress, Lady Bashful, who has resisted marriage ends up marrying the worthiest of her suitors. All three plots, however, are more about gender expectations than romances and comedies usually are; their happy endings are not as important or interesting as the questions they raise about what is valuable in the behavior of men and women.

There is some question about the degree of happiness achieved when the curtain falls. Lady Orphant, disguised as the heroic page Affectionata, energized by her pursuit of the man she has never seen but loves for his reputation alone, would seem to be a foil for Lady Bashful, who first appears to be afraid of any marriage. But as the action progresses the outcomes are called into question. Does Affectionata lose herself as she gains the love of Lord Singularity? What does Lady Bashful win? She freely agrees to marry Sir Serious Dumb, who is certainly a better partner than Sir Humphry Bold would be, but refuses to affirm the marriage with the usual wedding celebration. And how will the lives of Sir Peaceable Studious and his wife the Lady Ignorance be better now that they have agreed to shun fashionable society?

Bell in Campo is, among other things, a possible answer to some of the questions raised in *Loves Adventures*. Printed as the twelfth play in the 1662 volume in which *Loves Adventures* is the first, it also has three plots and three marriages, and although it would be wrong to see them as sequels, all of the marriages in the second play are of some duration, whereas those in *Loves Adventures* were just beginning. Lady Victoria is very much a possible avatar for a mature Lady Orphant. She does not masquerade as a man, but she does persuade her husband, Lord General, to take her to the battlefront, where she outperforms him in his own arena as the "Generaless" of a tightly trained army of "Heroickesses," winning back strongholds her husband and his troops have lost. Her successes do not finally reverse the seventeenth century's hierarchy of gender, but they do win some concessions for the women warriors that will carry over into their peacetime lives.

Meanwhile, each of the two subplots tells the story of a wife who stays at home. Madam Jantil stays in obedience to her husband's wishes, while Madam Passionate refuses when her husband suggests that she join Lady Victoria. Both women are widowed early in the play, so the two subplots are based on the women's very different modes of handling widowhood. Madam Jantil's choices are virtuous but deadly; Madam Passionate's are not so much vicious as foolish and, according to her, will probably lead to her death. All of Madam Jantil's long verse speeches mourning her dead husband are credited to "My Lord Marquiss of Newcastle," and she is as much praised by the members of her household as Madam Passionate is scorned by hers, suggesting that Madame Jantil's are the choices of a virtuous woman; still, Lady Victoria is the one who wins general praise while she is alive and the one whose fame will endure in public monuments and laws.

The Bridals, more like a typical Restoration comedy than most of Cavendish's plays, shares some characters with *The Convent of Pleasure.* These two pieces, though they are printed next to each other in the 1668 collection, are not a single play in two parts like *Loves Adventures* or *Bell in Campo*. Still, figuring out just how they do connect is a challenge. True to its title, *The Bridals* opens with two weddings and closes with a third, the marriage of the two young people whose fathers have tried to keep them apart. Until nearly the end of the second act the dialogue is dominated by the sort of innuendo and outright sexy talk licensed by any marriage celebration. Lady Coy, the bride of Sir Amorous, responds with an intense sexual bashfulness that arouses lust in Facil, one of the groomsmen, whereas Lady Vertue, the bride of Sir William Sage, responds with frankness and good sense, refusing to pretend a reluctance she does not feel but sensibly limiting the young men's wilder rituals. For example, when they claim the right to "rifle" for the brides' garters, she simply removes her garters herself and hands them over.

One plot, such as it is, depends on Facil's efforts to seduce Lady Coy, whose name, to match not only her husband's name but her own behavior after her wedding night, is changed to Lady Amorous. Another depends on the efforts of Sir Mercury Poet to marry Lady Fancy against the wishes of their rich fathers. The old men believe that the marriage of two such poetical young people will mean the end of their fortunes and family names, since such "great Wits" care nothing for money and seldom have "corporeal" children. But much stage time is occupied both by the free-floating, verbal trickster Mimick, who declares himself "the Lady Vertue's Mimick and the Lady Amorous fool," and by the trials of Courtly, another of the groomsmen, who is ruining himself as an escort for the many ladies of fashion who insist that he take them to all the stylish places of entertainment and pay for their pleasures. A hodgepodge, perhaps, at first glance, but it may be instructive to consider that "wit" itself, in many different forms, from creative intelligence to fashionable behavior, might be the protagonist of this play.

The Convent of Pleasure, the shortest complete work in *Plays, Never Before Printed*, contains several recurring motifs: cross-dressing, pageantry, a powerful woman as the central character, strong arguments by women against marriage, and some male behavior that makes the reader see why women might object to marrying. Like some of Cavendish's other plays, *The Convent of Pleasure* includes lyrics and lines written by her husband, now "My Lord Duke." The central argument of the play, that women are happier unmarried, is sustained even in the face of the conventional comic denouement: although Lady Happy does marry the Prince in the last act, she never recants her declaration that marriage is generally bad for women. Some developments within the drama suggest that her particular marriage might be a happy exception, while others suggest that it probably will not.

Lady Happy, made wealthy by her father's death and therefore pursued for her fortune by the "mode" men who were groomsmen in *The Bridals*, chooses to form a community exclusively of women, whom she supports. In the house left to her by her father she creates a place of physical, intellectual, and aesthetic pleasures. Descriptions of food and especially of interior decorations show the Convent to be modeled on the luxuries of life at court. But Cavendish goes beyond court precedent to make even the pleasures of courtship and special friendships available in the all-woman Convent; it becomes a custom for some of the women to dress and behave like masculine "servants" to others. The prince who will win Lady Happy enters the Convent disguised as "a great foreign princess of masculine aspect," only to cross-dress again as a man and become Lady Happy's servant in love. Participating in the pleasures of the Convent, they watch a series of plays within the play that illustrate the pains of marriage for rich and poor women alike, but when the skits are over the "princess" announces himself unconvinced, and Lady Happy lets the audience know that she is deeply attracted to this newcomer even though she believes him to be a woman.

After the skits there are two more performances, more like court masques than plays, in which the "princess" takes the main male role and Lady Happy the main but decidedly secondary female role. The first, a pastoral, ends with a shepherd's winning the hand of a reluctant shepherdess and pointing out that their marriage will be uncommonly happy because their courtship was uncommon. The shepherd does woo the shepherdess by praising her intellect and her lively curiosity; not once does he call her beautiful or mention her rich flocks. Still, in the final scene of this performance the celebrants dance around a phallic Maypole to lyrics, written by the playwright's husband, celebrating the shepherd for winning the "prize." The final performance is completely dominated by the "princess" in the role of Neptune, god of the sea. Neptune has the most lines, the last lines, and the designated kingdom. This god takes no notice of "a sea-goddess" played by Lady Happy. Instead Neptune declaims his own praises and the praises of the riches the sea has heaped upon him; the sea-goddess sings alone, and only of her relationship to the masculine sun. Right after this male-dominated tableau, events reveal the "princess" to be a prince. His wedding to Lady Happy occurs offstage at the end of act 4.

Although we next hear that "the State" is glad of the wedding, we never hear what Lady Happy thinks. Having spoken less and less to less and less notice throughout the play, by this point she has essentially fallen silent. Her few words in act 5, after her marriage, are spoken either directly to or in reference to Mimick, the moral but raunchy trickster of *The Bridals,* who suddenly appears and wheedles as a gift from the Prince, now the proprietor of his wife's entire fortune, the mansion that has housed the Convent of Pleasure. He does this by agreeing to create and speak the play's epilogue. Mimick's awkward speech, rather than a wedding celebration, takes center stage as the play ends.

All four of these plays, like all of Cavendish's dramatic works, contain complex representations of gender roles and gender expectations. The characters are alive and distinctive, far more nuanced than their humorous names suggest. Although some of her critics have dismissed the plays because they are too autobiographical (and who Sir William Sage and Lady Vertue represent is clear enough), they are so different from one another and even contradictory within themselves that they cannot all be autobiographies of anything but the multi-faceted and fascinating mind of a writer who wanted the world to remember her as a heroic man, a virtuous woman, a scientist, a philosopher, a poet, and a wit.

NOTES

1. See Margaret Cavendish, *Margaret Cavendish: Sociable Letters,* ed. James Fitz-maurice (New York: Garland, 1997), letter 131; and Cavendish's epistle "To His Grace the Duke of Newcastle," prefatory to the *Life of the Thrice Noble, High, and Puissant Prince William Cavendishe, Duke, Marquess, and Earl of Newcastle...* (London, 1667).

2. See Margaret Cavendish, *CCXI Sociable Letters* (1664; facs. reprint, New York: Scolar Press, 1969), letter 143.

3. William Cavendish, *La Methode nouvelle et invention extraordinaire de dresser les Chevaux...* (Antwerp, 1658). For the cost, see Henry Ten Eyck Perry, *The First Duchess of Newcastle and Her Husband as Figures in Literary History* (Cambridge: Harvard Univ. Press, 1918), 136.

4. See the bibliography for a complete list of her publications.

5. Margaret Cavendish, *Natures Pictures Drawn by Fancy from the Life* (London, 1656), 391.

6. See the duke's "Epistle to justifie the Lady Newcastle, and Truth against Falsehood; laying those false and malicious Aspersions of her, that she was not Author of her Books," prefatory to Margaret Cavendish, *Philosophical and Physical Opinions* (London, 1655); see also epistles 8 and 9 and the verse prologue prefatory to Margaret Cavendish *Playes* (London, 1662), and the dedication to the *Life* (1667).

7. Margaret Cavendish, *Observations Upon Experimental Philosophy, To which is added, the Description of a New Blazing World* (London, 1666), *Blazing World,* 25–26. See

also idem, *The Blazing World and Other Writings*, ed. Kate Lilley (London: Penguin, 1994), 218.

8. See Samuel Pepys, *Diary*, ed. E. B. Wheatley, vol. 6 (London: G. Bell, 1924), 233, 254, 274; John Evelyn, *Diary*, ed. E. S. DeBeer (Oxford, 1955), 478; and Mary Evelyn, "Letter to Mr. Bohun," in John Evelyn, *Diary and Correspondence of John Evelyn*, ed. William Bray, 2d ed., vol. 4 (London, 1857), 8.

9. Cavendish, *CCXI Sociable Letters*, letter 82.

10. Multiple editions and the listings by post–Great Fire publisher Anne Maxwell in the *Term Catalogues* (see *Term Catalogues*, ed. Edward Arber, 3 vols. [London: privately printed, 1903–6]), suggest that Cavendish's books may have made money.

11. See Elizabeth Brackley and Jane Cavendish, *The Concealed Fancies*, written in the early or mid 1640s, in *Renaissance Drama by Women: Texts and Documents*, ed. S. P. Cerasano and Marion Wynne-Davies (London: Routledge, 1996), 127–54. This play includes a foolish potential stepmother, Lady Tranquillity, sometimes identified with Cavendish, but Lady Tranquillity is a stock older woman satirized for her hopeless vanity, whereas Margaret Lucas was several years younger than her stepdaughters, who met her for the first time in 1660.

12. Gerard Langbaine, *An Account of the Dramatick Poets* (London, 1691), 386.

13. William Cavendish and Margaret Lucas, *The Phanseys of William Cavendish . . . Addressed to Margaret Lucas and Her Letters in Reply*, ed. Douglas Grant (London: Nonesuch, 1956), xxi–xxix.

14. "My affections were fixed on him, and he was the only person I was ever in love with: neither was I ashamed to own it, but gloried therein. For it was not an amorous love, I never was infected therewith. . . . But my love was honest and honourable, being placed upon merit, which affection joyed at the fame of his worth" (*Natures Pictures* [1656], 375). "Neither can I say I think the time tedious, when I am alone, so I be near My Lord, and know that he is well" (ibid., 386).

15. Dorothy Osborne, *The Letters of Dorothy Osborne to William Temple*, ed. G. C. Moore Smith (Oxford: Clarendon, 1928), 37 and 41. Bedlam was London's Bethlehem Hospital for the insane.

16. Cavendish paraphrases lines from the insulting poem in the front matter to *Poems and Fancies* (London, 1653) and in *CCXI Sociable Letters*, both times to insist on the appropriateness of her project and to anticipate male criticism: "And very likely they will say to me, as to the Lady that wrote the Romancy, '*Work*, Lady, *work, let writing books alone, / For surely* wiser Women *nere wrote one*'" ("To All Noble, and Worthy Ladies," prefatory to *Poems and Fancies*).

17. Mary Evelyn, "Letter to Mr. Bohun," 8–9.

18. Christopher, first viscount Hatton, *Hatton Correspondence*, ed. E. M. Thompson, vol. 1 (London, 1878), 47. See also Douglas Grant, *Margaret the First* (Toronto: Univ. of Toronto Press, 1957), 184. This sort of cross-dressing was practiced by a number of stylish ladies of both the court of Henrietta Maria before the Civil Wars and that of Anne of Denmark after the Restoration.

19. Grant, *Margaret the First*, 25–26.

20. A ballad by John Evelyn, a member of the Royal Society, is transcribed by Grant in *Margaret the First*, 24–26; an account of her visit can be found in S. I. Mintz, "The Duchess of Newcastle's Visit to the Royal Society," *Journal of English and Germanic Philosophy*, April 1952, 168–76.

21. Lamb's phrase is from "Mackery End" in *Essays of Elia* (London: Macmillan, 1903). In *The Life of Charles Lamb* (New York: G. P. Putnam's Sons, 1905) E. V. Lucas quotes William Hazlitt's account of a conversation about choosing people from the past to dine with: "Lamb declared for the duchess" (531).

22. Virginia Woolf, *A Room of One's Own* (1929; reprint, New York: Harcourt Brace Jovanovich, 1989), 62.

23. Grant, *Margaret the First*, 200.

24. Margaret Cavendish, "Preface to the Reader," *The Worlds Olio* (London, 1655).

25. Gallagher discusses Cavendish in "Embracing the Absolute: The Politics of the Female Subject in Seventeenth Century England," *Genders* 1 (spring 1988): 24–39.

26. James Fitzmaurice has suggested that *The Lotterie,* an unpublished play located in the University of Nottingham Library, can be assigned to Cavendish ("*The Lotterie* and *The Wits Triumvirate:* Literary Interactions of Margaret Cavendish and William Cavendish" [paper delivered at the Conference on Margaret Cavendish, University of East Anglia, Norwich, 1996]).

27. The duke was an alumnus of St. John's College, Cambridge.

28. *A Collection of Letters and Poems written by several Persons . . .* (London, 1678), 67–68.

29. *The First Duke and Duchess of Newcastle-upon-Tyne,* by the author of "A Life of Sir Kenelm Digby," "The Life of a Prig," etc. (London: Longman's, Green, 1910), 265. Longueville, however, undermines his own credibility by getting the number of her plays wrong, quoting Langbaine (1691) without correction that *Bell in Campo* is a tragedy, and declaring that the duchess's husband wrote the best lines in her poetry (249–51, 279). Longueville's book was reviewed all too gently by Virginia Woolf in the *Times Literary Supplement,* 12 February 1911, reprinted in *The Essays of Virginia Woolf,* ed. Andrew McNeillie, vol. 1 (London: Hogarth, 1986), 345–51.

30. Perry, *The First Duchess of Newcastle,* 230.

31. In her introduction to *The Blazing World and Other Writings* (London: Penguin, 1994) Kate Lilley appreciates Cavendish's copiousness and experimental challenges to genre in her other works but gives the plays only one sentence, dismissing them as "closet drama."

32. In fact, her longest, *Loves Adventures,* parts 1 and 2 (1662), is 74 folio pages of 12-point type, exactly the length of Jonson's *Volpone* in *Works* (London, 1616); *The Alchemist* is 72 pages long, 18 pages longer than the whole of *Bell in Campo.*

33. *CCXI Sociable Letters,* letter 173.

34. *Observations Upon Experimental Philosophy, To which is added, The Description of a New Blazing World, Blazing World,* 28–30. Lilley, 220–21.

35. Linda Payne develops this and other arguments for the stageability of at least some of Cavendish's plays in "Dramatic Dreamscape: Women's Dreams and Utopian Visions in the Works of Margaret Cavendish, Duchess of Newcastle," in *Curtain Calls: British and American Women and the Theater, 1660–1820,* ed. Mary Anne Schofield and Cecelia Macheski (Athens: Ohio Univ. Press, 1991), 18–33.

36. The best-known objection is that of Samuel Johnson in his 1765 *Preface to Shakespeare* (see *Johnson on Shakespeare,* ed. Arthur Sherbo, vol. 7 of *The Yale Edition of the Works of Samuel Johnson* [New Haven: Yale Univ. Press, 1968], 76–77).

37. Leo Salingar, "Comic Form in Ben Jonson: *Volpone* and the Philosopher's Stone," in *English Drama: Forms and Development,* ed. Marie Axton and Raymond Williams (Cambridge: Cambridge Univ. Press, 1977), 50–51.

Plays

Loves Adventures

Play

THE LORD FATHERLY	THE LADY BASHFULL
THE LORD SINGULARITY	THE LADY WAGTAILE
HIS SONNE	THE LADY AMOROUS
SIR SERIOUS DUMBE	MRS. ACQUAINTANCE
SIR TIMOTHY COMPLEMENT	NURSE FONDLY* FOSTER
SIR HUMPHRY BOLDE	TRUSTIES WIFE
SIR ROGER EXCEPTION	LADY ORPHANS' NURSE
SIR PEACEABLE STUDIOUS	MRS. REFORMER† WOMAN TO
FOSTER TRUSTY	THE LADY BASHFULL
THE LADY ORPHANT	TWO CHAMBER-MAYDES
THE LADY IGNORANT WIFE TO SIR	
PEACEABLE STUDIOUS	

PROLOGUE

Noble Spectators, you are come to see,
A Play, if good, perchance may clapped be;
And yet our Authoresse sayes that she hath heard,
Some playes, though good, hath not been so preferr'd;
As to be mounted up on high raised praise,
And to be Crown'd with Garlands of fresh bayes:
But the contrary have been hissed off,
Out from our Stage with many a censuring scoff;
But afterwards there understanding cleer'd,
They gave the praise, what they before had jeer'd.

---

* This read "Hondly" in the 1662 original.
† This read "Reformers" in the original.

The same she sayes may to her Play befall,
And your erroneous censures may recall:
But all such Playes as take not at first sight,
But afterwards the viewers takes delight:
It seemes there is more wit in such a Play,
Than can be understood in one whole day:
If soe, she is well content for her wits sake,
From ignorance repulses for to take;
For she had rather want those understanding braines,
Than that her Play should want wits flowing veynes.

ACT I

Scene 1

Enter the Lord FATHERLY, *and the Lord* SINGULARITY *his Son.*

LORD SINGULARITY. Pray, sir, do not force me to marry a childe, before you
   know whether she will prove vertuous, or discreet; when for the want of that
   knowledge, you may indanger the honour of your Line and Posterity with
   Cuckoldry and Bastardy.*

LORD FATHERLY. Son, you must leave that to fortune.

LORD SINGULARITY. A wise man, Sir, is to be the maker or spoiler of his own
   fortune.

LORD FATHERLY. Let me tell you Son, the wisest man that is, or ever was, may be
   deceived in the choosing a wife, for a woman is more obscure than nature
   her self, therefore you must trust to chance, for marriage is a Lottery, if you
   get a prize, you may live quietly and happily.

LORD SINGULARITY. But if I light of a blank, as a hundred to one, nay a
   thousand to one but I shall, which is on a Fool or a Whore, her Follies or
   Adulteries, instead of a praise, will sound out my disgrace.

LORD FATHERLY. Come, Come, she is Rich, she is Rich.

LORD SINGULARITY. Why Sir, guilded Horns are most visible.

LORD FATHERLY. 'Tis better, Son, to have a rich whore than a poor whore, but I
   hope Heaven hath made her Chast, and her Father being an honourable,

---

* Cuckoldry and Bastardy] A wife's unfaithfulness could lead to a "bastard," who would
nonetheless be her husband's legal child. The term *cuckold* derives from but reverses *cuckoo*, a bird
who lays its eggs in other birds' nests.

honest, and wise man, will breed her vertuously, and I make no question but you will be happy with her.

LORD SINGULARITY. But Sir, pray consider the inequality of our ages, she being but a Child, and I at mans Estate; by that time she is ready for the marriage bed: I shall be ready for the grave, and youths sharp appetites, will never rellish Age, wherefore she will seek to please her pallat else where.

LORD FATHERLY. Let me tell you, Son, should you marry a woman that were as many years older, than she is younger than you; it were a greater hazard, for first old women are more intemperate than young: and being older than the husband, they are apt to be jealouse, and being jealouse, they grow malitious, and malice seeks revenge, and revenge disgrace, therefore she would Cuckold you meerly to disgrace you.

LORD SINGULARITY. On the other side, those Women that are marryed young, Cuckholds there Husbands fames dishonouring them by their ignorant follyes, and Childish indiscretions, as much as with Adultery. And I should as soon choose to be a Cuckhold, as to be thought to be one: For my honour will suffer as much by the one as the other, if not more.

LORD FATHERLY. Heaven blesse the, Sonne, from jealousy, for thou art horrible afraid of being a Cuckhold.

LORD SINGULARITY. Can you blame me, Sir, since to be a Cuckhold is to be despised, scorned, laught, and pointed at, as a Monster worse than nature ever made, and all the Honour that my birth gave me and my education indued me, my vertue gained me, my industry got me; fortune bestowed on me, and fame inthron'd me for: may not only be lost by my wifes Adultery, but as I said by her indiscretion, which makes me wonder, how any man that hath a Noble Soul, dares marry since all his honour lyes or lives in the light heels of his wife, which every little passion is apt to kick away, wherefore good Sir, let me live a single life.

LORD FATHERLY. How Son, would you have me consent to extinguish the light of my Name, and to pull out the root of my posterity.

LORD SINGULARITY. Why Sir, it were better to lye in dark oblivion, than to have a false light to devulge your disgrace; and you had better pull out the root, than to have a branch of dishonour ingrafted therein.

LORD FATHERLY. All these Arguments against Marriage is, because you would injoy your Mistresses with freedom; fearing you should be disturbed by a wife.

LORD SINGULARITY. That needs not, for I observe, married Men takes as much liberty, if not more than Batchellors; for Batchellors are affraid they should challenge a promise of Marriage, and married Men are out of that danger.

LORD FATHER. Then that is the reason that Batchellors Court Married wives, and Married Men Courts Maides; but howsoever Son, if all Men should be of your mind, there would be no Marr[y]ing nor giving in Marriage; but all must be in Common.

LORD SINGULARITY. That were best Sir, for then there could be no Adultery committed, or Cuckolds made.

LORD FATHERLY. For shame take courage, and be not a fraid of a Woman.

LORD SINGULARITY. By Heaven Sir, I would sooner yield up my life to death, than venture my honour to a womans management.

LORD FATHER. Well Son, I shall not force you with threates or commands to marry against your will and good likeing; but I hope Heaven will turn your mind towards marriage, and sent {send} thee a loving, vertuous and discreet wife.

Scene 2

Enter the Lady WAGTAILE, *the Lady* AMOROUS, *Sir* TIMOTHY COMPLIMENT, *Sir* HUMPHREY BOLD, *and Sir* ROGER EXCEPTION.

SIR TIMOTHY COMPLIMENT. Bright beauty, may I be {your} Servant.

LADY AMOROUS. If I have any beauty, it was begot in your Eyes. And takes light from your commendations.

SIR TIMOTHY COMPLIMENT. You are Lady, the Starre of your Sex.

LADY AMOROUS. No truely, I am but a Meteor that soon goeth out.

LADY WAGTAILE. Preethy Sir *Timothy Compliment,* and Lady *Amorous,* do not stand prating here, but let us go a broad to some place to devert the time.

LADY AMOROUS. Dear *Wagtaile,* whether shall we goe?

SIR TIMOTHY COMPLIMENT. Faith let us go to a Play.

SIR HUMPHREY BOLD. Let's go to a Tavern.

SIR ROGER EXCEPTION. What with Ladyes!

SIR HUMPHREY BOLD. Why, Ladyes have been in Tavernes before now.

SIR ROGER EXCEPTION. It were as good to carry them to a Bawdy-house.*

SIR HUMPHREY BOLD. As good say you, faith now I think of it, better; it were the only place to pass a way idle time. Come Ladyes shall we go.

LADY AMOROUS. Whether?

SIR HUMPHREY BOLD. To a Bawdy-house.

LADY AMOROUS. O fye! fye! Sir *Humphrey Bold;* how wantonly you talk?

---

* Bawdy-house] house of prostitution.

LADY WAGTAILE. But would you carry us in good earnest to a Bawdy-house?

SIR HUMPHREY BOLD. Why, do you question it, when every house is a secret Bawdy-house. Na! Let me tell you, there be many Right Worshipfull, Nay, Right Honourable, and most Noble Pallaces made Bawdy-houses.

SIR ROGER EXCEPTION. Some perchance that are old and ruinous, and the right owners out.

SIR HUMPHREY BOLD. No, some that are new, large, and finely furnished; and the owners stately, proud, scornfull, and jeering, living therein.

SIR ROGER EXCEPTION. They should take heed of jeering, least they be jeered; and of being scornfull, least they be scorned.

SIR HUMPHREY BOLD. What say you Ladyes, are you resolved.

LADY WAGTAILE. No, No, we will not go with you to such places now; but I will carry you to a young Lady whose Father is newly dead, and hath left her all his Estate; and she is become a great heir.

SIR ROGER EXCEPTION. Perchance Lady she will not receive our visit, if her Father be newly dead.

LADY WAGTAILE. I perceive you are ignorant of Funerall customes, for widdowes, heires, and heiresses receives visits whilst the Corpes lyes above ground: And they will keep them so much the longer, to have so many more visitants: nay, sometimes they will keep them so long, as there dissembling is perceived, or so long as they stink above ground; for if they bury not the Corpes and set empty Coffins for want of imbalming, their miserableness will stench up the Nostrils of their vanity.

SIR ROGER EXCEPTION.* Nay by your favour Lady, there are some that are buried whilst they are steeming hot.

SIR HUMPHREY BOLD. Those are only such whose Executors, widdowes, or widdowers, feares they may revive again, and rather than that they should do so, they will bury them alive.

LADY WAGTAILE. You say rightly true, Sir *Humphrey Bold.*

SIR TIMOTHY COMPLIMENT. Sweet beautyes, let us go to see this Rich heiress.

LADY AMOROUS. Content.

SIR ROGER EXCEPTION. But Ladyes are you acquainted with her.

LADY WAGTAILE. O no! But you may know that all women rather than want visits, they will go to those they never saw, nor spoak to: but only heares of them, and where they live, and I can direct the Coachman to this Ladyes Lodging, wherefore let us go.

SIR HUMPHREY BOLD. I shall not deny to visit a Rich heiress.

---

* This read "Sir Roger Vanity" in the original.

SIR ROGER EXCEPTION. I shall waite upon you Ladyes, but—

LADY WAGTAILE. Nay, never make buts, but let's go.

LADY AMOROUS. Pray let us call Sir *Serious Dumb,* to go along with us.

LADY WAGTAILE. Faith *Amorous* you love his Company, because he can tell no tales.

SIR HUMPHREY BOLD. Pray call him not, but let him alone: for I dare sweare he is inventing of some useless and foolish Art.

SIR TIMOTHY COMPLIMENT. Is he so inventive say you, but if his inventions is useless, he invents in vain.

SIR ROGER EXCEPTION. Why may not a Dumb mans Inventions be as good as a blind, for the most usefullest Artes were invented, as the learned saith, by one born blind.

LADY WAGTAILE. Me thinkes a dumb man should not have much wit, for by my troath one that is dumb seemes to me like a fool; nay, one that speakes but little: I cannot for my life but condemn him, or her for an Ass.

SIR HUMPHREY BOLD. He may be a fool, although he may chance to light on some inventions; for Artes are oftner produced from chance than wit, but let us go and leave him.

LADY WAGTAILE *whispers to Sir* H. BOLD.

LADY WAGTAILE. Faith Sir *Humphrey Bold,* we must call him, or otherwise my friend *Amorous* will be out of humour.

SIR HUMPHREY BOLD. Doth she love silence so well.

LADY WAGTAILE. No, no, it is that she loves secrecy so well.

Exit.

CHORUS

In a minutes time is flown
From a Child, to Woman grown;
Some will smile, or laughing say;
This is but a foolish Play;
By Reason a Comedy, should of one dayes action be,
Let them Laugh and so will I
At there great simplicity;
I as other Poets brings
Severall Nations, Subjects, Kings
All to Act upon one stage,
So severall times in one Age.

Scene 3

Enter the Lady ORPHANT, *and Mrs.* ACQUAINTANCE.

MISTRISS ACQUAINTANCE. How do you know the Lord *Singularity* is such a gallant man? For he hath been out of the Kingdom this 7. yeares; wherefore, you could have no acquaintance, you being yet very young.

LADY ORPHANT. Although I have no acquaintance by sight, or experienced knowledge, yet by report I have: for I remembred I heard my Father say he was the honour of the Age, the glory of our Nation; and a pattern for all mankind to take a sample from, and that his person was answerable to his merits, for he said he was a very handsome man, of a Masculine presence, a Courtly garbe, and affable and courteous behaviour; and that his wit was answerable to his merits, person, and behaviour, as that he had a quick wit, a solid judgment, a ready tongue and a smooth speech.

MRS. ACQUAINTANCE. And did your Father proffer you to be his wife.

LADY ORPHANT. Yes, and I remember my father sighing said, he should have died in peace, and his soul would have rested in quiet, if he had been pleased to have accepted of me.

MRS. ACQUAINTANCE. When did your Father proffer you.

LADY ORPHANT. When I was but a Child.

MRS. ACQUAINTANCE. He is not married, and therefore he may chance to accept of you now, if you were profer'd.

LADY ORPHANT. That were but to be refused again, for I heare he is resolved never to marry, and it will be a greater disgrace to be refused now I am grown to womans Estate, than when I was but a Child, besides my Father is dead, and my marr[y]ing can give him no content in the grave; unless his soul could view the world and severall actions therein.

MRS. ACQUAINTANCE. So, is his Father dead.

LADY ORPHANT. Yes, and I here that is the cause he cares not to return into his native Country.

MRS. ACQUAINTANCE. I have a friend that hath his picture.

LADY ORPHANT. Is it a he or a she friend.

LADY ACQUAINTANCE. A she friend.

LADY ORPHANT. Pray be so much my friend, as to get your friends consent to shew me the Picture.

MRS. ACQUAINTANCE. Perchance I may get it to view it my selfe, but I shall never perswade her to lend it you, jealousy will forbid her.

LADY ORPHANT. She hath no cause to fear me, for I am not one to make an Amorous Mrs. and I have heard he will never marry.

MRS. ACQUAINTANCE. That is all one; woman hath hopes as much as feares, or doubts what ever men doth vow for, or against.

LADY ORPHANT. Pray send to her to lend it you, and then you may shew it me.

MRS. ACQUAINTANCE. I will try if she will trust me with it.

Exit.

LADY ORPHANT SOLUS {SOLA}. O Heaven, grant that the praise my Father gave this Lord whilst in the world he lived, prove not as curses to me his Child, so grieve his soul with my unhappy life.

Exit.

Scene 4

Enter the Lady BASHFULL, *and Mrs.* REFORMER *her woman; she being in yeares.*

MISTRISS REFORMER. Madam, now you are become a Mrs. of a Family, you must learn to entertain visitants, and not be so bashfull as you were wont to be, insomuch as you had not confidence to look a stranger in the face, were they never so mean persons.

LADY BASHFULL. Alas *Reformer,* it is neither their birth, breeding, wealth, or title, that puts me out of Countenance; for a poor Cobler will put me as much out of Countenance as a Prince; or a poor Semestress, as much as a great Lady.

MRS. REFORMER. What is it then?

LADY BASHFULL. Why there are unacustomated faces, and unacquainted humours.

MRS. REFORMER. By this reason, you may be as much out of countenance as {at} an unacustomed Dogg, or Cat, that you never saw before; or any other beast.

LADY BASHFULL. O no, for mankind is worse natured than beasts, and beasts better natured than men; besides beasts lookes not with censuring eyes, nor heares, or listens with inquisitive eares, nor speaks with detracting tongues, nor gives false judgement, or spitefull censures, or slandering reproaches, nor jeeres, nor laughs at innocent or harmless Errours, nor makes every little mistake a crime.

Enter the Lady BASHFULLS *Page.*

PAGE. Madam, there is a Coachfull of gallants allighted at the gate.

LADY BASHFULL. For heavens sake, say I have no desire to be seen.

REFORMER. No, say my Lady is full of grief and is not fit to receive visits.

Enter the Ladyes and Gentlemen. Whereat the Lady BASHFULL *stands trembling and shaking, and her eyes being cast to the ground, and her face as pale as death. They speak to* REFORMER.

Where is the Lady *Bashfull*, pray Gentlewoman tell her we are come to kiss her hands.

REFORMER *offers {not} to go forth.*

LADY WAGTAILE. Will you do us the favour old Gentlewoman, as to let the Lady know we are here.

REFORMER. If I am not so old as to be insensible, this is she.

LADY WAGTAILE. Is this she, alas good Lady, she is not well, for surely she hath a fit of an Ague upon her, she doth so shake, you should give her a *Carduss*-possit* and put her to bed.

LADY AMOROUS. Lady, are you sick.

She Answers not.

LADY WAGTAILE. She is sick indeed, if she be speechless.

REFORMER. Madam, pray pull up your spirits, and entertain this honourable Company.

LADY WAGTAILE. Why is the defect in her spirits.

REFORMER. She is young and bashfull.—

They all laugh except Sir ROGER EXCEPTION, *and Sir* SERIOUS DUMB. *Ha! Ha! She is out of countenance.*

SIR ROGER EXCEPTION. No she is angry, because we are strangers unknown unto her; and she takes it for a rudeness that we are come to visit her, therefore let us be gone.

LADY AMOROUS. Let me tell you, it is meer shamefacedness.

SIR ROGER EXCEPTION. I say no, for those that are angry will shake extreamly, and turn as pale as death.

SIR HUMPHREY BOLD. Lady, take courage, and look upon us with a confident brow.

All the while Sir SERIOUS DUMB *lookes on the Lady* BASHFULL *with fixt eyes. The Lady* BASHFULL *offers to speak to the Company, but cannot for stuttering; they all laugh again at her.*

REFORMER. Lord, Madam! will you make your self ridiculous.

LADY BASHFULL. I cannot help it, for my thoughts are consumed in the fiery flame of my blushes; and my words are smothered in the smoak of shame.

LADY WAGTAILE. O! she speakes, she speakes a little.

REFORMER. Pray Madam leave her at this time, and if you honour her with your Company again, she may chance to entertain you with some confidence.

LADY WAGTAILE. Pray let me and Sir *Humphrey Bold* come and visit her once a day, if it be but halfe an hour at a time, and we shall cure her I warrant thee.

---

* *Carduss*-possit] a drink of hot milk and spiced wine used to treat colds.

REFORMER. I wish she were cured of this imperfection.

SIR HUMPHREY BOLD. She must marry, she must marry, for there is no cure like a husband, for husbands beget confidence, and their wives are brought a bed with impudence.

LADY WAGTAILE. By your favour Sir *Humphrey Bold,* marriage must give way or place to courtship, for there are some wives as simply bashfull as Virgins; but when did you ever see, or know, or hear of courtly lovers, or Amorous courtships, to be bashfull: Their eyes are as piercing as light, and twinckles as Starrs, and their countenance as confident as day; and the discourses is freer than wind.

He imbraces her.

SIR HUMPHREY BOLD. And your imbraces are wondrous kind.

LADY WAGTAILE. In troth we women love you men but too well, that is the truth of it.

SIR ROGER EXCEPTION. Pray Madam let us go, and not stay to anger this young Lady as we do.

LADY WAGTAILE. Farewell friend, Sir *Humphry Bold* and I will visit your Lady to morrow.

As they were all going away, the Lady WAGTAILE *turnes back again.*

LADY WAGTAILE. Pray what may I call your name.

REFORMER. My name is *Reformer.*

LADY WAGTAILE. Good Mrs. *Reformer,* I am heartily glad to see you well.

REFORMER. I thank your Ladyship.

All goeth away but Sir SERIOUS DUMB, *and he stayes a little time to look upon the Lady* BASHFULL, *and then goeth out. Ex. The Lady* BASHFULL SOLA, *and after they were all gone she stretches up her self.*

LADY BASHFULL. O in what a torment I have been in; hell is not like it.

Exit.

Scene 5

Enter the Lady ORPHANT, *and Mrs.* ACQUAINTANCE.

LADY ORPHANT. Have you got the Picture?

MRS. ACQUAINTANCE. Yes, but I have seen handsomer men in my opinion than this Picture doth represent.

The Lady ORPHANT *takes the Picture and views it with a stedfast eye.*

LADY ORPHANT. I perceive you have no judgment in the Originall, nor skill in the Copy; for this Picture is most naturally penselled, the Painter hath drawn it so lively. That one may perceive his noble Soul to appear through his lovely, and lively Countenance; do but observe it well, and you will see as much as I.

MRS. ACQUAINTANCE. That is impossible, unless I had your heart, for though my skill of the Copy, or shadow, may be as much as yours, yet my affections to the Originall is less; which makes my eyes not partiall.

LADY ORPHANT. What will the owner take for that Picture?

MRS. ACQUAINTANCE. She will not sell it at any rate.

LADY ORPHANT. I wish she would, for I would buy it at any price.

MRS. ACQUAINTANCE. She prizes it as highly as you, loving him as much; or well (as you do.)

LADY ORPHANT. How know you that?

MRS. ACQUAINTANCE. Because I know she hath given him proofs of her love, which I believe you never did.

LADY ORPHANT. You mistake lust for love, ambition, for merit, I love not for the bodyes sake, but for the soules pure spirit.

Ex.

ACT II

Scene 6

Enter two Merchants.

1. MERCHANT. I hear the Lord *Singularity* hath given the Turkes a great defeat, he is both a wise, prudent, and valiant man.

2. MERCHANT. Methinks our Nation should not suffer such a person as he, to hazard his life in the service of other Countryes.

1. MERCHANT. O it is an honour to our Nation, to let the world know what gallant men it breeds, besides our nation is in peace with all the world; and he being active, hates to live idly, and dully at home, although he have a great estate, and is well beloved in his Country.

2. MERCHANT. What command doth the *Venetians* give him?

1. MERCHANT. He is a Generall, for he commands a great Army.

2. MERCHANT. Is he married?

1. MERCHANT. No, and it is reported he never will marry, but he loves Mistrisses well, which all Souldiers doth for the most part.

2. MERCHANT. Then *Italy* is the best Countrey in the world for a souldier, there being the greatest store and most variety of *Curtezans*, for many of the *Italians* are, as many are in other Nations, rather Carpet Knights, then

fighting souldiers, they have more skill in setting musicall notes, than pitching a battle; in kissing a Mistrisses hand with a good grace, than shooting of a Cannon bullet with a great courage; they can take better aime at a window, than of an enemy. And though they often receive woundes, yet they are from fair *Venus,** not from cruell *Mars.*

1. MERCHANT. But *Mars* souldiers when they skirmish in loves duels, receives woundes as often from fair *Venus,* as other men; and *Italy* hath as many gallant valliant men, bred and born in her, as any other Nation, and there are as many Carpet Knights in other Nations, as in *Italy,* and if valiant, and gallant men be indued with vertue {virtuous}, they are not the less to be esteemed; and as for *Curtizans,* all Nations is stored as much as *Italy,* but they do not so openly prefess it, as those in *Italy* doth.

2. MERCHANT. For my part, I cannot think they are so good Souldiers as they were in *Caesars* time.

1. MERCHANT. That may be, for there is no such souldiers as *Caesars* souldiers were, no not in the world; that is, there are no men so patient, obedient, carefull, industrious, laborious, daring, adventurous, resolute, and active, in these Warrs, in this age, as the *Romans* were in *Caesars* time; and of all the souldiers, *Caesars* souldiers were the best, and of all commanders *Caesar* himself, yet those warriers was not less courtly to the feminine sex, than these of this age; and if you did talk with an understanding Souldier, he would tell you that *Amors* gave an edge to courage, and that it is a mark of a gallant man, and a brave souldier to be an *Amarato;* and as for the *Curtizans* of *Italy,* if there can be an honest act in a dishonest life, it is that the *Curtizans* in *Italy* professes what they are; so that men are not deceived by them, nor betrayed into marriage; wherein other Nations men are cozened with counterfeit modesty, and drawn into marriage by pretended chastity, and then dishonoured by foul adultery, or shamed by marrying a private *Curtizan,* not knowing she was so.

2. MERCHANT. I perceive by thee, that Merchants loves a Mistriss as well as a Souldier.

1. MERCHANT. Surely by thy talk thou art ignorant of thy own profession, which is to trade, and traffick into all Nations, and with all sorts; but yet, Merchants may be Souldiers if they will, and Souldiers may be Merchants if they please; but the truth is all men in the world are Merchants.

2. MERCHANT. No, beggars are not.

---

* *Venus . . . Mars]* Venus was the Roman goddess of love and beauty; Mars was the Roman god of war.

1. MERCHANT. But they are, for they traffick with prayers and praises for almes.

2. MERCHANT. The best Merchants I know are Priests, for they trade into Heaven; and traffick with *Jove.*

1. MERCHANT. That makes them so poor, for heavens commoditie are not saleable on earth.

Ex.

Scene 7

Enter the Lady ORPHANT, *Nurse* FONDLY, FOSTER TRUSTY

LADY ORPHANT. Dear Nurse and *Foster* Father, grant to my desires and assist my designs.

NURSE FONDLY. What to let you wander about the world like a Vagabond, besides it is against the modesty of your Sex.

LADY ORPHANT. Are holy Pilgrimes Vagabonds, or is it immodest for the bodies of devout soules to travell to the sacred Tombe to offer penetentiall tears.

NURSE FONDLY. Why, you are no Pilgrime, nor is your journey to a godly end.

LADY ORPHANT. My journey will be to an honest end, for though I am loves Pilgrime, yet I shall travell to an honest heart; there to offer my pure affections.

NURSE FONDLY. To a deboist* man, there to offer your Virginity.

LADY ORPHANT. Mistake me not, for though I love beyond a common rate, even to an extream degree, yet I am chastly honest, and so shall ever be; my grave shall witness my constancy.

The Lady ORPHANT *weeping. Ex.*

FOSTER TRUSTY. Beshrew your tongue wife for speaking so sharply to our young Lady, she was left to our trust, care, and tender usage, and not to be snapt and quarrelled with.

NURSE FONDLY. Yes, and you would betray your trust to her childish folly.

FOSTER TRUSTY. No that I would not, neither would I venture or yield up her life to loves melancholly.

NURSE FONDLY. Come, come husband, you humour her too much, and that will spoile her I am sure.

Ex.

Scene 8

Enter Sir PEACEABLE STUDIOUS *with a Book in his hand; a Table being set out, whereon is Pen, Ink, and Paper. After he hath walked a turn or two, with his eyes*

---

* deboist] debauched; damaged by evil living.

fixt upon the ground, he sits down to the Table, and begins to write. Enter the Lady IGNORANT *his Wife.*

LADY IGNORANT. Lord Husband! I can never have your company, for you are at all times writing, or reading, or turning your Globes, or peaking thorough your Prospective Glasse,* or repeating Verses, or speaking Speeches to your self.

SIR P. STUDIOUS. Why wife, you may have my company at any time; Nay, never to be from me if you please, for I am alwaies at home.

LADY IGNORANT. 'Tis true, your person is alwaies at home, and fixt to one place, your Closet as a dull dead statue to the side of a wall, but your mind and thoughts are alwaies abroad.

SIR P. STUDIOUS. The truth is, my mind sometimes sends out my thoughts like Coye† ducks, to bring more understanding in.

LADY IGNORANT. You mistake Husband, for your thoughts are like vain, or rather like false *Scouts* that deceives your understanding, imprisons your senses, and betrayes your life to a dull solitariness.

SIR P. STUDIOUS. 'Tis better to live a quiet solitary life, than a troublesome and an uneasie life.

LADY IGNORANT. What is a man born for, but to serve his Countrey, side with his friends, and to please the effeminate Sex.

SIR P. STUDIOUS. You say right wife, and to serve his Countrey, is to finde out such inventions as is usefull either in Peace or War; and to form, order and settle Common-wealths by devizing‡ Laws, which none but studious brains e're did, or can do. Tis true, practice doth pollish beauty and adorn, but neither layes the Foundation, nor brings the Materials, nor builds the walls thereof; and to side with friends, is to defend Right and Truth with sound arguments and strong proofs, from the tyrannical usurpation of false opinions, vain phantasms, malicious satires, and flattering oratorie, and to please the effeminate Sex, is to praise their beauty, wit, vertue and good graces in soft Numbers, and smooth Language, building up Piramides of poetical praises, Printing their fame thereon, by which they live to After-ages.

LADY IGNORANT. Prithy Husband mistake us not, for women cares not for wide mouthed fame; and we take more delight to speak our selves whilst we

---

* Prospective Glasse] telescope.
† Coye] decoy.
‡ This word was "Denizing" in the original, but denizing laws are laws that confer rights of residency; "devizing" makes sense here.

live, than to be talked of when we are dead, and to take our present pleasures, than to abstain our selves for After-ages.

SIR P. STUDEOUS. Well wife, what would you have me do?

LADY IGNORANCE.* Why, I would have you so sociable, as to sit and discourse with our friends and acquaintance, and play the good fellow amongst them.

SIR P. STUDIOUS. What need we to have any other friends than our selves; our studies, books and thoughts.

LADY IGNORANCE. Your studies, books and thoughts, are but dull acquaintance, melancholly companions, and weak friends.

SIR P. STUDIOUS. You do not wife consider their worth; for books are conversable, yet silent acquaintance, and study, is a wise Counsellor; and kind friends, and poetical thoughts are witty Companions, wherein other Societies and Companies are great inconveniences, and oftimes produces evil effects, as Jealousie, Adulterie, Quarrels, Duels, and Death, besides slanders, backbitings and the like.

LADY IGNORANCE. Truly Husband, you are strangely mistaken; for those Societies as I would have you frequent, doth Sing, Dance, Rallie, make Balls, Masks, Playes, Feasts, and the like, and also makes Frollicks or Rubices, or Playes at Questions and Commands, Purposes or Ridles, and twenty such like Pastimes and fine sports they have.

SIR P. STUDIOUS. But surely Wife you would not like this kind of life, nor I neither; especially if we were in one and the same Company; for perchance you may hear wanton Songs sung, and see amorous glances or rude or immodest Actions, and when you dance, have a secret nip, and gentle gripe of the hand silently to declare their amorous affections; and when you are at Questions or Commands, you will be commanded to kiss the men, or they you, which I shall not like, neither should you; or if they are commanded to pull of your Garter, which no chast and modest woman will suffer, nor no gallant man, or honourable husband will indure to stand by to see, and if you refuse you disturb the rest of the Company, and then the women falls out with you in their own defence, and the men takes it as an affront, and disgrace, by reason none refuses but you; This causes quarrels with Strangers, or quarrels betwixt our selves.

LADY IGNORANT. 'Tis true, if the Company were not Persons of Quality which were civilly bred; but there is no rude Actions, or immodest behaviours

---

* The change from "Ignorant" (specific) to "Ignorance" (general) is maintained to the end of this couple's story in part 2.

offered or seen amongst them; Besides, if you do not like those sports, you may play at Cardes or Dice to pass away the time.

SIR P. STUDIOUS. But Wife, let me examine you, have or do you frequent these Societies that you speak so Knowingly, Learnedly and Affectionately of?

LADY IGNORANCE. No otherwise Husband, but as I have heard, which reports makes me desire to be acquainted with them.

SIR P. STUDIOUS. Well, you shall, and I will bear you company, to be an Eye-witness how well you behave your self, and how you profit thereby.

LADY IGNORANCE. Pray Husband do, for it will divert you from your too serious studies, and deep thoughts, which feeds upon the health of your body, which will shorten your life; and I love you so well, as I would not have you dye, for this I perswade you to, is for your good.

SIR P. STUDIOUS. We will try how good it is.

Ex.

Scene 9

Enter Nurse FONDLY, *and* FOSTER TRUSTY *her Husband.*

NURSE FONDLY. How shall I keep your Journey secret, but that every body will know of it.

FOSTER TRUSTY. We will give out that such a deep melancholly have seized on her, since her Fathers death, as she hath made a vow not to see any creature besides your self for two years; As for me, I have lived so solitary a life with my solitary Master, this Ladies Father, that I have few or no acquaintance; besides, I will pretend some business into some other parts of the Kingdom, and I having but a little Estate, few will inquire after me.

NURSE FONDLY. So in the mean time I must live solitary, all alone, without my Husband, or Nurse-childe, which Childe, Heaven knows, I love better, than if I had one living of my own.

FOSTER TRUSTY. I am as fond of her, as you are, and Heaven knows, would most willingly sacrifice my old life, could it do her any service.

NURSE FONDLY. But we indanger her life, by the consenting to this journey, for she that hath been bred with tenderness and delicateness, can never indure the coldes and heats, the dirt and dust that Travellers are subject to; Besides, to be disturbed and broaken of her sleep, and to have ill Lodging, or perhaps none at all, and then to travel a foot like a Pilgrim: Her tender feet will never indure the hard ground; nor her young legs never able to bear her body so long a journey.

FOSTER TRUSTY. Tis true, this journey may very much incommode her, yet if she doth not go to satisfie her mind, I* cannot perceive any hopes of life, but do foresee her certain death, for her mind is so restless, and her thoughts works so much upon her body, as it begins to waste, for she is become lean and pale.

NURSE FONDLY. Well! Heaven bless you both, and prosper your journey, but pray let me hear often from you, for I shall be in great frights and fears.

FOSTER TRUSTY. If we should write, it may chance to discover us, if our Letters should be opened, wherefore you must have patience.

Ex.

Scene 10

Enter the Lady BASHFULL, *and* REFORMER *her Woman.*

LADY BASHFULL. *Reformer,* I am little beholding to you.

REFORMER. Why Madam.

LADY BASHFULL. Why, you might have told a lye for me once in your life, for if you had not spoke the truth by saying I was the Lady, they came to see, they would never have guest I had been she, for they expected me to have been a free bold Entertainer, as they were Visitors, which is, as I do perceive, to be rudely familiar at first sight.

REFORMER. But to have told a lye, had been to commit a sin.

LADY BASHFULL. In my conscience the Gods would have forgiven you, nay, they would have blest you; For it is a most pious and charitable act in helping the distressed; Besides, you had not only helped a present distress, but released a whole life out of misery; for as long as I live my thoughts will torment me: O! They wound my very soul already, they will hinder my pious devotions; For when I pray, I shall think more of my bashful behaviour, and the disgrace I have received thereby, than of Heaven; Besides, they will starve me, not suffering the meat to go down my throat, or else to choke me, causing it to go awry, or else they will cause a Feaver; for in my conscience I shall blush even in my sleep, if I can sleep; For certainly I shall dream of my disgrace, which will be as bad as a waking memory: O! that I had *Opium,* I would take it, that I might forget all things; For as long as I have memory, I shall remember my simple behaviour, and as for my Page, he shall go, I am resolved to turn him away.

REFORMER. Why madam?

---

* Emended from italics. I have silently emended subsequent randomly italicized *I*'s in this play.

LADY BASHFULL. Because he let them come in.

REFORMER. He could not help it, for they followed him at the heels, they never stayed for an answer from you, or to know whether you were within or no, and there were a great many of them.

LADY BASHFULL. I think there was a Legion of them.

REFORMER. You speak as if they were a Legion of Angels.

LADY BASHFULL. Nay, they proved a Legion of Divels to me.

REFORMER. There was one that seemed to be a fine Gentleman, but he spake not a word.

LADY BASHFULL. They may be all what you will make them, or describe them, for I could make no distinction whether they were men or women, or beasts, nor heard no articulated sound, only a humming noise.

REFORMER. They spake loud enough to have pierced your ears, if strength of noise could have done it, but the Gentleman that did not speak, looked so earnestly at you, as if he would have looked you thorough.

LADY BASHFULL. O that his eyes had that piercing faculty, for then perchance he might have seen; I am not so simple as my behaviour made me appear.

Ex.

Scene 11

Enter Sir PEACEABLE STUDIOUS, *and the Lady* IGNORANCE *his Wife.*

SIR PEACEABLE STUDIOUS. I have lost 500. pounds since you went in with the Ladies.

LADY IGNORANCE. 500. Pounds in so short a time.

SIR P. STUDIOUS. 'Tis well I lost no more: But yet, that 500. pounds would have bought you a new Coach, or Bed, or Silver Plate, or Cabinets, or Gowns, or fine Flanders-laces, and now its gone, and we have no pleasure nor credit for it, but it is no matter, I have health for it, therefore I will call to my Steward to bring me some more.

LADY IGNORANCE. No, do not so, for after the rate you have lost, you will lose all your Estate in short time.

SIR P. STUDIOUS. Faith let it go, 'tis but begging or starving after it is gone, for I have no trade to live by, unless you have a way to get a living, have you any.

LADY IGNORANCE. No truly Husband, I am a shiftless creature.

SIR P. STUDIOUS. Yes, but you may play the Whore, and I the Shark, so live by couzening* and cheating.

---

* couzening] swindling.

LADY IGNORANCE. Heaven defend Husband.

SIR P. STUDIOUS. Or perchance some will be so charitable to give us suck'd bones from stinking breaths, and rotten teeth, or greasie scraps from fowl hands; But go wife, prithy bid my Steward send me 500. pounds more, or let it alone; I will run on the score, and pay my losings at a lump.

LADY IGNORANCE. No dear Husband, play no more.

SIR P. STUDIOUS. How! not play any more say you, shall I break good Company with sitting out; Besides, it is a question whether I have power to leave off, now I have once begun; for Play is Witch-craft, it inchants temperance, prudence, patience, reason and judgment and it kicks away time, and bids him go as an old bald-pated fellow as he is, also it chains the life with fears, cares and griefs of losing to a pair of Cards and set of Dice.

LADY IGNORANCE. For Heaven sake pitty me! If you consider not your self.

SIR P. STUDIOUS. Can you think a Husband considers his wife, when he forgets, or regards not himself, when all loves is self-love, for a man would have his Wife to be loving and chaste for his honours sake, to be thrifty for his profit sake, to be patient for quiet sake, to be cleanly, witty and beautifull for his pleasure sake, and being thus, he loves her; For if she be false, unkind, prodigal, froward, sluttish, foolish, and ill-favoured, he hates her.

LADY IGNORANT. But if a Husband loves his wife, he will be carefull to please her, prudent for her subsistence,* industrious for her convenience, valiant to protect her, and conversable to entertain her, and wise to direct and guide her.

SIR P. STUDIOUS. To rule and govern her, you mean wife.

LADY IGNORANCE. Yes, but a Husbands follies will be but corrupt Tutors, and ill Examples for a wife to follow; wherefore dear Husband, play no more, but come amongst the effeminate Societie, you will find more pleasure at less charges.

SIR P. STUDIOUS. Well wife, You shall perswade me for this time.

LADY IGNORANCE. I thank you Husband.

Ex.

Scene 12

Enter the Lady ORPHANT, *and* FOSTER TRUSTY, *as two Pilgrims.*

FOSTER TRUSTY. My childe, you were best sit and rest your self, you cannot chose but be very weary, for we have travelled a great journey to day.

---

* In the original there was a comma following *her*.

LADY ORPHANT. Truly I am as fresh, and my spirits are as lively, as if I had not trod a step to day.

FOSTER TRUSTY. I perceive love can work Miracles.

LADY ORPHANT. Are not you Father a weary?

FOSTER TRUSTY. It were a shame for me to be weary, when you are not; But my childe, we must change these Pilgrims weeds, when we are out of our own Countrey; as when we are in *Italy*, otherwise we cannot pretend to stay in the Venetian Armie, but must travel as Pilgrims do to *Jerusalem:* But it were best we put our selves into Beggers garments until we come into the Armie, for fear we should be strip'd by Thieves; for I have heard, Thieves will strip Travellers, if their cloths be not all ragges.

LADY ORPHANT. 'Tis true, and Thieves as I have heard, will rob Pilgrims soonest, finding many good Pilladge, wherefore we will accoutre our selves like to ragged Beggers.

Ex.

ACT III

Scene 13

Enter the Lady BASHFULL, *as in a melancholly humour, and* REFORMER *her Woman.*

REFORMER. Lord Madam! I hope you are not seriously troubled for being out of Countenance.

LADY BASHFULL. Yes truely.

REFORMER. What? as to make you melancholly!

LADY BASHFULL. Yes, very melancholly, when I think I have made my self a scorn, and hath indangered my reputation.

REFORMER. Your reputation! Heaven bless you, but your life is so innocent, harmless, chaste, pure and sweet, and your actions so just and honest, as all the Divels in Hell cannot indanger your reputation.

LADY BASHFULL. But spitefull tongues, which are worse than Divels, may hurt my reputation.

REFORMER. But spite cannot have any thing to say.

LADY BASHFULL. Spite will lye, rather than not speak, for envie is the mother of spite, and slander is the Mid-wife.

REFORMER. Why, what can they say?

LADY BASHFULL. They will say I am guilty of some immodest act, or at least thoughts, or else of some heynous and horrid crime, otherwise I could not be ashamed, or out of countenance, if I were innocent.

REFORMER. They cannot say ill, or think ill, but if they could, and did, what are you the worse, as long as you are innocent.

LADY BASHFULL. Yes truely, for I desire to live in a pure esteem, and an honourable respect in every breast, and to have a good report spoke on me, since I deserve no other.

REFORMER. There is an old saying, that opinion travels without a Passe-port, and they that would have every ones good opinion, must live in every mans age: But I am very confident, there is none lives or dyes without censures, or detraction; even the Gods themselves, that made man, hath given man power and free will to speak, at least to think what they will; That makes so many Athiests in thought, and so many several factions by disputation, and since the Gods cannot, or will not be free from censures, why should you trouble your self with what others say, wherefore pray put off this indiscreet and troublesome humour, for if you would not regard censure, you would be more confident.

LADY BASHFULL. I will do what I can to mend.

Scene 14

Enter the Lady ORPHANT, *and* FOSTER TRUSTY, *like two poor Beggers.*

FOSTER. Childe, you must beg of every one that comes by, otherwise we shall not seem right Beggers.

LADY ORPHANT. If our necessities were according to our outward appearance, we were but in a sad condition; for I shall never get any thing by begging, for I have neither learn'd the tone, nor the Beggers phrase to move pity or charity.

FOSTER TRUSTY. Few Beggers move pity, they get more by importunity, than by their oratorie, or the givers charity.

Enter 2. Gentlemen. She goeth to them and beggs.

LADY ORPHANT. Noble Gentlemen, pity the shiftless youth, and infirm old age that hath no means to live, but what compassionate charity will bestow.

1. GENTLEMAN. You are a young boy, and may get your living by learning to work.

LADY ORPHANT. But my Father being very old, is past working, and I am so young, as I have not arrived to a learning degree of age, and by that time I have learn'd to get my living, my Father may be starved for want of food.

2. GENT. Why, your Father may beg for himself whilst you learn to work.

LADY ORPHANT. My Father's feeble legs can never run after the flying speed of pityless hearts, nor can he stand so long to wait for conscience almes, nor knock so hard to make devotion hear.

1. GENT. I perceive you have learn'd to beg well, though not to work, and because you shall know my devotion is not deaf, there is something for your Father and you.

2. GENT. Nay, faith boy, thou shalt have some of the scraps of my charity to, there is for thee.

LADY ORPHANT. Heaven bless you; and grant to you, all your good desires.

Gentlemen Ex. Enter a Lady and Servants.

LADY ORPHANT. Honourable Lady, let the mouth of necessity suck the breast of your charity to feed the hungry Beggers.

LADY. Away you rogue, a young boy and beg! You should be strip'd, whip'd, and set to work.

LADY ORPHANT. Alas Madam, naked poverty is alwaies under the lash of miserie, which forceth us to work in the quarries of stony hearts, but we finde the mineral so hard, as we cannot get out enough to build up a livelyhood.

LADY. Imploy your selves upon some other work then.

Lady Ex. Enter a mean Trades-man.

LADY ORPHANT. Good Sir relieve a poor begger.

TRADES-MAN. Faith boy, I am so poor, as I want relief my self; yet of what I have, thou shalt share with me; there is a peny of my two pence, which is all I have, and Heaven do thee good with it.

Trades-man Exit.

LADY ORPHANT. I perceive poverty pities poverty, as feeling the like miserie, where riches is cruel, and hard-hearted, not knowing what want is.

FOSTER TRUSTY. I perceive wit can work upon every thing, and can form it self into what shape it please, and thy wit playes the Begger so well, as we needed not to have stored our selves from our own Stocks, but have lived upon the Stocks of others.

LADY ORPHANT. But if all Stocks were as insipid* as the Ladies, we should have starved, if we had not brought sap from our own home; But Father, I am weighed down with the peny the poor *Trades-man* gave me.

FOSTER TRUSTY. Why, it is not so heavy.

LADY ORPHANT. It is so heavy, as it burthens my conscience, and I shall never be at ease, nor be able to travel any farther, until I have restored the peny to the giver again.

---

* insipid] boring, flat-tasting; Cavendish makes a pun on soup stock.

FOSTER TRUSTY. How should we do that, for it is as hard and difficult to find out that man, as to finde out the first cause of effects.

LADY ORPH. Well, I will play the Philosopher, and search for him.

FOSTER TRUSTY.* But if you should meet him, perchance you will not know he was he.

LADY ORPH. O yes, for his extraordinary charity made me take particular notice of him.

Enter the Trades-man as returning back.

LADY ORPH. Most charitable and—

TRADES-MAN. What boy, wouldst thou have the other peny,

LADY ORPH. Most noble Sir, I have received from a bountifull hand, a summe of money, and since you were so charitable to divide the half of your store to me, so I desire I may do the like to you.

TRADES-MAN. No boy, keep it for thy self, and thy old Father; I have a Trade, and shall get more.

LADY ORPH. Pray take it for luck-sake, otherwise I shall never thrive.

TRADES-MAN. Faith I finde boy, thou art not as most of the World are; the more riches they get, the more covetous they grow.

LADY ORPH. Sir, pray take this.

TRADES-MAN. What do you give me here, a piece of Gold?

LADY ORPH. Yes Sir.

TRADES-MAN. That were extortion, to take a pound for a peny.

LADY ORPH. No, it is not extortion, since I can better spare this pound now, than you could your peny, when you gave it me; wherefore it is but justice,

TRADES-MAN. Well, I will keep it for thee, and when you want it, come to me again, and you shall have it: I live in the next street, at the signe of the *Holy-lamb*.

LADY ORPHANT. Pray make use of it, for I may chance never to see you more.

Exeunt.

Scene 15

Enter Sir STUDIOUS, *and the Lady* IGNORANCE *his Wife.*

SIR P. STUDIOUS. Faith Wife, with sipping of your Gossiping-cups, I am half drunk.

LADY IGNORANCE. Lord Husband! There were some of the Ladies that drank twice as much as you did, and were not drunk, and to prove they were not drunk, was that they talked as much before they drunk, as after; For there

---

* In the original this read "Foster Nurse."

was such a confusion of words, as they could not understand each other, and they did no more, when they had drunk a great quantity of Wine.

SIR P. STUDIOUS. That was a signe they were drunk, that they talked less, but how chance that you drank so little.

LADY IGNORANCE. Truly, Wine is so nauseous to my taste, and so hatefull to my nostrils, as I was sick when the cup was brought to me.

SIR P. STUDIOUS. I know not what it was to you, but to me it was pleasant, for your Ladies were so gamesome, merry and kind, as they have fired me with amorous love ever since.

Enter the Lady IGNORANCE's *maid.*

MAID. Madam, the Lady *Wagtail,* and other Ladies, have sent to know if your Ladyship were within, that they might come and wait upon you.

Sir PEACEABLE STUDIOUS *chiks the maid under the Chin, and kisses her.*

SIR P. STUDIOUS. Faith *Nan,* thou art a pretty wench.

LADY IGNORANCE. What Husband? Do you kiss my maid before my face.

SIR P. STUDIOUS. Why not Wife, as well as one of your sociable Ladies in a frollick, as you kiss me, I kiss *Nan.*

LADY IGNORANCE. So, and when *Nan* kisses your Barber, he must kiss me.

SIR P. STUDIOUS. Right, this is the kissing frollick, and then comes the stricking frollick, for you strike *Nan, Nan* gently strikes me, and I justly beat you, and end the frollicks with a—{divorce}*

Enter the Lady WAGTAIL, *and other Ladies of the Societie, with the Lady* AMOROUS.

LADY WAGTAIL. What? a man and his Wife dully alone together! Fie for shame.

LADY AMOROUS. Lawfull love is the dullest and drouziest companion that is, for Wives are never thought fair, nor Husbands witty.

SIR P. STUDIOUS. Your Ladyship is learned in loves Societies.

LADY AMOROUS. Yes that I am, for I have observed, that if there be a match'd company, every man having a woman, their conversation is dull, every mans tongue whispering in his Mistriss eare, whilst the women are mute, listening to that which is whispered unto them; but let there be but one man amongst a company of women, and then their tongues runs races, striving with each other, which shall catch that one man, as the only prize, when the weaker wits runs themselves straite out of breath.

SIR P. STUDIOUS. And must not {that} one man run against them all.

---

* Murals in Bolsover Castle, one of the homes of the duke of Newcastle, depict such erotic play.

LADY AMOROUS. O yes? and many times his wit beats them all.

SIR P. STUDIOUS. Faith Lady? They must not be such strong winded wits as yours is, which is able to beat a dozen Masculine wits out of the field.

LADY AMOROUS. You are pleased to give me a complement.

The Lady IGNORANCE *seems melancholly.*

LADY WAGTAILE. The merry God have mercy on you? What makes you so melancholly.

LADY IGNORANCE. I am not well to day.

LADY WAGTAIL. If you are troubled with melancholly vapours, arising from crude humours, you must take as soon as you wake after your first sleep, a draught of Wormwood-wine, then lye to sleep again, and then half an hour before you rise, drink a draught of Jelley-broth, and after you have been up an hour and a half, eate a White-wine-caudle, then a little before a dinner, take a Toste and Sack, and at your meals, two or three good glasses of Clarret-wine; as for your Meats, you must eate those of light digestion, as Pheasant, Partridges, Cocks, Snipes, Chickens, young Turkies, Pea-chickens and the like; And in the After-noon, about four or five a clock, you must take Naples-bisket dip'd in Ippocrass,* which helps digestion much, and revives the spirits, and makes one full of discourse, and not only to discourse, but to discourse wittily, and makes one such good company, as invites acquaintance, and ties friendship.

The whilst the Lady WAGTAIL *talks to the Lady* IGNORANCE, *she eyes her Husband, who seems to court the Lady* AMOROUS.

LADY AMOROUS. Faith I will tell your Wife what you say.

LADY WAGTAIL. That is fowl play, and not done like one of the Society, especially when my Lady is not well.

LADY AMOROUS. What? Is she sick! I lay my life she hath eate too much Branne Sturgeon, or Sammon without muskadine or Sack, or Neats-tongues, Bakon and Anchoves, Caveare, or Lobsters, without Rhenish-wines, or Oysters, or Sausages without Clarret-wine, or hath she eaten Potatoe-pies without dates, Ringo-roots, Marrow and Chestnuts,† have you not? i faith confess.

---

* Wormwood-wine . . . Ippocrass] Wormwood-vine would be vermouth or absinthe; Jelley-broth, consomme; White-wine-caudle, milk mixed with white wine; Sack, sweet sherry; Snipes, fowl, possibly ibis; Naples-bisket, oval-shaped cookie; and Ippocras, wine flavored with spices.

† Branne Sturgeon . . . Chestnuts] Branne Sturgeon, sturgeon stuffed with bran; muskadine, sweet wine made from muscadine grapes; Neats-tongues, ox tongues; Ringo-roots, roots of the eryngo, or sea holly, usually candied, regarded as an aphrodisiac; Marrow, either the fatty substance found inside bones or a gourdlike vegetable. The point seems to be an array of exciting and luxurious foods.

LADY IGNORANCE. No indeed.

LADY AMOROUS. Why? I hope you have not taken a surfeit of White-meats, those childish meats, or with Water-grewel, Ponado, Barley-grewel, those Hodge-podgely meats.*

LADY IGNORANCE. Neither.—

LADY AMOROUS. Why, then you have over-heated your self with dancing or fretting and vexing your self at your ill fortune at Cards; or your Tayler hath spoiled some Gown, or your Coach-man was out of the way when you would go abroad; is it not so.

LADY IGNORANCE. No.

LADY AMOROUS. Why? Then your Husband hath crost some design, or hath angered you some other way.

The Lady IGNORANCE *blushes. They all laugh, and speak at one time; She blushes, She blushes.*

LADY WAGTAIL. Faith *Amorous,* thou hast found it out! Sir *Peaceable Studious* you are to be chidden to anger your Wife; wherefore tell us how you did anger her, when you did anger her, and for what you did anger her.

SIR P. STUDIOUS. Dear, sweet, fine, fair Ladies! be not so cruel to me, as to lay my Wives indisposition to my charge.

LADY WAGTAILE. But we will, and we will draw up an Accusation against you, unless you confess, and ask pardon.

SIR P. STUDIOUS. Will you accuse me without a Witness?

LADY WAGTAIL. Yes, and condemne you too.

SIR P. STUDIOUS. That were unjust! if Ladies could be unjust.

LADY AMOROUS. O Madam! we have a witness? her blushing is a sufficient witness to accuse him; Besides, her melancholly silence will help to condemn him.

LADY IGNORANCE. Pardon me Ladies, for when any of our Sex is offended, or angered, whether they have cause or not, they will rail louder than *Joves*† thunder.

LADY AMOROUS. So will you in time.

LADY WAGTAIL. Let us jumble her abroad; Come Madam! we will put you out of your dull humour.

---

* White-meats . . . Hodge-podgely meats] White-meats, food prepared with milk; Ponado, bread boiled in water; Hodge-podgely meats, unappetizing mixtures, in this case bland and dull.

† *Joves*] Jove was the Roman king of the gods.

LADY IGNORANCE. No Madam? Pray excuse me to day; in truth I am not well.

LADY AMOROUS. No, let us let my Lady alone, but let us take her Husband, and tutour him.

SIR P. STUDIOUS. Ladies, give me leave to praise my self, and let me tell you? I am as apt a Scholar, as ever you met with, and as willing to learn.

LADY AMOROUS. Farewell Madam, we will order Sir *P. Studious,* and try what disposition he is of, and how apt to be instructed.

LADY IGNORANCE. Pray do Madam, he promiseth well.

Ex.

Scene 16

Enter FOSTER TRUSTY, *and the Lady* ORPHANT.

LADY ORPHANT. Now we are come into the Armie, how shall we demean our selves like poor Beggers.

FOSTER TRUSTY. By no means, for though you beg well yet you will never get what you come for with begging, for there is an old saying, that although all charity is love, yet all love is not charity.

LADY ORPHANT. It were the greatest charity in the World, for him to love me; for without his love, I shall be more miserable than poverty can make me.

FOSTER TRUSTY. But poverty is so scorned and hated, that no person is accepted which she presents; Nay, poverty is shunn'd more than the Plague.

LADY ORPHANT. Why? it is not infectious.

FOSTER TRUSTY. Yes faith, for the relieving of necessity, is the way to be impoverished.

LADY ORPH. But their rewards are the greater in Heaven.

FOSTER TRUSTY. 'Tis true, but their Estates are less on earth.

LADY ORPHANT. But blessings are more to be desired than wealth.

FOSTER TRUSTY. Well? Heaven bless us, and send us such fortune, that our long journey may prove successfull, and not profitless, and because Heaven never gives blessings, unless we use a prudent industry; you shall put your self into good clothes, and I will mix my self with his followers and servants, and tell them, as I may truely, that you are my Son, for no mans Son but mine you are, was so importunate, as you will never let me rest, until I brought you to see the Lord *Singularity,* and they will tell him, to let him know his fame is such, as even young children adore him, taking a Pilgrimage to see him, and he out of a vain-glory will desire to see you.

LADY ORPHANT. But what advantage shall I get by that.

Enter the Lord SINGULARITY, *and many Commanders attending him.*

FOSTER TRUSTY. Peace! here is the General.

COMMANDER. The enemie is so beaten, as now they will give us some time to breath our selves.

GENERAL. They are more out of breath than we are, but the States are generous enemies, if they give them leave to fetch their wind, and gather strength again.

LADY ORPHANT. Father, stand you by, and let me speak.

She goeth to the General, and speaks to him:

Heaven bless your Excellencie.

LORD GENERAL. From whence comest thou boy?

LADY ORPH. From your native Countrey.

GENERAL. Cam'st thou lately?

LADY ORPH. I am newly arrived.

GENERAL. Pray how is my Countrey, and Countrey-men, live they still in happy peace, and flourishing with plenty.

LADY ORPH. There is no noise of war, or fear of famine.

GENERAL. Pray *Jove* continue it.

LADY ORPHANT. It is likely so to continue, unless their pride and luxurie begets a factious childe, that is born with war, and fed with ruine.

GENERAL. Do you know what faction is?

LADY ORPH. There is no man that lives, and feels it not, the very thoughts are factious in the mind, and in Rebellious passions arises warring against the soul.

GENERAL. Thou canst not speak thus by experience boy, thou art too young, not yet at mans Estate.

LADY ORPHANT. But children have thoughts, and said to have a rational soul, as much as those that are grown up to men; but if souls grow as bodies doth, and thoughts increases with their years, then may the wars within the mind be like to School-boys quarrels, that falls out for a toy, and for a toy are friends.

GENERAL. Thou speakest like a Tutour, what boyish thoughts so ever thou hast; but tell me boy? what mad'st thee travel so great a journey.

LADY ORPH. For to see you.

GENERAL. To see me boy!

LADY ORPH. Yes, to see you Sir, for the Trumpet of your praise did sound so loud, it struck my ears, broke open my heart, and let desire run forth, which restless grew until I travelled hither.

GENERAL. I wish I had merits to equal thy weary steps, or means for to reward them.

LADY ORPH. Your presence hath sufficiently rewarded me.

GENERAL. Could I do thee any service boy?

LADY ORPH. A bounteous favour you might do me Sir?

GENERAL. What is that boy?

LADY ORPH. To let me serve you, Sir.

GENERAL. I should be ingratefull to refuse thee, chose thy place.

LADY ORPH. Your Page, Sir, if you please.

GENERAL. I accept of thee most willingly.

CAPTAIN. But Sir? may not this boy be a lying, couzening, flattering dissembling, treacherous boy.

GENERAL. Why Captain, there is no man that keeps many servants, but some are lyers, and some treacherous, and all flatterers; and a Master receives as much injurie from each particular, as if they were joyned in one.

LADY ORPH. I can bring none that will witness for my truth, or be bound for my honesty, but my own words.

GENERAL. I desire none, boy, for thy tongue sounds so sweetly, and thy face looks so honestly, as I cannot but take, and trust thee.

LADY ORPH. Heaven bless your Excellence, and fortune prosper you, for your bounty hath been above my hopes, and equal to my wishes.

GENERAL. What is thy name?

LADY ORPH. *Affectionata* my Noble Lord.

GENERAL. Then follow me *Affectionata*.

Ex.

ACT IV

Scene 17

Enter the Lady BASHFULL, *and* REFORMER *her woman. Enter Page.*

PAGE. Madam, there was a Gentleman gave me this Letter, to deliver to your Ladyships hands.

LADY BASHFULL. A Letter! Pray *Reformer* open it, and read it, for I will not receive Letters privately.

Page Exit.

REFORMER. The superscription is for the Right Honourable, the Lady *Bashfull;* these present.

THE LETTER

MADAM,

Since I have had the honour to see you, I have had the unhappiness to think my self miserable, by reason I am deprived of speech, that should plead my suit, but if an affectionate soul, chaste thoughts, lawfull desires, and a fervent heart can plead without speech, let me beg your favour to accept of me for your servant; and what I want in Language, my industrious observance, and diligent service shall supply; I am a Gentleman, my breeding hath been according to my birth, and my Estate is sufficient to maintain me according to both; As for your Estate, I consider it not, for were you so poor of fortunes goods, as you had nothing to maintain you, but what your merit might challenge out of every purse; yet if you were mine, I should esteem you richer than the whole World, and I should love you, as Saints love Heaven, and adore you equal to a Dietie; for I saw so much sweetness of nature, nobleness of soul, purity of thoughts, and innocency of life, thorough your Bashfull countenance, as my soul is wedded thereunto, and my mind so restless; therefore, that unless I may have hopes to injoy you for my Wife; I shall dye,

Your distracted Servant,
SERIOUS DUMB.

LADY BASHFULL. Now *Reformer,* what say you to this Letter?

REFORMER. I say it is a good honest, hearty affectionate Letter, and upon my life, it is the Gentleman I commended so; he that looked so seriously on you; and your Ladyship may remember, I said he viewed you, as if he would have looked you thorough, and you made answer, that you wished he could, that he might see you were not so simple, as your behaviour made you appear, and now your wish is absolved.

LADY BASHFULL. What counsel will you give me in this cause?

REFORMER. Why? write him a civil answer.

LADY BASHFULL. Why should I hold corespondence with any man, either by Letter, or any other way, since I do not intend to marry.

REFORMER. Not marry?

LADY BASHFULL. No, not marry.

REFORMER. Why so?

LADY BASHFULL. Because I am now Mistriss of my self, and fortunes, and have a free liberty; and who that is free, if they be wise, will make themselves slaves, subjecting themselves to anothers humour, unless they were fools, or mad, and knew not how to chose the best and happiest life.

REFORMER. You will change this opinion, and marry, I dare swear.

LADY BASHFULL. Indeed I will not swear, but I think I shall not, for I love an easie, peaceable and solitary life, which none injoys but single persons; for in marriage, the life is disturbed with noise and company, troublesome imployments, vex'd with crosses, and restless with cares; Besides, I could not indure to have Parteners to share of him, whom my affections had set a price upon, or my merit, or beauty, or wealth, or vertue had bought.

REFORMER. So, I perceive you would be jealouse, if you were married.

LADY BASHFULL. Perchance I might have reason, but to prevent all inconveniences, and discontents, I will live a single life.

REFORMER. Do what likes you best, for I dare not perswade you any way, for fear my advice should not prove to the best.

Exeunt.

Scene 18

Enter AFFECTIONATA, *and* FOSTER TRUSTY.

FOSTER TRUSTY. Now you are placed according to your desire, what wil you command me to do?

AFFECTIONATA. Dear *Foster* Father, although I am loth to part from you, yet by reason I shall suffer in my estate, I must intreat you to return home, for my Nurse your wife, hath not skill to manage the fortune my Father left me; for she knows not how to let Leases, to set Lands, to receive Rents, to repair Ruins, to disburst Charges, and to order those affairs as they should be ordered; which your knowledge, industry and wisdom will dispose and order for my advantage.

FOSTER TRUSTY. But how if you be discovered.

AFFECTIONATA. Why, if I should, as I hope I shall not, yet the *Lord Singularity* is so noble a person, as he will neither use me uncivily, nor cruelly.

FOSTER TRUSTY. All that I fear, if you should be discovered, he should use you too civilly.

AFFECTIONATA. That were to use me rudely, which I am confident he will not do, and I am confident that you do believe I will receive no more civillity (if you call it so) than what honour will allow and approve of.

FOSTER TRUSTY. But jealousie will creep into the most confident breasts sometimes, yet I dare trust you, though I fear him.

AFFECTIONATA. I hope there is no cause to fear him, or doubt me, wherefore dear Father, let us go and settle our affairs here, that you may return home to order those there.

Scene 19

Enter Sir PEACEABLE STUDIOUS, *and the Lady* IGNORANCE *his Wife, She being undrest, her mantle about her, as being not well.*

SIR P. STUDIOUS. In truth wife, it is a great misfortune you should be sick this Term-time, when the Society is so much increast, as it is become a little Common-wealth.

LADY IGNORANCE. If there be so many, they may the better spare me.

SIR P. STUDIOUS. 'Tis true, they can spare your company, but how can you want their companies.

LADY IGNORANCE. You shall be my Intelligencer of their pastimes.

SIR P. STUDIOUS. That I will wife, but it will be but a dull recreation, only to hear a bare relation.

LADY IGNORANCE. As long as you partake of their present pleasures, and pleasant actions, what need you take care of me.

SIR P. STUDIOUS. Yes, but I must in Justice, for since you have cured me of my studious Lethargie, I ought to do my indeavour to divert your melancholly; and there is no such remedy as the Society; wherefore dear wife, fling off this melancholly sickness, or sick melancholly, and go amongst them; for surely your sickness is in your mind, not in your body.

She cries.

SIR P. STUDIOUS. What, do you cry Wife, who hath angered you?

LADY IGNORANCE. Why you.

SIR P. STUDIOUS. Who, I anger'd you! why I would not anger a woman, no, not my Wife for the whole World, If I could possible avoid it, which I fear cannot be avoided, for if I should please one of your Sex, I should be sure to displease another:—But that is my comfort, it is not my fault; but dear Wife, how have I offended you.

LADY IGNORANCE. Why did you kiss my maid before my face.

SIR P. STUDIOUS. Why did you perswade me.

LADY IGNORANCE. Did I perswade you to kiss my maid.

SIR P. STUDIOUS. No, but you did perswade me to be one of the Society, and there is kissing, and I though it was as well to kiss your maid before your face, as a sociable Lady before your face.

LADY IGNORANCE. And why do you make love to the Ladies, since I suffer none to make love to me.

SIR P. STUDIOUS. No, for if you did, I would fling you to death, to be imbraced in his cold arms; Besides, those actions that are allowable and seemly, as manly in men, are condemned in women, as immodest, and unbecoming, and dishonourable; but talking to you, I shall miss of the pleasant sports, and therefore, if you will go, come, the Coach is ready.

LADY IGNORANCE. No, I will not go.

SIR P. STUDIOUS. Then I will go without you.

LADY IGNORANCE. No, pray Husband go no more thither.

SIR P. STUDIOUS. How! not to go? nor to go no more, would you desire {disswade} me from that which you perswaded me to; Nay, so much as I could never be quiet, disturbing my harmless studies, and happy mind, crossing my pleasing thoughts with complaining words, but I perceive you grow jealouse, and now you are acquainted, you have no more use of me, but would be glad to quit my company, that you may be free abroad.

LADY IGNORANCE. No Husband, truly I will never go abroad, but will in-ancor* my self in my own house, so you will stay at home, and be as you were before, for I see my own follies, and am ashamed of my self, that you should prove me such a fool.

SIR P. STUDIOUS. Do you think me so wise and temperate a man, as I can on a sudden quit vain pleasures, and lawfull follies.

LADY IGNORANCE. Yes, or else you have studied to little purpose.

SIR P. STUDIOUS. Well, for this day I will stay at home, and for the future-time I will consider.

Exeunt.

Scene 20

Enter two Servants of the Generals.

1. SERVANT. This boy that came but the other day, hath got more of my Lords affection, than we that have served him this many years.

2. SERVANT. New-comers are alwaies more favoured than old waiters; for Masters regards old Servants no more, than the Imagerie in an old suit of Hangings, which are grown threed-bare with time, and out of fashion with change; Besides, new Servants are more industrious and diligent than old; but when he hath been here a little while, he will be as lazie as the rest, and then he will be as we are.

1. SERVANT. I perceive my Lord delights to hear him talk, for he will listen very a tentively to him, but when we offer to speak, he bids us to be silent.

---

* inancor] become an anchoret or anchoress, a holy hermit usually "anchored" to a particular sanctuary.

2. SERVANT. I wonder he should, for when we speak, it is with gravity, and our discourse is sententious, but his is meer squibs.*

Enter AFFECTIONATA.

AFFECTIONATA. Gentlemen, my Lord would have one of you to come to him.

1. SERVANT. Why, I thought you could supply all our places, for when you are with him, he seems to have no use of us.

AFFECTIONATA. It shall not be for want of will, but ability, if I do not serve him in every honest office.

1. SERVANT. So you will make some of us knaves.

AFFECTIONATA. I cannot make you knaves, unless you be willing to be knaves your selves.

2. SERVANT. What, do you call me knave?

AFFECTIONATA. I do not call you so.

Ex.

2. SERVANT. Well, I will be revenged, if I live.

Ex.

Scene 21

Enter the Lady BASHFULL, *and* REFORMER *her woman.*

REFORMER. Madam, I have inquired what this Sir *Serious Dumb* is, and 'tis said he is one of the finest Gentlemen in this Kingdom, and that his valour hath been proved in the wars, and that he is one that is very active and dexterous in all manly exercises, as riding, fencing, vaulting, swimming, and the like, Also that he is full of inventions, and a rare Poet, and that he hath a great Estate, only that he is dumb, and hath been so this twelve years and upwards.

LADY BASHFULL. *Reformer.* What makes you so industrious to inquire after him, surely thou art in love withim.

REFORMER. In my conscience I liked him very well, when he was to see you.

LADY BASHFULL. The truth is, he cannot weary you with words, nor anger you in his discourse, but pray do not inquire after him, nor speak of him; for people will think I have some designe of marriage.

REFORMER. I shall obey you, Madam.

Exeunt.

Scene 22

Enter the Lord SINGULARITY, *and* AFFECTIONATA. *He strokes* AFFECTIONATA*'s head.*

---

* squibs] firecrackers.

LORD SINGULARITY. *Affectionata,* Thou art one of the diligent'st boys that {ever I} had.

AFFECTIONATA. How can I be otherwise, Sir, since you are the Governour of my soul, that commands the Fort of my passion, and the Castle of my imaginations, which are the heart, and the head.

LORD SINGULARITY. Do you love me so much?

AFFECTIONATA. So well my Lord, as you are the archetectour of my mind, the foundation of my thoughts, and the gates of my memorie, for your will is the form, your happiness the level,* and your actions the treasurie.

LORD SINGULARITY. Thy wit delights me more, than thy flattery perswades; for I cannot believe a boy can love so much; Besides, you have not served me so long, as to beget love.

AFFECTIONATA. I have loved you from my infancy, for as I suck'd life from my Nurses breath, so did I love from fames, drawing your praises forth, as I did milk, which nourished my affections.

LORD SINGULARITY. I shall strive, boy, to requite thy love.

AFFECTIONATA. To requite, is to return love for love.

LORD SINGULARITY. By Heaven? I love thee, as a Father loves a son.

AFFECTIONATA. Then I am blest,

Exeunt.

Scene 23

Enter two Souldiers.

1. SOULDIER. What is this boy that our General is so taken with.

2. SOULDIER. A poor Begger-boy!

1. SOULDIER. Can a poor Begger-boy merit his affections?

2. SOULDIER. He is a pretty boy, and waites very diligently.

1. SOULDIER. So doth other boys, as well as he, but I believe he is a young Pimp, and carries, and conveys Love-letters.

2. SOULDIER. Like enough to, for boys are strangely crafty in those imploy-ments, and so industrious, as they will let no times nor opportunities slip them, but they will find waies to deliver their Letters and messages.

Exeunt.

Scene 24

Enter the Lady BASHFULLS *Page, and Sir* SERIOUS DUMB, *who gives a Note to the Page to read.*

---

* level] a flat tract of land suitable for building; Cavendish makes a pun on moral standard.

PAGE. Sir, I dare not direct you to my Lady, as you desire me in this Note, and if I should tell her, here is a Gentleman that desired to visit her, she would refuse your visit.

DUMB *gives the young Page four or five pieces of Gold.*

PAGE. I will direct you to the room wherein my Lady is, but I must not be seen, nor confess I shewed you the way.

Page, and Sir SERIOUS DUMB *Exeunt.*

Scene 25

Enter the Lord SINGULARITY, *and* AFFECTIONATA.

LORD SINGULARITY. Come *Affectionata,* sit down and entertain me with thy sweet discourse, which makes all other company troublesome, and tedious to me, thine only doth delight me.

AFFECTIONATA. My Noble Lord? I wish the plat-form of my brain were a Garden of wit, and then perchance my tongue might present your Excellencies with a Posie of flowery Rhethorick, but my poor brain is barren, wanting the {maturity of time; yet what it doth afford, although but bracks or mosse; if you command, I shall present them to you.}

LORD SINGULARITY. Thou hast an eloquent tongue, (and a gentle soul.)

AFFECTIONATA. My Noble Lord, I have hardly learn'd my native words, much less the eloquence of Language, and as for the souls of all mankind, they are like Common-wealths, where the several vertues, and the good graces are the Citizens therein, and the natural subjects thereof; but vices and follies, as thievish Borderers, and Neighbour-enemies, which makes inrodes, factions, mutinies, intrudes and usurps Authority, and if the follies be more than the good graces, and the vices too strong for the vertues, the Monarchy of a good life falls to ruine, also it is indangered by Civil-wars amongst the passions.

LORD SINGULARITY. What passions indangers it most?

AFFECTIONATA. Anger, malice, and despair.

LORD SINGULARITY. Were you never angry?

AFFECTIONATA. I am of too melancholly a nature, to be very angry.

LORD SINGULARITY. Why? Are melancholly persons never angry?

AFFECTIONATA. Very seldom, my Lord, for those that are naturally melancholly, doth rather grieve, than fret, they sooner wast into sighes, than fly about with fury; more tears flows thorough their eyes, than words pass thorough their lips.

LORD SINGULARITY. Why should you be melancholly?

AFFECTIONATA. Alas, nature hath made me so; Besides, I find there is not much reason to joy, for what we love, perchance it loves not us, and if it doth, we cannot keep it long, for pleasures passeth like a dream; when pains doth stay, as if eternal were.

LORD SINGULARITY. Thou art composed with such harmonie, as thy discourse is as delightfull musick, wherein the soul takes pleasure.

Exeunt.

Scene 26

Enter the Lady BASHFULL, *Sir* SERIOUS DUMB *following her, where* REFORMER *her Woman meets them.*

REFORMER. Madam, now the Gentleman is here, you must use him civilly, and not strive to run away from him, wherefore pray turn, and entertain him.

The Lady BASHFULL *turns to him, but is so out of countenance, and trembles so much, as she cannot speak, but stands still and mute; All the while he fixes his eyes upon her.*

REFORMER. Pray speak to him, Madam, and not stand trembling, as if you were like to fall.

LADY BASHFULL. My spirits is seized on by my bashfull and innocent fears, insomuch, as they have not strength to support my body without trembling.

REFORMER. Sweet Madam, try to speak to him?

LADY BASHFULL. Honourable Sir? give me leave to tell you, that my bashfullness doth smother the senses and reason in my brain, and chokes the words in my throat I should utter, but pray do not think it proceeds from crimes, but an imperfection of nature, which I have strove against, but cannot as yet rectifie.

Sir SERIOUS DUMB *Civily bows to her, then gives* REFORMER *his Table-book to read. She reads.*

Madam,

He hath writ here, that had his tongue liberty to speak, all that he could say, would be so far below, and inferiour to what might be said in your praise, as he should not adventure to presume to speak.

LADY BASHFULL. I will presume to break my brain, but I will invent some ways to be rid of his company.

He follows her, Exeunt.

ACT V

Scene 27

Enter the General, and sits in a melancholly posture. Enters AFFECTIONATA, *and stands with a sad countenance. The General sees him.*

LORD SINGULARITY. What makes thee look so sad, my boy?

AFFECTIONATA. To see you sit so melancholly.

LORD SINGUL. Clear up thy countenance, for its not a deadly melancholly, though it is a troublesome one.

AFFECTIONATA. May I be so bold to ask the cause of it.

LORD SINGUL. The cause is, a cruel Mistriss.

AFFECTIONATA. Have you a Mistriss, and can she be cruel?

LORD SINGULARITY. O! Women are Tyrants, they draw* us on to love, and then denies our suits.

AFFECTIONATA. Will not you think me rude, if I should question you?

LORD SINGUL. No, for thy questions delights me more, than my Mistriss denials grieves me.

AFFECTIONATA. Then give me leave to ask you, whether your suit be just.

LORD SINGUL. Just, to a Lovers desires.

AFFECTIONATA. What is your desire?

LORD SINGUL. To lye with her.

AFFECTIONATA. After you† have married her?

LORD SINGULARITY. Marry her saist thou, I had rather be banish'd from that Sex for ever, than to marry one, and yet I love them well.

AFFECTIONATA. Why have you such an adversion to marriage, being lawfull and honest.

LORD SINGUL. Because I am affraid to be a Cuckold!

AFFECTIONATA. Do you think there is no chaste women?

LORD SINGULARITY. Faith boy, I believe very few, and those that are men, knows not where to find them out, for all that are not married, professes chastity, speaks soberly, and looks modestly, but when they are marryed, they are more wild than *Bachalins,* far worse than *Satyres*‡ making their Husbands horns far greater than a Stags, having more branches sprouts thereon.

AFFECTIONATA. And doth he never cast those horns?

LORD SINGUL. Yes, if he be a Widower, he casts his horns, only the marks remains, otherwise he bears them to his grave.

---

* This read "daw" in the original.

† This read "yon" in the original; turned letters are common in early printed books.

‡ *Bachalins . . . Satyres*] Bacchanalians, worshipers of the god Bacchus, who celebrate their god in a drunken frenzy; satyres, mythic creatures, half man, half goat, and entirely horny, though not female as would be necessary in this context, since it is an unfaithful wife who gives her husband cuckold's horns.

AFFECTIONATA. But put the case you did know a woman that was chaste; would not you marry her?

LORD SINGUL. That is a question not to be resolved, for no man can be resolved, whether a woman can be chaste or not.

Affectionata fetches a great sighe.

Lord Singul. Why do you sighe, my boy?

AFFECTIONATA. Because all women are false, or thought to be so, that wise men dares not trust them.

LORD SINGULARITY. But they are fools, that will not try, and make use of them, if they can have them; wherefore I will go, and try my Mistriss once again.

Exeunt.

Scene 28

Enter the Lady IGNORANCE, *and her Maid. She hears a noise.*

LADY IGNORANCE. What a noise they make below, they will disturb my Husbands study; go and tell those of my Servants, that I will turn them away for their carelessness, as that they cannot place, set, or hold things sure, but let them fall to make such a noise.

MAID. I shall.

maid Ex.

LADY IGNORANCE. It shall be my study how to order my house without noise wherefore all my Servants shall be dumb, although not deaf, and I will take none, but such as have corns on their feet, that they may tread gently, and all my Houshold-vessel shall be of wood, for wood makes not such a noise when it chance to fall, or is hit against a wall, as metal doth, which rings like bells, when it is but touched, neither will I have Houshold-vessels of Earth, for earthen-pots, pans and the like; when they fall and break, sounds as if a stonewall fell.

Ex.

Scene 29

Enter the General, and three or four Commanders.

GENERAL. On my soul Gentlemen, the boy is an honest boy, and no wayes guilty of this you tax him for.

COMMANDERS. Pardon us, my Lord, for giving your Excellence notice that the States are jealouse of him for a Spie, but we do not any wayes accuse him.

GENERAL. Will the States examine him, say you?

COMMANDERS. So we hear, my Lord.

GENERAL. Well Gentlemen, pray leave me for this time, and I will take care the boy shall be forth-coming, whensoever the States shall require him.

COMMANDERS. Your Lordships humble Servants—

Commanders Ex. The General solus.

GENERAL. A Spie, it cannot be, for he is neither covetous, nor malicious, revengefull, nor irreligious, but I will try him.

Exit.

Scene 30

Enter the Lady BASHFULLS *Chamber-maid, and Mrs.* REFORMER *her Gentle-woman.*

CHAMBER-MAID. Mrs. *Reformer,* pray tell me who that handsome Gentleman is, which follows my Lady about?

REFORMER. He is one that is Noble, and Rich, and is in love with my Lady.

CHAMBER-MAID. Truly it is the strangest way of wooing, that ever was, for my Lady goeth blushing out of one room into another, and he follows her at the heels: In my conscience my Lady is ashamed to sit down, or to bid him leave her company, and surely they must needs be both very weary of walking, but sure he will leave her, when it is time to go to bed.

REFORMER. It is to be hoped he will.

Enter the Lady BASHFULL, *and Sir* SERIOUS DUMB *following her.*

REFORMER. Madam, you will tire your self and the Gentleman, with walking about your house; wherefore pray sit down.

LADY BASHFULL. What! To have him gaze upon my face.

REFORMER. Why, your face is a handsome face, and the owner of it is honest, wherefore you need not be ashamed, but pray rest your self.—

LADY BASHFULL. Pray perswade him to leave me, and then I will.

REFORMER. Sir, my Lady intreats you to leave her to her self.

Sir SERIOUS DUMB *writes then, and gives* REFORMER *his Table-book to read.*

REFORMER. He writes he cannot leave you, for if his body should depart, his soul will remain still with you.

LADY BASHFULL. That will not put me out of countenance, because I shall not be sensible of its presence, wherefore I am content he should leave his soul, so that he will take his body away.

He writes, and gives REFORMER *the Book.*

REFORMER *reads.* He writes, that if you will give him leave once a day to see you, that he will depart, and that he will not disturb your thoughts, he will only wait upon your person for the time he lives, he cannot keep himself long from you.

LADY BASHFULL. But I would be alone.

REFORMER. But if he will follow you, you must indure that with patience, you cannot avoid.

Sir SERIOUS DUMB *goeth to the Lady* BASHFULL, *and kisseth her hand, and Ex.*

REFORMER. You see he is so civil, as he is unwilling to displease you.

LADY BASHFULL. Rather than I will be troubled thus; I will go to some other parts of the World.

REFORMER. In my conscience, Madam, he will follow you, wheresoever you go.

LADY BASHFULL. But I will have him shut out of my house.

REFORMER. Then he will lye at your gates, and so all the Town will take notice of it.

LADY BASHFULL. Why so, they will howsoever, by his often visits.

REFORMER. But not so publick.

Exeunt.

Scene 31

Enter the GENERAL, *and* AFFECTIONATA.

LORD SINGULARITY. *Affectionata.* Thou must carry a Letter from me, to my Mistriss.

AFFECTIONATA. You will not marry her, you say.

LORD SINGUL. No.

AFFECTIONATA. Then pardon me, my Lord, for though I would assist your honest love by any service I can do, yet I shall never be so base an Instrument, as to produce a crime.

LORD SINGUL. Come, come, thou shalt carry it, and I will give thee 500. pounds for thy service.

AFFECTIONATA. Excuse me, my Lord.

LORD SINGULARITY. I will give thee a thousand pounds.

AFFECTIONATA. I shall not take it, my Lord.

LORD SINGUL. I will give thee five thousand, nay ten thousand pounds.

AFFECTIONATA. I am not covetous, my Lord.

LORD SINGULARITY. Will make thee Master of my whole Estate, for without thy assistance, I cannot injoy my Mistris, by reason she will trust none with our Loves, but thee.

AFFECTIONATA. Could you make me Master of the whole World, it could not tempt me to do an action base, for though I am poor, I am honest, and so honest, as I cannot be corrupted, or bribed there-from.

LORD SINGULARITY. You said you loved me?

AFFECTIONATA. Heaven knows I do above my life, and would do any service that honour did allow of.

LORD SINGULARITY. You are more scrupulous than wise.

AFFECTIONATA. There is an old saying, my Lord, that to be wise, is to be honest. *Exeunt.*

Scene 32

Enter Sir PEACEABLE STUDIOUS, *And meets his Ladies maid.*

SIR P. STUDIOUS. Where is your Lady?

MAID. In her Chamber, Sir.

SIR P. STUDIOUS. Pray her to come to me?

MAID. Yes Sir.

Sir P. Studious Exit. Enter another Maid to the first.

1. MAID. Lord, Lord! What a creature my Master has become, since he fell into his musing again, he looks like a melancholly Ghost, that walks in the shades of Moon-shine, or if there be no Ghost, such as we fancie, just such a one seems her {he}, when a week since, he was as fine a Gentleman as one should see amongst a thousand.

2. MAID. That was because he kiss'd you, *Nan.*

1. MAID. Faith it was but a dull clownish part, to meet a Maid that is not ill-favoured, and not make much of her, who perchance have watch'd to meet him, for which he might have clap'd her on the cheek, or have chuck'd her under the chin, or have kiss'd her, but to do or say nothing, but bid me call my Lady, was such a churlish part? Besides, it seemed neither manly, gallantly, nor civilly.

2. MAID. But it shewed him temperate and wise, not minding such frivilous and troublesome creatures as women are.

1. MAID. Prithy, it shews him to be a miserable, proud, dull fool.

2. MAID. Peace, some body will hear you, and then you will be turn'd away.

1. MAID. I care not, for if they will not turn me away, I will turn my self away, and seek another service, for I hate to live in the house with a Stoick.*

Scene 33

Enter the GENERAL, *and* AFFECTIONATA.

AFFECTIONATA. By your face, Sir, there seems a trouble in your mind, and I am restless until I know your griefs.

---

* Stoick] one who lives very simply; the term is derived from an ancient Greek philosophy that emphasizes restraint and self-denial.

LORD SINGULARITY. It is a secret I dare not trust the aire with!

AFFECTIONATA. I shall be more secret than the aire, for the aire is apt to divulge by retorting Echoes* back, but I shall be as silent as the Grave.

LORD SINGUL. But you may be tortured to confess the truth.

AFFECTIONATA. But I will not confess the truth, if the confession may any wayes hurt, or disadvantage you; for though I will not belye truth by speaking falsely, yet I will conceal a truth, rather than betray a friend. Especially, my Lord and Master: But howsoever, since your trouble is of such concern, I shall not wish to know it, for though I dare trust my self, yet perchance you dare not trust me, but if my honest fidelity can serve you any wayes, you may imploy it, and if it be to keep a secret, all the torment that nature hath made, or art invented, shall never draw it from me.

LORD SINGUL. Then let me tell thee, that to conceal it, would damn thy soul.

AFFECTIONATA. Heaven bless me! But sure, my Lord, you cannot be guilty of such sins, that those that doth barely hear, or know them shall be damned.

LORD SINGUL. But to conceal them, is to be an Actor.

AFFECTIONATA. For Heaven sake then keep them close from me, if either they be base or wicked, for though love prompt me to inquire, hoping to give you ease in bearing part of the burthen, yet Heaven knows, I thought my love so honourable placed on such a worthy person, and guiltless soul, as I might love and serve without a scandal, or a deadly sin.

LORD SINGULARITY. Come, you shall know it.

AFFECTIONATA. I'l rather stop my ears with death.

LORD SINGUL. Go, thou art a false boy.

AFFECTIONATA. How false a boy howsoever you think me, I have an honest soul and heart that is ready to serve you in any honest way, but since I am deceived, and couzened into love by false reports, finding the best of mankind basely wicked, and all the World so bad, that praise nothing good, and strives to poyson vertue; I will inancor my self, and live on Antidotes of prayers, for fear of the infection.

LORD SINGUL. And will not you pray for me?

AFFECTIONATA. I cannot chose, my Lord, for gratitude inforces me; First, because I have loved you, next because I have served you; and give me leave to kiss your hand, and then there drop some tears at my departure.

Weeping kneels down, and kisses his† hand.

---

* This was spelled "Ecohes" in the original.
† This read "her" in the original.

LORD SINGULARITY. Rise, you must not go away untill you have cleared your
self from being a spie.
AFFECTIONATA. I fear no accusations.
Exeunt.

Finis

The Second Part of *Loves Adventures*

THE LORD SINGULARITY

SIR SERIOUS DUMB

SIR TIMOTHY COMPLIMENT

SIR HUMPHRY BOLD

SIR ROGER EXCEPTION

SIR PEACEABLE STUDIOUS

FOSTER TRUSTY

COLLONELS, CAPTAINS, LIEUTEN-
ANTS AND CORPORALS

PETITIONERS

OFFICERS. MESSENGERS

JUDGES. JURIES

SERVANTS

THE LADY ORPHANT

LADY BASHFULL

LADY IGNORANCE

LADY WAGTAIL

LADY AMOROUS

NURSE FONDLY

MISTRISS REFORMER, LADY
BASHFULLS WOMAN

CHAMBER-MAIDS

EPILOGUE*

Noble Spectators, you have spent this day;
Not only for to see, but judge our Play:
Our Authoress *sayes, she thinks her Play is good,*
If not, 'tis none of her fault, for she writ
The Acts, *the* Scenes, *the* Language *and the* Wit;
Wherefore she sayes, that she is not your Debtor;
But you are hers, until you write a better;
Of even terms to be she understands
Impossible, except you clap your hands.

---

* An epilogue usually comes at the end of a play, and judging from the language of this one, it was probably meant to.

The Second Part

ACT I

Scene 1

Enter the Lady BASHFULLS *Chamber-maid, and Mrs.* REFORMER *her woman.*

REFORMER. This dumb Lover is the most diligent'st servant that ever was, and methinks my Lady is somewhat more confident than she was; for she will sit and read whilst he sits by.

MAID. Doth she read to him?

REFORMER. No, she reads to herself.

MAID. There comes abundance of Gallants to visit my Lady every day, and they have all one answer, that is, she is not willing to receive visits, and they all go civilly away, unless Sir Humphry Bold and he rails horribly.

REFORMER. I have received from several Gentlemen, above 20. Letters a day, and as fast as they come, she makes me burn them.

MAID. But she reads them first.

REFORMER. No, I read them to her.

MAID. And doth she answer all those Letters?

REFORMER. She never answered one in her life, and I dare swear, she never will.

The Lady BASHFULL *calls, from another Room.*

REFORMER. Madam!—

Exeunt.

Scene 2

Enter the Lord SINGULARITY, *and* AFFECTIONATA.

LORD SINGULARITY. *Affectionata,* Hast thou forgiven me my fault of doubting of thy vertue, so much as to put it to a Tryal.

AFFECTIONATA. My Noble Lord; have you forgiven my facility and wavering faith that could so easily, and in so short a time believe you could be wicked, although you did accuse your self.

LORD SINGULARITY. Nay *Affectionata,* I did not accuse my self, though I did try thee.

AFFECTIONATA. Then I have committed a treble fault through my mistake, which requires a treble forgiveness.

LORD SINGULARITY. Thou art so vertuous, thou canst not commit a fault, and therefore needs no forgiveness.

Exeunt.

Scene 3

Enter the Lady WAGTAIL, *and Sir* HUMPHRY BOLD.

SIR HUMPHRY BOLD. Madam, You have been pleased to profess a friendship to me, and I shall desire you will do a friendly part for me.

LADY WAGTAIL. Any thing that lyes in my power, good Sir *Humphry Bold*.

SIR HUMPHRY BOLD. Then pray, Madam, speak to the Lady Bashfull in my behalf, that I may be her Husband.

LADY WAGTAIL. I will Sir *Humphry,* but she is bashfull, yet I was there Yesterday, and she entertained me indifferently well, but seemed to be wonderfull coy; but howsoever I will do my poor indeavour, Sir *Humphry.*

SIR HUMPHRY BOLD. Pray do, Madam.

Exeunt.

Scene 4

Enter AFFECTIONATA, *walking in a melancholly posture; his Hat pulled over his brows, and his arms inter-folded; To him enters the Lord* SINGULARITY.

LORD SINGULARITY. My *Affectionata,* Why walks thou so melancholly?

He pulls of his Hat to his Lord, and Bows.

AFFECTIONATA. The cause is not that I lye under aspersion, by reason I lye not under a crime; But truly, my Lord, I am troubled that I am threatened to be tormented, for I would not willingly indure pain, though I could willingly receive death; but as for the aspersions, I am no wayes concerned; for I make no question, but my honest life, my just actions, and the truth of my words, will so clear me at the last, as I shall appear as innocent to the World, as Angels doth in Heaven.

LORD SINGULARITY. Comfort your self, for I will rather suffer death, than you shall suffer pain.

AFFECTIONATA. Heaven defend you, my Lord, whatsoever I suffer,

Ex.

Scene 5

Enter the Lady WAGTAIL, *and Mistriss* REFORMER.

LADY WAGTAIL. Pray Mistriss *Reformer,* be Sir *Humphry Bold*'s friend to thy Lady, and I protest to thee, he shall be thy friend, as long as he and you live, and I do not see any reason your Lady should refuse him; for he is both as proper and stout a man, as any is living this day in the Land.

REFORMER. Indeed Madam, I dare not mention it to my Lady, for she is so adverse against marriage, as she takes those for her enemies as doth but mention it.

LADY WAGTAIL. Then surely she is not a woman, for there is none of the effeminate Sex, but takes it for a disgrace to live an old maid, and rather than dye one, they will marry any man that will have them; and the very fear of not marrying, is so terrible to them, as whilst they are so young, as they are not fit to make wives, they will miserably cast away themselves to the first that makes a proffer, although they be poor, base or mean, rather than venture to try out their fortunes.

REFORMER. But my Lady is not of that humour.

LADY WAGTAIL. Come, come, I know thou canst perswade thy Lady if thou wouldst, and if you will, Sir *Humphry Bold* will give thee 500 *l.** to buy thee a Husband, for thou hast lived too long a maid I faith.

REFORMER. I am not a maid, Madam, I am a widow.

LADY WAGTAIL. What, a musty widow!

REFORMER. I know not whether I am musty, but I am a widow.

LADY WAGTAIL. Let mee tell thee, that it is as great a disgrace to live a widow, as an old maid; wherefore take thee 500 *l.* to get thee a second Husband.

REFORMER. Truly I would not sell my Lady for all the World, much less for 500 *l.*, neither would I marry again, if I were young, and might have my choyce.

LADY WAGTAIL. Lord bless me, and send me out of this house, least it should infect me; for let me tell thee, were my Husband dead to morrow, I would marry the day after his Funeral, if I could get any man to marry me, and so I would serve 20. Husbands one after another.

REFORMER. Your best way were to have 20. Husbands at one time, so that your Ladyship might not be a day without.

LADY WAGTAIL. O fie! If women might have twenty Husbands, they would have no room for courtly Servants; but prithy help Sir *Humphry Bold,* and take his offer, and let me speak with the Lady my self.

REFORMER. That your Ladyship cannot at this time, for my Lady is not well.

LADY WAGTAIL. Then pray remember my most humble service, and tell her, I will come to morrow, and if she be sick, I will talk her well.

LADY WAGTAIL *Ex.* REFORMER *alone.*

REFORMER. Dead you would talk her, for thou hast an endless tongue; Oh! what man is so miserable that is her Husband.

REFORMER *Exit.*

* *l.*] pounds.

Scene 6

Enter two or three Commanders.

1. COMMANDER. It is reported that our Generals Page hath behaved himself so handsomly, spoke so wittily, defended his cause so prudently, declared his innocence so clearly, and carried his business so wisely, as the *Venetian* States have not only quitted him freely, but doth applaud him wonderfully, extolls him highly, and offers him any satisfaction for the injurie and disgrace that hath been done him; but he only desires, that the man that had accused him, which man, was one of the Generals men, should be pardoned, and not punished.

2. COMMANDER. I hope our General is well pleased, that his beloved boy is not only cleared, but applauded.

1. COMMANDER. O! He doth nothing but imbrace him, and kiss him, as if he were his only son, yet he did gently chide him that he asked pardon for his accusers; for said he, if all false accusers should be pardoned, no honest man would escape free from censure.

3. COMMANDER. But I hear the States have given order to our General to meet the *Turkes* again, for it is reported by intelligences that they have recruited into a numerous body.

2. COMMANDER. Faith I think the *Turkes* are like the tale of the Gyant, that when his head was cut off there rise two in the place.

1. COMMANDER. I think they are like the vegetable that is named threefold, the more it is cut the faster it growes.*

3. COMMANDER. I would the Devil had them for me.

2. COMMANDER. We do what we can to send them to Hell; but whether they will quit thee, I cannot tell.

Exeunt.

Scene 7

Enter the Lord General, and AFFECTIONATA.

LORD SINGULARITY. My *Affectionata* I wonder you could suffer an accusation so patiently knowing you were accused falsly.

AFFECTIONATA. The clearnesse of my innocency needed not the fury of a violent passion to defend it, neither could passion have rectified an injury.

---

* tale of the Gyant . . . growes] images from folktales, though the giant may be related to the Hydra of Greek mythology, killed by the hero Hercules as the second of twelve almost impossible labors.

LORD SINGULARITY. Tis true, yet passion is apt to rise in defence of innocency, and honour.

AFFECTIONATA. And many times passion (my Lord) destroyes the life in striving to maintain the truth, and defend the innocent; but I find a passionate sorrow that your Lordship must go to indanger your life in the warrs again.

LORD SINGULARITY. The warrs is pastime to me, for I hate idleness, and no imployment pleases me better than fighting, so it be in a good cause; but you shall stay.

AFFECTIONATA. Why my Lord, are you weary of my service?

LORD SINGUL. Know I am carefull of thy safety, thy rest and peace, for shouldst thou not come near danger, yet the very tragical aspect will terrefie thee to death, thou art of so tender a nature, so soft and sweet a disposition.

AFFECTIONATA. Truly my Lord, if you leave me behind you, the very fear of your life will kill me, where if your Lordship* will let me go, love will give me courage.

LORD SINGUL. Then let me tell you, you must not go, for I have adopted you my Son, and I have setled all my Estate upon thee, where, if I am killed, you shall be my Heir, for I had rather vertue should inherit my Estate than birth; yet I charge thee take my Name upon thee, as well as my Estate unto thee.

AFFECTIONATA. My noble Lord, I should be prouder to bear your name, than to be Master of the whole World, but I shall never be so base to keep my self in safety, in hope of your Estate, wherefore must intreat your leave to go with you.

LORD SINGUL. I will not give you leave, but command you to the contrary, which is to stay.

AFFECTIONATA. I cannot obey you in this, for love will force me to run after you.

LORD SINGUL. I will have you lash'd, if you offer to go.

AFFECTIONATA. Stripes cannot stay me!

LORD SINGUL. I will have you tyed, and kept by force.

AFFECTIONATA. By Heaven, my Lord, i'l tear my flesh, and break my bones to get lose, and if I have not legs to run, i'l creep thorough the Earth like worms, for though I shall move but slowly, yet it will be a satisfaction to my soul, that I am travelling after you.

LORD SINGULARITY. *Affectionata,* You anger me very much.

AFFECTIONATA. Indeed my Lord, you grieve me more than I can anger you.

---

* This read "Lordyship" in the original.

AFFECTIONATA *weeps.*

LORD SINGULARITY. What, do you crie! and yet desire to be a souldier?

AFFECTIONATA. A valiant heart, my Lord, may have a weeping eye to keep it company.

LORD SINGULARITY. If no perswasion can stay you, you must go along with me.

AFFECTIONATA *bows, as giving his Lord thanks. Exeunt.*

Scene 8

Enter the Lady WAGTAIL, *the Lady* AMOROUS, *Sir* HUMPHRY BOLD, *Sir* TIMOTHY COMPLIMENT, *to the Lady* BASHFULL, *who hangs down her head, as out of countenance.*

LADY WAGTAIL. Faith Lady *Bashfull*, we will have you abroad to Balls and publick meetings, to learn you a confident behaviour, and a bold speech; Fie! You must not be bashfull.

LADY AMOROUS. Our visiting her sometimes, hath made her so, as she is not altogether so bashfull as she was.

Enter Sir SERIOUS DUMB, *who bows first to the Lady* BASHFULL, *then to the rest of the Company, and then goeth behind the Lady* BASHFULL, *and stands close by Mistriss* REFORMER.

LADY AMOROUS. Surely Sir *Serious Dumb* is a domestick servant here, he stands and waits as one.

He bows with an aknowledging face.

SIR HUMPHRY BOLD. If she wil entertain such servants as he, she is not so modest as she appears. Lady, perchance if I had come privately alone, I had been entertained with more freedom, and not have had my suit denied, and my person neglected with scorn, and he received with respect.

Sir SERIOUS DUMB *comes and gives him a box on the eare, they both draw their swords, all the women runs away squeeking, only the Lady* BASHFULL *stayes, and runs betwixt their swords, and parts them; Sir* TIMOTHY COMPLIMENT *looks on as affraid to stir.*

LADY BASHFULL. For Heaven sake! fight not here, to affright me with your quarrels.

SIR HUMPHRY BOLD. I will have his heart-bloud.

LADY BASHFULL. Good Sir *Serious Dumb*, and Sir *Humphry Bold*, leave off fighting.

Sir SERIOUS DUMB *draws back.*

LADY BASHFULL. Pray Sir *Humphry Bold*, give me your sword, that I may be sure you will not fight.

SIR HUMPHRY BOLD. What, yield my sword up! I will dye first.

Enter the Ladies again. All speak at one time, who is kill'd, who is kill'd.

Sir HUMPHRY BOLD *presses towards Sir* SERIOUS DUMB.

LADY BASHFULL. Good Ladies, hold Sir *Humphry Bold*, and I will try to perswade Sir *Serious Dumb.*

They hold Sir HUMPHRY BOLD.

LADY WAGTAIL. What, you shall not stir, I am sure you will not oppose us women.

LADY BASHFULL. Noble Sir, to give me an assurance you will not fight, give me your sword.

Sir SERIOUS DUMB *kisses the hilt of his sword, then gives it her.*

Sir HUMPHRY BOLD *gets lose from the Ladies, and goeth to assault Sir* SERIOUS DUMB; *He being unarmed, the Lady* BASHFULL *seeing him, steps betwixt them, and with Sir* SERIOUS DUMB's *sword, strikes at Sir* HUMPHRY BOLD, *and stikes his sword out of his hand.*

LADY BASHFULL. What, are you not ashamed to assault an unarmed man.

Sir HUMPHRY BOLD *runs to take up his sword, she also runs and sets her foot upon it.*

LADY BASHFULL. Let the sword alone, for it is my prize; and by Heaven, if you touch it, I will run you thorough with this sword in my hand.

Sir HUMPHRY BOLD *runs, and catcheth Sir* TIMOTHY COMPLIMENTS *sword, and offers to make a thrust at Sir* SERIOUS DUMB, *who puts the sword by, and beats it down with one hand, and with the other strikes it aside, then closes with him, and being skillfull at Wrestling trips up his heels, then gets upon him and having both his hands at liberty, wrings out Sir* Humphry Bold's *sword out of his hand, then ariseth and gives the sword to the right owner, who all the time trembled for fear,* The women in the mean time squeeks. *and never durst strive to part them.*

SIR HUMPHRY BOLD. Hell take me, but I will be revenged: Lady, I hope you will give me my sword again.

LADY BASHFULL. Never to fight against a woman, but my victorious spoils, I will deliver to this gallant Gentleman, who delivered up his life and honour into my hand, when he gave me his sword, and I indangered the loss of both by taking it, for which my gratitude hath nothing to return him but my self and my fortunes, if he please to accept of that and me.

Sir SERIOUS DUMB *bows with respect, and kisses her hand.*

LADY BASHFULL. Sir, I wish my person were more beautifull than it is, for your sake, and my fortune greater, with more certainty of continuance, as neither

being subject to time or accident, but this certainly I promise you, which is,
my chaste and honest life; Now Sir, pray take these two
swords, this was yours, fear gave me confidence, this I won,
love gave me courage.

Gives him the two swords.

Sir SERIOUS DUMB *leads out his Mistriss. Exit.*

SIR HUMPHRY BOLD. I will be revenged.

Omnes Exeunt.

ACT II

Scene 9

Enter the Lord General, and AFFECTIONATA.

LORD SINGUL. *Affectionata,* I hear thou has brought Arms, I am sure thou canst
not fight.

AFFECTIONATA. I am sure I will do my indeavour, my Lord.

LORD SINGULARITY. Why, the very weight of thy Arms will sink thee down.

AFFECTIONATA. O no, my Lord, my desire shall bear them up.

LORD SINGUL. Alas, thou hast no strength to fight?

AFFECTIONATA. What strength my active body wants, my vigorous spirits shall
make good.

LORD SINGUL. Prethee, my boy, do not adventure thy self, but stay in my Tent.

AFFECTIONATA. That would be a shame for me, and a dishonour to you, since`
you have adopted me your son, wherefore the World shall never say, you
have bestowed your favour and your love upon a coward.

LORD SINGULARITY. I well perceive I have adopted a very willful boy?

AFFECTIONATA. Indeed, my Lord, I have no will, but what doth follow you.

The General Strokes AFFECTIONATA *on the cheek. Exeunt.*

Scene 10

Enter Sir SERIOUS DUMB, *and his Mistriss the Lady* BASHFULL.

SIR SERIOUS DUMB. The time I vowed to silence is expir'd, and though my
thoughts not gloriously attired with Eloquence, for Rhetorick I have none,
yet civil words, fit for to wait upon a modest Lady, and to entertain an honest
mind with words of truth, though plain? For 'tis not Rhetorick makes a
happy life, but sweet society, that's void of strife.

LADY BASHFULL. Sir, Rhetorick is rather for sound than sense, for words than
reason.

SIR SERIOUS DUMB. Yet my sweet Mistriss, I wish my voice were tune to your eare, and every word set as a pleasing note to make such musick as might delight your mind.

LADY BASHFULL. Your words flow thorough my ears, as smooth, clear, pure, water from the spring of *Hellicon*,* which doth not only refresh, but inrich my dull insipid brain.

Scene 11

Enter a Captain and his Corporal.

CORPORAL. The Turks never received such a blow, as they have this time?

CAPTAIN. A pox of them, they have made us sweat?

CORPORAL. Why Captain, sweating will cure the Pox,† and though you curse the Turks, yet it is we that live in *Italy,* that is diseased with them.

CAPTAIN. The truth is, we lost more health in the *Venetian* service, than we gain wealth.

CORPORAL. Nay faith Captain, we do not only lose our health, but wast our wealth, for what booties we get from the Turks, the Courtezans gets from us.

CAPTAIN. For that cause now I have gotten a good bootie, I will return with mine own Country, and buy a—

CORPORAL. A what Captain?

CAPTAIN. An Office in civil Government.

CORPORAL. But you will never be civil in your Office.

CAPTAIN. That needs not to be, for though all Magisterial Offices bear civil Authority, yet the Officers and Magistrates therein, are more cruel and ravenous than common souldiers.

CORPORAL. Verily Captain, I think common Souldiers are more mercifull and just than they.

CAPTAIN. Verely Corporal, I think you will become a *Puritan* Preacher.

CORPORAL. Why should you think so, Captain.

CAPTAIN. First, because you have got the Pox, and that will make you Preach in their tone, which is, to speak thorough the nose; the next is, you have left the ranting Oaths that Souldiers use to swear, and use their phrases; as verily my beloved brethren, which brethrens souls, they care not for, nor thinks thereof, for though they speak to the brethren, they Preach to the sisters, which edifies wonderfully by their Doctrine, and they gain and receive as

---

* *Hellicon*] Helicon, a mountain in Boeotia, said to be sacred to the muses who inspire art and poetry.

† Pox] syphilis, which causes eruptions that pit the skin as smallpox does.

wonderfull from their female flocks, for those *Puritan* Preachers have more Tithes out of the Marriage-bed, than from the Parish-stock.

CORPORAL. If it be so beneficial, Captain, I had rather be a *Puritan* Preacher, than an Atheistical States-man.

CAPTAIN. Faith Corporal, I think there is not much Religion in either, but if there be, it lies in the States-man, for he keeps Peace, the other makes War.

CORPORAL. If they make wars, they are our friends, for we live by the spoils of our enemies.

CAPTAIN. 'Tis true, when as we get a victory, or else our enemies lives on the spoil of us, for though we have no goods to lose, yet we venture our lives, neither do we live on the spoil of our enemies, but only in foreign wars, for in civil wars we live by the spoil of our Friends, and the ruining of our Country.

CORPORAL. Then we are only obliged to Preachers for civil wars.

CAPTAIN. Faith Corporal, we are obliged to them for both; for as their factious Doctrine causes a Rebellion by railing on the Governours and Governments, so their flattering Sermons sets a Prince on fire, who burns in hot ambition to conquer all the World.

CORPORAL. These latter Preachers you mention, Captain, are not *Puritan* Preachers, but Royal Preachers.

CAPTAIN. You are right Corporal, for they are divided in two parts, although their Doctrine meets at one end, which is in war.

CORPORAL. Captain, you have discovered so fully of Preachers, that if you will give me leave, I will preach to our Company.

CAPTAIN. Out you rogue, will you raise a war amongst our selves, causing a mutinie to cut one anothers throats?

CORPORAL. Why Captain, it is the fashion and practice of Souldiers to Preach now adayes.

CAPTAIN. That is amongst the Rebel party to keep up their faction, and so strengthen the flank thereof, but amongst the Royal party, the Preaching Ministers turn fighting Souldiers, incouraging their good example, as by their valliant onsets, and not the Souldiers Preaching Ministers.

CORPORAL. Why Captain, the Royal party needs no incouragement, the justice of their cause is sufficient.

CAPTAIN. You say right, they want not courage to fight, but they want conscience to plunder; Besides, the Royal party is apt to give quarter, which should not be, for Souldiers should destroy all they take in Civil-wars, by reason there is no gain to be made of their Prisoners, as by the way of

Ransoms, but if we stay from our Company, our General will preach such a Sermon, as may put us into despair of his favour, and indanger our lives at the Council of war.

Exeunt.

Scene 12

Enter three or four Commanders.

1. COMMANDER. I think our Generals new made son is a spirit; for when the General was surrounded with the Turks, this adopted Son of his flew about like lightning, and made such a massacre of the Turks, as they lay as thick upon the ground, as if they had been mushrooms.

2. COMMANDER. Certainly the General had been take Prisoner, if his Son had not rescued him, for the General had adventured too far into the enemies body.

1. COMMANDER. 'Tis strange, and doth amaze me with wonder, to think how such a Willow-twig could bore so many mortal holes in such strong timber'd bodies as the Turks.

2. COMMANDER. By him one would believe miracles were not ceast.

3. COMMANDER. Well, for my part I will ask pardon of my General for condemning him privately in my thoughts, for I did not think him the most fond, (I will not say what) for adopting a poor Beggar-boy for his son, and setled all his Estate, which is, a very great one upon him.

1. COMMANDER. The truth is, he is a very gallant youth, and if he lives and continues in the wars, he will prove a most excellent Souldier.

2. COMMANDER. Certainly he sprung from a Noble Stock, either by his Fathers side, or by his Mothers.

1. COMMANDER. By his behaviour he seems Nobly born from both.

3. COMMANDER. And by his poverty, Nobly born from neither.

1. COMMANDER. Mean persons may have wealth, and Noble births be Beggars.

Exeunt.

Scene 13

Enter AFFECTIONATA *in brave cloths, Hat and Feather, and a Sword by his side, and a great many Commanders following and attending him, with their Hats off, the whilst he holds off his Hat to them.*

AFFECTIONATA. Gentlemen, I beseech you, use not this ceremonie to me, it belongs only to my Lord General.

COMMANDERS. Your merits and gallant actions deserves it from us; Besides, it is your due, as being the Generals adopted Son.

AFFECTIONATA. My Lords favour may place a value on me, though I am poor in worth, and no wayes deserves this respect.

1. COMMANDER. Faith Sir, had it not been for you, we had lost the battel.

AFFECTIONATA. Alas, my weak arm could never make a conquest, although my will was good, and my desire strong to do a service.

2. COMMANDER. Sir, the service was great, when you rescued our General, for when a General is taken or kill'd, the Armies are put to rout, for then the common Souldiers runs away, never stayes to fight it out.

AFFECTIONATA. I beseech you Gentlemen, take not the honour from my Lord to give it me, for he was his own defence, and ruine to his enemies; for his valiant spirits shot {fire} thorouh his eyes, and struck them dead, thus his own courage was his own safety, and the *Venetians* victory.

Enter a Messenger from the VENETIAN-*States to* AFFECTIONATA, *he bows to him.*

MESSENGER. Noble Sir, the *Venetian*-States hath made you Lieutenant-General of the whole Armie, and one of the Council of War, where they desire your presence.

AFFECTIONATA. The honours they have given me, is beyond my management.

Messenger Exit. As AFFECTIONATA *was going forth, enters some poor Souldiers Wives with Petitions, offers to present them to* AFFECTIONATA.

1. WIFE. Good your Honour, speak in the behalf of my Petition.

2. WIFE. And mine.

3. WIFE. And mine.

AFFECTIONATA. Good women, I cannot do you service, for if your Petitions are just, my Lord the General will grant your request, and if they be unjust, he will not be unjust in granting them for my intreatie, nor will I intreat therefore.

WIVES. If it please your Honour, we implore Mercy, not Justice.

AFFECTIONATA. Where Justice and Wisdom will give leave for Mercy, I am sure my Lord will grant it, otherwise, what you call mercy, will prove cruelty, and cause ruine and destruction.

WIVES. We beseech your Honour then, but to deliver our Petitions.

AFFECTIONATA. For what are they?

WIVES. For the lives of our Husbands.

AFFECTIONATA. Are they to be executed?

WIVES. They are condemned, and to be hanged to morrow, unless the General gives them pardons.

AFFECTIONATA. What are their crimes?

1. WIFE. My Husband is to be hanged for plundering a few old rotten Household-goods.

AFFECTIONATA. Give me your Petition, necessity might inforce him.

2. WIFE. My Husband is to be hanged for disobeying his Captain when he was drunk.

AFFECTIONATA. When which was drunk? your Husband or his Captain?

2. WIFE. My Husband.

AFFECTIONATA. Disobedience ought to be severely punished, yet because his reason was drowned in drink, and his understanding smothered with the vapour therof, whereby he knew not what he did, I will deliver your Petition.

AFFECTIONATA. And what is yours?

3. WIFE. My Husband is to be hanged for ravishing a Virgin.

AFFECTIONATA. I will never deliver a Petition for those that are Violaters of Virginity, I will sooner act the Hang-mans part my self to strangle hm.

AFFECTIONATA. What is your Husbands crime?

4. WIFE. My Husband is to be hanged for murther.

AFFECTIONATA. O horrid! They that murther, ought to have no mercy given to them, since they could give no mercy to others.

WIVES. Good your Honour.

AFFECTIONATA. Nay, never press me, for I will never deliver your Petition.

Wives Exeunt. Enter Commanders that were to be Cashiered (to Petition AF-FECTIONATA.)

1. CAPTAIN. Noble Sir, I come to intreat you to be my friend, to speak to the General in my behalf that I may remain in my place, for I am to be cashierd.

AFFECTIONATA. For what?

1. CAPTAIN. For a small fault, Sir, for when the battel was begun, I had such a cholick took me in the stomach, as I was forced to go aside, and untruss a point.

AFFECTIONATA. It had been more for your honour, Captain, to had let nature discharge it self in your breeches. And what, are you cashiered Captain?

2. CAPTAIN. Marry, for my good service, for when the battel begun, my Souldiers run away, and I run after to call them back, they run, and I rid so long, as we were gotten ten miles from the Armie, but I could not get them, untill such time as the battel was won.

AFFECTIONATA. It had been more honour for you to have fought single alone without your Souldiers, than to have followed your Souldiers, although to make them stay, and you would have done more service with your standing still than your running; and what, are you to be cashiered?

3. CAPTAIN. Why Sir, my company wanted Powder, and I went to fetch or give order; for some to be brought, and before I returned to my Company, the battel was won.

AFFECTIONATA. It had been more for your honour and good service, to have stayed and incouraged your Souldiers by your example with fighting with your sword, for the sword makes a greater execution than the shot; but since they were not wilfull, nor malicious faults, I shall do you what service I can, for fear sometimes may seize the valiantest man. And what were your faults Colonel?

1. COLONEL. Mine was for betraying a Fort.

AFFECTIONATA. O base! He that betrays a Fort, ventures to betray a Kingdom, which is millions of degrees worse than to betray a life, or a particular friend; for those that betrays a Kingdom, betrays numbers of lifes, and those that betrays their native Country, betrays that which gave them nourishing strength, and you have had great mercy in giving you your life, although you lose your place. And what was your fault?

COMMANDER. Mine was for neglecting the Watch.

AFFECTIONATA. That is as bad as to give leave for the enemie to surprize, only the one betrays through carelesness, the other through covetousness. And what was your fault *Colonel?*

COLONEL. Mine was for disobeying the Generals Orders.

AFFECTIONATA. Let me tell you Colonel, he that will not obey, is not fit to command; and those that commits careless, stubborn, malicious and wicked crimes; I will never deliver their Petition, nor speak in their behalf.

Commanders Exeunt. Enter a poor Souldier.

SOULDIER. Good your Honour save me from punishment.

AFFECTIONATA. What are you to be punished for?

SOULDIER. I am to be punished, because I said my Captain was a coward.

AFFECTIONATA. What reason had you to say so?

SOULDIER. The reason was, because he sung and whistled when he went to fight.

AFFECTIONATA. That might be to shew his courage.

SOULDIER. O no, it was to hide his fear.

AFFECTIONATA. But you ought not to have called your Captain coward, had he been so; for the faults of Superiours are to be winked at, and obscured, and not to be divulged: Besides, yours was but a supposition, unless he ran away.

SOULDIER. No Sir, he fought.

AFFECTIONATA. Then you were too blame for judging so.

SOULDIER. I confess it, Sir, wherefore pray speak for me.

AFFECTIONATA. Indeed I cannot, for to call a man coward, is to kill, at least to wound his reputation, which is far worse, than if you had kill'd the life of his body; by how much honour is to be preferred before life; but if you can make your peace with your Captain by asking his pardon; I will then speak to the General, that the sentence for your punishment may be taken off, wherefore let me advise you to go to your Captain, and in the most humblest and sorrowfulst manner ask forgiveness of him.

SOULDIER. I shall, and it please your Honour.

Exeunt.

Scene 14

Enter Sir PEACEABLE STUDIOUS *solus.*

SIR PEACEABLE STUDIOUS.
How happy is a private life to me;
Wherein my thoughts ran easily and free;
And not disturb'd with vanities and toyes,
On which the senses gazes, as young boys
On watery bubbles in the aire blown,
Which when they break, doth vanish and are gone.

Enter the Lady Ignorance.

LADY IGNORANCE. I doubt I disturb your Poetry?

SIR P. STUDIOUS. No wife, you rather give life and fire to my muse, being chaste, fair and vertuous, which are the chief theams for Poets fancies to work on.

LADY IGNORANCE. But that wife that is despised by her Husband, and not loved, is dejected in her own thoughts, and her mind is so disquietted, as it masks her beauty, and vails, and obscures her vertues.

SIR P. STUDIOUS. The truth is, wife, that if my affections to you, had not been firmely setled; your indiscretion and effeminate follies had ruined it, but my love is so true, as you have no cause to be jealous; but I confess you made me sad, to think that your humour could not sympathize with mine, as to walk in the same course of life as I did, but you were ignorant and would not believe me, untill you had found experience by practice, by which practice you have found my words to be true, do you not?

LADY IGNORANCE. Yes, so true, as I shall never doubt them more; But pray Husband, tell me what discourse you had with the Ladies, when you went abroad with them?

SIR P. STUDIOUS. Why, they railed against good Husbands, called them Uxorious Fools, Clowns, Blocks, Stocks, and that they were only fit to be made Cuckolds through their confident fondness, and that kind Husbands appeared like simple Asses; I answered, that those Husbands that were Cuckolds, appeared not only like silly *Asses,* but base Cowards, that would suffer their wives to be courted, and themselves dishonoured when they ought to destroy their wives Gallants, if visibly known, and to part from their wives, at least to inancor them, and not only for being false, but for the suspition caused by their indiscretions; otherwise said I, a kind Husband shews himself a Gallant, Noble, Generous, Just, Wise man, and contrary, he is a base man, that will strive to disgrace himself, by disgracing his wife with neglects and disrespects; and a coward, to tyranize only over the weak, tender, and helpless Sex; for women being tender, shiftless, and timorous creatures by nature, is the cause they joyn themselves by chaste Wedlock to us men for their safety, protection, honour and livelyhood, and when a man takes a woman to his wife, he is an unworthy and treacherous person, if he betrays her to scorns, or yields her to scoffs, or leaves her to poverty; and he is a base man that makes his wife sigh and weep with unkindness either by words or actions, wherefore said I, it is wisdom for men to respect their wives with a civil behaviour, and sober regard, and it is heroick to defend, protect and guard their lives and vertues, to be constant to their vows, promises and protestations, and it is generous to cherish their health, to attend them in their sickness, to comply with their harmless humours, to entertain their discourses, to accompany their persons, to yield to their lawfull desires, and to commend their good graces, and that man which is a Husband, and doth not do thus, is worthy to be shamed, and not to be kept company with, which is not called an Uxorious Husband, for said I, an Uxorious Husband I understand to be, a honest, carefull and wise Husband.

LADY IGNORANCE. And what said they, after you said this?

SIR P. STUDIOUS. They laugh'd and said, my flowery Rhetorick was strewed upon a dirty ground; I answered, it was not dirty where I lived, for my wife was beautifull, chaste and cleanly, and I wished every man the like, and after they perceived that neither the railing, nor laughing at good Husbands could not temper me for their palats, they began to play and sport with one another, and sung wanton songs, and when all their baits failed, they quarreled with me, and said I was uncivil, and that I did not entertain them well, and that I was not good Company, having not a conversable wit, nor a gentle behaviour, and that I was not a gallant Cavalier, and a world of those reproches and idle discourses, as it would tire me to repeat it, and you to hear it.

LADY IGNORANCE. Pray resolve me one question more, what was it you said to the Lady *Amorous,* when she threatened to tell me?

SIR P. STUDIOUS. I only said nature was unkind to our Sex, in making the beautifull females cruel.

LADY IGNORANCE. Was that all, I thought you had pleaded as a courtly Sutor for loves favours.

SIR P. STUDIOUS. No indeed, but let me tell you, and so inform you, wife, that those humour'd women, take as great a pleasure to make wives jealouse of their Husbands, and Husbands jealouse of their wives, and to seperate their affections, and to make a disorder in their Families, as to plot and design to intice men to court them, & Cuckold their Husband, also let me tell you, that much company, and continual resort, brings great inconveniences for its apt to corrupt the mind, and make the thoughts wild, the behaviour bold, the words vain, the discourse either flattering, rude or tedious, their actions extravagant, their persons cheap, being commonly accompanyed, or their company common. Besides, much variety of Company, creates amorous luxurie, vanity, prodigality, jealousie, envie, malice, slander, envie, treachery, quarrels, revenge and many other evils, as laying plots to insnare the Honourable, to accuse the Innocent, to deceive the Honest, to corrupt the Chaste, to deboyst the Temperate, to pick the purse of the Rich, to inslave the poor, to pull down the lawfull Authority, and to break just Laws; but when a man lives to himself within his own Familie, and without recourse, after a solitary manner, he lives free, without controul, not troubled with company, but entertains himself with himself, which make the soul wise, the mind sober, the thoughts industrious, the understanding learned, the heart honest, the senses quiet, the appetites temperate, the body healthfull, the actions just and prudent, the behaviour civil and sober; He governs orderly, eats peaceably, sleeps quietly, lives contentedly, and most commonly, plentifully and pleasantly, ruling and governing his little Family to his own humour, wherein he commands with love, and is obeyed with duty, and who that is wise, and is not mad, would quit this heavenly life to live in hellish Societies, and what can an honest Husband and wife desire more, than love, peace and plenty, and when they have this, and is not content, 'tis a sign they stand upon a Quagmire, or rotten Foundation, that will never hold or indure, that is, they are neither grounded on honesty, nor supported with honour.

LADY IGNORANCE. Well Husband, I will not interupt your studies any longer, but as you study Phylosophie, Wisdom and Invention, so I will study obedience, discretion and Houswifery.

Omnes Exeunt.

ACT III

Scene 15

Enter the General, and AFFECTIONATA.

LORD SINGULARITY. *Affectionata*, Were you never bred to the Discipline of War?

AFFECTIONATA. Never, my Lord, but what I have been since I came to you.

LORD SINGULARITY. Why, thou didst speak at the Council of War, as if thou hadst been an old experienced souldier, having had the practice of fourty years, which did so astonish the grave Senators and old Souldiers, that they grew dumb, and for a while did only gaze on thee.

AFFECTIONATA. Indeed, my Lord, my young years, and your grave Counsel did not suit together.

LORD SINGULARITY. But let me tell thee, my boy, thy rational and wise speeches, and that grave counsels was not mis-match'd.

AFFECTIONATA. Pray Heaven I may prove so, as your favours, and your love may not be though misplaced.

LORD SINGULARITY. My Love thinks thee worthy of more than I can give thee, had I more power than *Caesar* had.

Exeunt.

Scene 16

Enter some Commanders.

1. COMMANDER. I heart that the Duke of *Venice* is so taken with our Generals adopted Son, as he will adopt him his Son.

2. COMMANDER. Hay-day! I have heard that a Father hath had many Sons, but never that one Son hath had so many Fathers; but contrary, many Sons wants fathering.

3. COMMANDER. 'Tis true, some Sons hath the misfortune not to be owned, but let me tell you Lieutenant, there be few children that hath not many such Fathers; as one begets a childe, a second owns the childe, a third keeps the childe, which inherits as the right Heir; and if a fourth will adopt the childe; a fift, or more may do the like, if they please.

1. COMMANDER. So amongst all his Fathers, the right Father is lost.

3. COMMANDER. Faith, the right Father of any childe is seldome known, by reason that women takes as much delight in deceiving the World, and dissembling with particularly men, as in the cuckolding their Husbands.

2. COMMANDER. The truth is, every several Lover cuckolds one another.

1. COMMANDER. Perchance that is the reason that women strives to have so many Lovers; for women takes pleasure to make Cuckolds.

3. COMMANDER. And Cuckolds to own children.

Exeunt.

Scene 17

Enter AFFECTIONATA, *then enters to him, two or three* VENETIAN *Gentlemen, as Embassadors from the Duke of* VENICE.

1. GENTLEMAN. Noble Sir, the great Duke of *Venice* hath sent us to let you know he hath adopted you his Son, and desires your company.

AFFECTIONATA. Pray return the great Duke thanks, and tell him those favours are too great for such a one as I; but if he could, and would adopt me, as *Augustus Caesar* did *Tiberius,* and make me master of the whole World; by Heaven I would refuse it, and rather chose to live in a poor Cottage, with my most Noble Lord.

2. GENTLEMAN. But you must not deny him; Besides, he will have you.

AFFECTIONATA. I will dye first, and rather chose to bury my self in my own tears, than build a Throne with ingratitude.

1. GENTLEMAN. But it is ungratefull to deny the Duke.

AFFECTIONATA. O no, but I should be the ingrate of ingratitude, should I leave my Noble Lord, who from a low despised poor mean degree, advanced me to Respect and Dignity:

Whose favours I will keep close in my heart,
And from his person I will never part.
For though I dye, my soul will still attend,
And wait upon him, as his faithfull friend.

He offers to go away in a melancholly posture and humour, so as not considering the Gentlemen. Whereupon one of them follows him, and catches hold of his Cloak.

2. GENTLEMAN. Noble Sir, will not you send the Duke an answer?

AFFECTIONATA. Have not I answered? Then pray present my thanks in the most humblest manner to the great Duke, and tell him he may force the presence of my person, but if he doth, it will be but as a dead carcase without a living soul; for tell him, when I am from my Lord,

I withering vade, as flowers from Sun sight;
His presence is to me, as Heavens light.

AFFECTIONATA *Exit.*

1. GENTLEMAN. 'Tis strange that such an honour cannot perswade a boy!

2. GENTLEMAN. That proves him a boy, for if he had been at mans estate, he

would not have refused it, but have been ambitious of it, and proud to receive it.

1. GENTL. Indeed youth is foolish, and knows not how to chose.

2. GENTL. When he comes to be a man, he will repent the folly of his youth.

Exeunt.

Scene 18

Enter the Lady BASHFULL, *and Lady* WAGTAIL *not knowing Sir* SERIOUS *could speak.*

LADY WAGTAIL. Pray Madam, let me perswade you, not to cast your self away, to marry a dumb man, for my troth, all those that are dumb, are meer fools; for who can be witty or wise that cannot speak, or will not speak, which is as bad.

LADY BASHFULL. Why Madam? Wisdome nor wit, doth noth not {doth not} live nor lye in words, for prudence, fortitude and temperance, expresses wisdom and capacity; ingenuity and fancie expresseth wit, and not words.

LADY WAGTAIL. But let me advise you to chose Sir *Humphry Bold,* he is worth a thousand of Sir *Serious Dumb;* besides, he is a more learned man by half, and speaks several Languages.

LADY BASHFULL. Perchance so, and yet not so wise; for Parrots will learn Languages, and yet not know how to be wise, nor what wisdome is, which is to have a sound judgement, a clear understanding, and a prudent forecast.

LADY WAGTAIL. Faith all the World will condemn you to have no forecast, if you marry Sir *Serious Dumb.*

LADY BASHFULL. Let them speak their worst, I care not, as not fearing their censures.

LADY WAGTAIL. You were fearfull and bashfull.

LADY BASHFULL. 'Tis true, but now am grown so confident with honest love, I care not if all the World did know of it; nay, I wish it were published to all ears.

The Lady BASHFULL *offers to go away.*

LADY WAGTAIL. Nay, you must not go, untill you have granted my suit in the behalf of Sir *Humphry Bold.*

LADY BASHFULL. Pray let me go, for I hate him more, than Heaven hates Hell.

LADY WAGTAIL. Nay, then I will leave you.

Exeunt.

Scene 19

Enter AFFECTIONATA, *who weeps. Enter the Lord* SINGULARITY.

LORD SINGULARITY. Why weepest thou *Affectionata?*

AFFECTIONATA. Alas, my Lord, I am in such a passion, as I shall dye, unless it
flows thorough mine eyes, and runs from off my tongue.
For like as vapours from the Earth doth rise,
And gather into clouds beneath the skies;
Contracts to water, swelling like moist veins,
When over-fill'd, falls down in showering rains:
So thoughts, which from a grieved mind are sent,
Ariseth in a vaporous discontent.
Contracts to melancholly, which heavy lies
Untill it melts, and runs forth through the eyes;
Unless the Sun of comfort, dry doth drink
Those watery tears that lyes at the eyes brink;
Or that the rayes of joy, which streams bright out
Which active heat disperseth them about.

LORD SINGULARITY. Faith *Affectionata*, I am no good Poet, but thy passion
moves so sweetly in numbers and stops, so just with rhimes, as I cannot but
answer thee,
Like as the Sun beauty streams rayes about,
A smiling countenance like day breaks out:
And though a frown obscures sweet beauties sight,
Yet beauties beams makes cloudy frowns more bright:
But melancholly beauty doth appear
As pleasing shades, or Summers evenings clear.
So doth thine *Affectionata*, but prethee do not wast thy breath into sighs, nor
distill thy life into tears.

AFFECTIONATA. I wish I might here breath my last, and close my eyes for ever.

LORD SINGULARITY. I perceive *Affectionata*, you take it unkindly I did perswade you to take the Dukes offer; But if you think I did it out of any other
design than a true affection to you; By Heaven, you do me wrong by false
interpretation.

AFFECTIONATA. If you, my Lord, did love but half so well as I, you would rather
chose to dye, than part with me.

LORD SINGULARITY. I love thee beyond my own interest or delight, for what is
best for thee, I account as the greatest blessing, should it bring me any other
wayes a curse.

AFFECTIONATA. Then let me still live with you, for that is best for me.

LORD SINGULARITY. Here I do vow to Heaven, to do my indeavour with my life
to keep thee with me, or to be alwayes where thou art.

AFFECTIONATA. O! what a weight you have taken from my soul, wherein my thoughts like wet-winged-birds sate heavy; my senses like as blinking Lamps which vaporous damps of grief had neer put out.

LORD SINGULARITY. Let me tell thee *Affectionata,* I have travelled far, observed much, and have had divers incounters, but I never met such vertue, found such truth, nor incountered such an affection as thine.

imbraces him.

> *And thus I do imbrace thee, and do wish our souls may twine,*
> *As our each bodyes thus together joyn.* *

Exeunt.

Scene 20

Enter Sir SERIOUS DUMB, *and his Mistriss the Lady* BASHFULL.

SIR SERIOUS DUMB. Dear Mistriss, do not you repent your favours, and wish your promise never made; doth not your affection vade?

LADY BASHFULL. No, it cannot, for never was any love placed upon a Nobler soul than my love is, which is on yours, insomuch, as I do glory in my affection, and grow self-conceited of its judgement.

SIR SERIOUS DUMB. And will you be constant?

LADY BASHFULL. Let not your humble thoughts raise a doubt of jealousie; for I am fixt, as time is to eternity.

SIR SERIOUS DUMB. Then I thank nature for your Creation, honour for your Breeding, and heaven for your Vertue, and fortune that hath given you to me, for I can own nothing of that worth that could deserve you.

LADY BASHFULL. I cannot condemn jealousie, because it proceeds from pure love, and love melts into kinds {kindness} on a constant heart, but flames like Oyle on a false one, which sets the whole life on fire.

SIR SERIOUS DUMB. But now I cannot doubt your love nor constancies, since you have promised your heart to me; for true Lovers are like the light and the Sun, inseparable.

Exeunt.

Scene 21

Enter some Commanders.

1. COMMANDER. Come fellow-souldiers, are you ready to march?

2. COMMANDER. Whether?

1. COMMANDER. Into our own native Country, for our General is sent for home.

---

* This speech is italicized in the 1662 text.

3. COMMANDER. Except there be wars in our own Country, we cannot go with him.

1. COMMANDER. I know not whether there be wars or peace, but he obeys, for he is preparing for his journey.

2. COMMANDER. Who shall be General when he is gone?

3. COMMANDER. I know not, but I hear the States offers to make our young Lieutenant-General, General, but he refuseth it.

2. COMMANDER. Would they would make me General?

3. COMMANDER. If thou wert General, thou wouldst put all method out of order.

1. COMMANDER. Faith Gentlemen, I would lead you most prudently, and give you leave to plunder most unanimously.

3. COMMANDER.* And we would fight couragiously, to keep what we plunder.

2. COMMANDER. Come, let us go, and inquire how our affairs goeth.

Exeunt.

Scene 22

Enter the Lord SINGULARITY *and* AFFECTIONATA.

LORD SINGULARITY. Now *Affectionata*, we have taken our leave of the States: I hope thy mind is at peace, and freed from fears of being staid.

AFFECTIONATA. Yes my† Lord.

LORD SINGULARITY. They did perswade thee much to stay.

AFFECTIONATA. They seemed much troubled for your Lordships departure.

LORD SINGULARITY. Truly I will say thus much for my self, that I have done them good service, and I must say thus much for them, that they have rewarded me well.

AFFECTIONATA. I have heard, my Lord, that States seldom rewards a service done; wherefore I believe, they hope you will return again, and fees you for that end.

LORD SINGULARITY. I shall not be unwilling when my Country hath no imployment for me.

AFFECTIONATA. Methinks, my Lord, since you have gotten a fame abroad, you should desire to live a setled life at home.

LORD SINGULARITY. A setled life would seem but dull to me that hath no wife nor children.

AFFECTIONATA. You may have both, If you please, my Lord.

---

* his read "1. Commander" in the original.
† This read "my my" in the original.

LORD SINGULARITY. For children I desire none, since I have thee, and wives I care not for, but what are other mens.

Enter a Messenger with a Letter to the Lord SINGULARITY.

LORD SINGULARITY. From whence comest thou friend?

MESSENGER. From *Rome,* my Lord.

LORD SINGULARITY. If you please to stay in the next room, I shall speak to you presently.

Messenger Exit. The Lord SINGULARITY *breaks up the Letter and reads.*

LORD SINGULARITY. *Affectionata,* From whence do you think this Letter comes?

AFFECTIONATA. I cannot guess, my Lord.

LORD SINGULARITY. From the Pope, who hath heard so much of thy youth, vertue, wit and courage, as he desires me to pass thorough *Rome* in* my journey home, that he might see thee.

AFFECTIONATA. Pray Heaven his Holynesse doth not put me into a Monastery, and force me to stay behind you.

LORD SINGULARITY. If he should, I would take the habit, and be incloistered with thee; but he will not inforce a youth that hath no will thereto.

AFFECTIONATA. Truly my Lord, I have no will to be a Fryer.

LORD SINGULARITY. Indeed it is somewhat too lazie a life, which all heroick Spirits shame {shun}, for those loves liberty and action: But I will go and dispatch this Messenger, and to morrow we will begin our journey.

Exeunt.

Scene 23

Enter the Lady WAGTAIL, *and the Lady* AMOROUS.

LADY WAGTAIL. Faith *Amorous,* it had been a victory indeed worth the bragging off, if we could have taken Sir *Peacable Studious* Loves prisoner, and could have infettered him in *Cupid*'s bonds.

LADY AMOROUS. It had been a victory indeed, for I will undertake to inslave five Courtiers, and ten Souldiers, sooner, and in less time than one studious Scholar.

LADY WAGTAIL. But some Scholars are more easily taken than the luxurious Courtiers, or deboist Souldiers.

LADY AMOROUS. O no! for Luxurie and Rapine begets lively Spirits, but a study quenches them out.

LADY WAGTAIL. One would think so by Sir *Peaceable Studious,* but not by some other Scholars that I am acquainted with.

---

* This read "im" in the original.

LADY AMOROUS. But confess, Lady *Wagtail*, do not you find a studious Scholar dull company, in respect of a vain Courtier, and a rough Souldier.

LADY WAGTAIL. I must confess, they that study Philosophy, are little too much inclined to morality, but those that study Theologie, are not so restringent.*

LADY AMOROUS. Well, for my part, since I have been acquainted with Sir *Peaceable Studious*, I hate all Scholars.

Exeunt.

Scene 24

Enter three Men, as the Inhabitants of ROME.

1. MAN.† Tis wonderful such a youth as Lord *Singularity*'s Son is, should have so great a wit, as to be able to dispute with so many Cardinals.

2. MAN. The greater wonder is; that he should have the better of them!

1. MAN. 'Tis said the *Pope* doth admire him! and is extreamly taken with him.

2. MAN. If *Jove* had so much admired him, he would have made him his *Ganimed*.‡

1. MAN. He offered to make him a living Saint, but he thanked his Holyness, and said, he might Saint him, but not make him holy enough to be a Saint, for said he, I am unfit to have Prayers offered to me, that cannot offer Prayers as I ought, or live as I should; then he offered him a Cardinals hat, but he refused it; saying he was neither wise enough, nor old enough for to accept of it; for said he, I want *Ulisses*§ head, and *Nestors*‖ years to be Cardinal, for though less devotion will serve a Cardinal than a Saint, yet politick wisdome is required.

3. MAN. Pray Neighbours tell me which way, and by what means I may see this wonderful youth; for I have been out of the Town, and not heard of him.

2. MAN. You cannot see him now, unless you will follow him where he is gone.

1. MAN. Why, whether is he gone?

2. MAN. Into his own Country, and hath been gone above this week.

3. MAN. Nay, I cannot follow him thither.

Exeunt.

---

* restringent] constipated.

† "Man" added by this editor.

‡ *Ganimed*] Ganymede, a beautiful boy taken as a lover by the king of the gods in Greek and Roman mythology.

§ *Ulisses*] Ulysses, Latin name of Odysseus, the wise and wily hero of Homer's *Odyssey*.

‖ *Nestors*] Nestor was the oldest of the Greek generals in Homer's *Iliad*, celebrated for his wisdom.

Scene 25

Enter the Lord SINGULARITY, *and* AFFECTIONATA, *as being in the Country.*

LORD SINGULARITY. *Affectionata,* you have promised me to be ruled by me in every thing, so that you may not part from me.

AFFECTIONATA. I have, my Lord, and will obey all your commands, so far as I am able.

LORD SINGULARITY. Then I am resolved now I am returned into my own Country, to get thee a wife, that thy fame and worthy acts may live in thy Posterity.

AFFECTIONATA. Jove bless me, a wife! by Heaven, my Lord, I am not man enough to marry!

LORD SINGUL. There is many as young as you, that have been Fathers, and have had children.

AFFECTIONATA. If they were such as I am, they might father Children, but never get them.

LORD SINGULARITY. Thou art modest, *Affectionata,* but I will have you marry, and I will chose thee such a wife, as modest as thy self.

AFFECTIONATA. Then we never shall have children, Sir.

LORD SINGUL. Love and acquaintance will give you confidence; but tell me truly, *Affectionata,* didst thou never court a Mistriss?

AFFECTIONATA. No truly, Sir.

LORD SINGULARITY. Well, I will have you practice Courtship, and though I will not directly be your Baud or Pimp, yet I will send you amongst the effeminate Sex, where you may learn to sport with Ladies, as well as fight with *Turks.*

AFFECTIONATA *speaks softly to her self; pray* JOVE *they do not search me. Exeunt.*

Scene 26

Enter the Lady WAGTAIL, *and the Lady* AMOROUS.

LADY WAGTAIL. I can tell you news?

LADY AMOROUS. What news?

LADY WAGTAIL. Sir *Serious Dumb* can speak again!

LADY AMOROUS. I am sorrow for that, for now he may tell tales out of School.

LADY WAGTAIL. If he do, we will whip him with the rods of tongues, which is more sharp than the rods of wyer.

LADY AMOROUS. We may whip him with words, but we our selves shall feel the smart of reproch.

LADY WAGTAIL. How simply you talk, as if reproch could hurt a woman; when reproch is born with us, and dyes with us.

LADY AMOROUS. If reproch have no power of our Sex, why are all women so carefull to cover their faults, and so fearfull to have their crimes divulged.

LADY WAGTAIL. Out of two reasons; first, because those of the masculine Sex, which have power, as Fathers, Uncles, Brothers and Husbands; would cut their throats, if they received any disgrace by them; for disgrace belongs more to men than women: The other reason is, that naturally women loves secrets, yet there is nothing they can keep secret, but their own particular faults, neither do they think pleasure sweet, but what is stollen.

LADY AMOROUS. By your favour, women cannot keep their own faults secret.

LADY WAGTAIL. O yes, those faults that may ruine them if divulged, but they cannot keep a secret that is delivered to their trust; for naturally women are unfit for trust, or council.

LADY AMOROUS. But we are fit for faction.

LADY WAGTAIL. The World would be but a dull World, if it were not for industrious factions.

LADY AMOROUS. The truth is, that if it were not for faction, the World would lye in the cradle of Peace, and be rock'd into a quiet sleep of security.

LADY WAGTAIL. Prethee talk not of quiet, and peace, and rest, for I hate them as bad as death.

LADY AMOROUS. Indeed they resemble death, for in death there is no wars nor noise.

LADY WAGTAIL. Wherefore it is natural for life, neither to have rest nor peace, being cantrary to death.

Exeunt.

ACT IV

Enter the Lord SINGULARITY, *and* AFFECTIONATA.

AFFECTIONATA. My Lord, I hear the King hath invited you to attend him in his progress this Summer.

LORD SINGULARITY. Yes, but I have made my excuse, and have got leave to stay at home; for I will tell thee truly, that I had rather march ten miles with an Artillery, than travel one with a Court; and I had rather fight a battel, than be bound to ceremony, or flattery, which must be practiced if one live at Court: Besides, I have been bred to lead an Armie, and not to follow a Court; And the custom of the one have made me unacquainted, and so unfit for the other; for though I may truly say I am a good Souldier, yet I will confess ingenuously to thee, I am a very ill Courtier.

AFFECTIONATA. I think they are the most happiest, that are least acquainted with a great Monarchs Court.

LORD SINGULARITY. I will tell thee a discourse upon this theam in the time of *Henry* the eighth of *England,* there were many Courtiers of all degrees about him, and the theam of their discourse was, who was the happiest man in *England;* So all the Nobles and inferior Courtiers agreed unanimously it was his Majesty, and it could be no man else; and they all said, that their judgements was so clear in that point, that it could not admit of a contradiction, or dispute: Said *Henry* the eighth, by the body of the Lord, you are all mistaken, then said one of the Courtiers, I beseech your Majesty to tell us who is the happiest man; By the Lord, said the King, that Gentleman that lives to his profit, and dare moderately spend for his pleasure, and that neither knows me, nor I know him, he is the happiest man in the Kingdom; and I am of *Henry* the eights opinion; but howsoever, it were better to be such a one that goeth with the bagge and baggage of an Armie, than one of the tail of a Court.

AFFECTIONATA. But your Lordship would not refuse to be as the chief, as to be a Favourite; for a Favourite is more sought, feared and flattered, than the King himself.

LORD SINGULARITY. I think I should not refuse to be a Favourite, by reason a Favourite is a General to command, Martial and Conduct in all affairs, both at home and abroad, in peace and in war, and all by the power and authority of the commission of Favourites.

AFFECTIONATA. Which Commission hath a greater and larger extent than any other Commission.

LORD SINGULARITY. You say right, for it extends as far as the Kings power.

Exeunt.

Scene 27

Enter the Lady BASHFULL, *and* REFORMER *her woman.*

REFORMER. Madam, shall your wedding be private, or publick?

LADY BASHFULL. Private.

REFORMER. I wonder you will have it private.

LADY BASHFULL. Why do you wonder?

REFORMER. Because the wedding-day is the only triumphant day of a young maids life.

LADY BASHFULL. If my whole life were triumphant, it would be but as one day when it was past, or rather as no day nor time; for what is past, is as if it never were; and for one day I will never put my self to that ceremonious trouble, which belongs to feasting; revelling, dressing and the like.

REFORMER. I perceive your Ladyship desires to be undrest upon the Wedding-day.

LADY BASHFULL. No, that I do not, but as I will not be carelessly undrest, so I will not be drest for a Pageant show.

Exeunt.

Scene 28

Enter the Lord SINGULARITY *and* AFFECTIONATA.

AFFECTIONATA. I think there is no Family more methodically ordered, prudently governed than your Lordships.

LORD SINGULARITY. It were a disgrace to my profession, if I should not well know how to command; for a good Commander in the field, can tell how to be a good Manager in his private Family, although a prudent Master of a Family knows not how to be a skillfull Commander in the field; but a prudent Master must have a trusty Steward, so a knowing General must have a carefull and skilfull Lieutenant-General, or else he will be very much troubled; also both Master and General must have other Officers, or else they will not find their Accounts or Conquests as he hopes or expects, For neither General nor Master can order every particular command, nor rectifie every particular errour himself; for a Generals Office, is only to direct, order and command the chief Officers, and not the common Souldiers; So the Master of a Family, is only to direct, order and command his Steward, he the rest of the Officers, and the common servants, every one must order those that belongs to their several Offices.

AFFECTIONATA. Then the common Servants are like the common Souldiers.

LORD SINGULARITY. They are so, and are as apt to mutiny, if they be not used with strickt discipline: Thus, if a Master of a Family have the right way in the management of his particular affairs, he may thrive easily, have plenty, live peaceably, be happy, and carry an honourable port with an indifferent Estate, when those of much greater Estates, which knows not, nor practices the right method, or rules and governs not with strictness, his servants shall grow factious, mutinous, and be alwaies in bruleries,* by which disorders his Estate shall waste invisible, his servants cozen egregiously; he lives in penurie, his

---

* bruleries] northern and Scots dialect for broils, quarrels, or disturbances.

servants in riot, alwaies spending, yet alwaies wanting, forced to borrow, and yet hath so much, that if it were ordered with prudence, might be able to lend, when by his imprudence, he is troubled with stores, yet vex'd with necessity.

AFFECTIONATA. I should think that no man ought to be a Master of a Family, but those that can govern orderly and peaceably.

LORD SINGULARITY. You say right, for every Master of a Family are petty-Kings, and when they have rebellions in their own small Monarchies, they are apt to disturb the general Peace of the whole Kingdom or State they live in; for those that cannot tell how to command their own Domesticks, and prudently order their* own affairs, are not only uselesse to the Common-wealth, but they are pernicious and dangerous, as not knowing the benefit and necessity of obedience and method.

Exeunt.

Scene 29

Enter the Lady WAGTAIL, *and the Lady* AMOROUS.

LADY WAGTAIL. The Lord Singularity hath brought home the sweetest, and most beautifullest young Cavalier, as ever I saw.

LADY AMOROUS. Faith he appears like *Adonas*.†

LADY WAGTAIL. Did you ever see *Adonas?*

LADY AMOROUS. No, but I have heard the Poets describe him.

LADY WAGTAIL. *Venus* and *Adonas* are only two poetical *Ideas,* or two *Ideas* in poetical brains.

LADY AMOROUS. Why, *Ideas* hath no names.

LADY WAGTAIL. O yes, for Poets christens their *Ideas* with names, as orderly as Christians Fathers doth their children.

LADY AMOROUS. Well, I wish I were a *Venus* for his sake.

LADY WAGTAIL. But if you were only a poetical *Venus,* you would have little pleasure with your *Adonas.*

LADY AMOROUS. Hay ho! He is a sweet youth.

LADY WAGTAIL. And you have sweet thoughts of the sweet youth.

LADY AMOROUS. My thoughts are like Mirtle-groves to entertain the *Idea* of the Lord *Singularity*'s Son.

LADY WAGTAIL. Take heed there be not a wild-boar in your Mirtle Imagenarie Grove, that may destroy your *Adonas Idea.*

---

* Misspelled as "rheir" in the original.

† *Adonas*] Adonis, the beautiful young hunter loved by the goddess Venus, was killed by a boar; the myrtle tree, sacred to the goddess, has strong sexual implications.

LADY AMOROUS. There is no beast there, only sweet singing-birds called *Nightingals.*

Exeunt.

Scene 30

Enter the Lord SINGULARITY *and* AFFECTIONATA.

AFFECTIONATA. Pray, my Lord, what Lady is that you make such inquiry for?

LORD SINGULARITY. She is a Lady I would have thee marry; One that my Father did much desire I should marry, although she was very young, and may be now about thy years. I hear her Father is dead, but where the Lady is, I cannot find out.

AFFECTIONATA. Perchance she is married, my Lord.

LORD SINGULARITY. Then we should find her out, by hearing who she hath marryed.

AFFECTIONATA. But if she be not marryed, she being as old as I, I am too young for her, for Husbands should be older than their wives.

LORD SINGULARITY. But she is one that is well born, well bred, and very rich; and though thou art young in years, yet thou art an aged man in judgment, prudence, understanding, and for wit, as in thy flourishing strength.

AFFECTIONATA. Perchance, my Lord, she will not like me, as neither my years, my person, nor my birth.

LORD SINGULARITY. As for thy years, youth is alwayes accepted by the effeminate Sex; and thy person she cannot dislike, for thou art very handsom, and for thy birth, although thou art meanly born, thou hast a noble nature, a sweet disposition, a vertuous soul, and a heroick spirit; Besides, I have adopted thee my Son, and the King hath promised to place my Titles on thee, and hath made thee Heir of my whole Estate, for to maintain thee according to those Dignities.

AFFECTIONATA. But I had rather live unmarried, my Lord, if you will give consent.

LORD SINGULARITY. But I will never consent to that, and if you be dutifull to me, you will marry such a one as I shall chose for you.

AFFECTIONATA. I shall obey whatsoever you command, for I have nothing but my obedience to return for all your favours.

LORD SINGULARITY. Well, I will go and make a strickt inquiry for this Lady.

LORD SINGULARITY *exit.* AFFECTIONATA *alone.*

AFFECTIONATA. Hay ho! what will this come to, I would I were in my Grave; for love and fear doth torture my poor life; Heaven strike me dead! or make me this Lords wife.

Exeunt.

Scene 31

Enter the Lady WAGTAIL, *and the Lady* AMOROUS.

LADY AMOROUS. How shall we compass the acquaintance of Lord *Singularity*'s Son?

LADY WAGTAIL. Faith *Amorous,* thou lovest boys, but I love men; wherefore I would be acquainted with the Lord Singularity himself; Besides, his adopted Son was a poor Beggar-boy 'tis said, and I cannot love one that is basely born.

LADY AMOROUS. His birth may be honourably, though poor, and of low and mean descent; for if he was born in honest wedlock, and of honest Parents, his birth cannot be base.

LADY WAGTAIL. O yes, for those that are not born from Gentry, are like course brown bread, when Gentry of ancient descent, are like flower often boulted to make white manchet.*

LADY AMOROUS. By that rule, surely he came from a Noble and Ancient Race; for I never saw any person more white and finely shap'd in my life than he is; and if fame speaks true, his actions have proved he hath a Gentlemans soul; But say he were meanly born, as being born from a Cottager, yet he is not be despised nor disliked, nor to be lesse esteemed, or beloved, or to be thought the worse of, for was *Lucan* lesse esteemed for being a *Stone-Cutter,* or his wit lesse esteemed; or was King *David* lesse esteemed or obeyed, for being a *Shepheard;* or the *Apostles* lesse esteemed or believed, for being *Fishermen, Tent-makers* or the like; or the man that was chosen from the Plough, to be made Emperour; I say, was he lesse esteemed for being a Plough-man? No, he was rather admired the more; or was *Horace*† esteemed, or his Poems thought the worse, for being Son to a freed man, which had been a slave; or was *Homer* lesse admired, or thought the worse Poet, for being a poor blind man, and many hundred that I cannot name, that hath gained fame, and their memories lives with Honour and Admiration in every Age, and in

---

* boulted . . . manchet] sifted to make fine wheat bread.

† *Lucan* . . . *Horace*] Lucan, Roman author of the epic *Civil War* and nephew of the Stoic philosopher Seneca; King David, author of the Psalms; the man chosen from the plough to be made emperor, Cincinnatus; Horace, a Roman poet, son of a freed slave, especially admired and imitated for his odes and satires.

every Nation, Kingdom, Country and Family, and it is more worthy, and those persons ought to have more love and respect, that have merit, than those that have only Dignity, either from favour of Princes, or descended from their Ancestors; for all derived Honours, are poor and mean, in respect of self-creating honour, and they only are to be accounted mean and base, that are so in themselves; but those that are born from low and humble Parents, when they have merits, and have done worthy actions, they are placed higher in fames Court, and hath more honour by fames report, which sounds their praises louder than those of greater descent, although of equal worth and merit, and justly, for it is more praise-worthy, when those that were the lowest, and are as it were trod into the earth, or was born, as the phrase is, from the Dunghill, should raise themselves equal to the highest, who keeps but where they were placed by birth; but many times they keep not their place, but fall from the Dignity of their birth, into the myer of baseness, treachery and treason, when the other rises as the Sun out of a cloud of darkness, darting forth glorious beams thorough all that Hemisphere.

LADY WAGTAIL. I perceive by your discourse, Lovers are the best Disputers; Orators, and as I have heard, the best Poets; But I never heard you discourse so well, nor speak so honourably in all my life, wherefore I am confident, 'twas love spake, not you.

Exeunt.

ACT V

Scene 32

Enter AFFECTIONATA, *Nurse* FONDLY, *and* FOSTER TRUSTY *her Husband.*

NURSE FONDLY. My child, we can no longer conceal you, for we are accused of murthering you, and are summoned to appear before a Judge and Jury.

AFFECTIONATA. For Heaven sake, conceal me as long as you can; for if I be known, I shall be utterly ruined with disgrace.

NURSE FONDLY. Whose fault was it? I did advise you otherwise, but you would not be ruled, nor counselled by me; and my Husband like an unwise man, did assist your childish desires.

FOSTER TRUSTY. Well wife, setting aside your wisdom, let us advise what is best to be done in this case.

NURSE FONDLY. In this case we are either to be hanged, or she is to be disgraced; and for my part, I had rather be hanged, for I am old, and cannot live long.

FOSTER TRUSTY. If you were a young wench, thou mightest chance to escape hanging, the Judges would have taken pity on thee, but being old, will condemn thee without mercy.

NURSE FONDLY. If I were not a pretty wench, and the Jurie amorous men, at least the Judges so, I should be hanged neverthelesse.

AFFECTIONATA. Come, come, *Foster Father*, and *Nurse*, let us go and advise. *Exeunt.*

Scene 33

Enter the Lady WAGTAIL, *and a Captain.*

LADY WAGTAIL. Pray tell me, what manner of Country is *Italy?*

CAPTAIN. In short, Madam, there is more Summer than Winter, more Fruit than Meat, and more meat than Hospitality.

LADY WAGTAIL. Why Captain, fruit is meat.

CAPTAIN. I mean flesh-meat.

LADY WAGTAIL. Out upon that Country, that hath neither Flesh nor Hospitality! But captain, what are the natures, dispositions, and manners of the Italians?

CAPTAIN. In general, Madam, thus, their natures, dispositions, and manners are, as generally all other people of every other Nation are, for the generality of every Nation are alike, in natures, dispositions and person; that is, some are of good, and some are of bad, some handsom and some ill-favoured; but for the most part, there are more ill-favoured than handsom, more foul than fair, and the general manner of the whole World is, to offer more than present, to promise more than perform, to be more faigning than real, more courtly than friendly, more treacherous than trusty, more covetous than generous, and yet more prodigal than covetous; but as for the *Italians*, they are more luxurious* than gluttonous, and they love pleasures more than Heaven.

LADY WAGTAIL. They have reason, by my troth; for who can tell whether in *Joves* Mansion, there are so many sweet and delightful pleasures, as in this World: But Captain, you do not tell me what pleasure the women have in *Italy?*

CAPTAIN. Those woman that are married, are restrain'd and barr'd from all courtly pleasure, or as I may say, the pleasure of Courtships; but the Courtezans have liberty to please themselves, and to be their own carvers.†

---

* luxurious] lecherous.

† carvers] those who can choose for themselves; a figure of speech probably derived from carving a roast, since the carver gets first choice of the meat, though the word's heavy repetition in this exchange is sexually suggestive.

LADY WAGTAIL. And there is nothing I love so well, as to carve both for my self and others.

CAPTAIN. And there is no Nation in the World, so curious, and ingenuous in the art of carving, as the *Italians.*

LADY WAGTAIL. I am resolved to go into *Italy,* if it be but to learn the art of carving, but I will leave my Husband behind me; for you say, wives have not that free liberty of carving, and if I leave my Husband, I may pass for a Widow, though not for a maid.

CAPTAIN. But Madam, you are past your travelling years, for the best time for women to travel, is about twenty.

LADY WAGTAIL. By your favour, Sir, a woman never grows old, if she can but conceal her age, and say she is young.

CAPTAIN. But she must often repeat it.

LADY WAGTAIL. She must so, which she may easily do, talking much, for women wants not words, neither are we sparing of them; But Captain, I must intreat your company, for you are acquainted with the Country, and hath the experience of the humours and natures of that people, and having been a Souldier and a Traveller, will not be to seek in the wayes of our journey.

CAPTAIN. I shall wait upon you, Madam.

LADY WAGTAIL. No Captain, you shall be as Master, to command, and I will be your Servant to obey.

CAPTAIN. You shall command me, Madam.

Exeunt.

Scene 34

Enter AFFECTIONATA *alone.*

O! How my soul is tormented with love, shame, grief and fear *(she stops a little)* I am in love, but am ashamed to make it known, Besides I have given the World cause to censure me, not only in concealing of my Sex, and changing of my habit, but being alwaies in the company of Men, acting a masculine part upon the Worlds great Stage,* and to the publick view: but could I live thus concealed, I should be happy, and free from censure: But O curst fortune! that pleasure takes in crossing Lovers, and busie time that makes all things as restless as it self, doth strive to divulge my acts, when I have no defence, or honest means for to conceal them; for if I do oppose, I

---

* In *CCXI Sociable Letters,* letter 195, Cavendish writes of her delight in an actress she saw in Antwerp, who played male characters very convincingly.

shall become a Murtherer, and bear a guilty conscience to my grave, which may torment my soul, when as my body is turn'd to dust.

Stops.

But since there is no remedy, i'l weep my sorrows forth, and with the water of my tears, i'l strive to quench the blushing heat, that like quick lightning, flashes in my face.

Enter the Lord SINGULARITY, *finding* AFFECTIONATA *weeping.*

LORD SINGULARITY. My dear *Affectionata,* What makes thee so melancholly, as to be alwaies weeping?

AFFECTIONATA. I must confess, my Lord, here of late my eyes have been like *Egypt,* when it is over-flown with *Nilus,* and all my thoughts like *Crockodiles.*

LORD SINGULARITY. What is the cause?

AFFECTIONATA. Alas, my Lord, causes lyes so obscure, they are seldom found.

LORD SINGULARITY. But the effects may give us light to judge what causes are.

AFFECTIONATA. Effects deceives, and often cozens us, by reason one effect may be produced from many several causes, and several effects proceeds from one cause.

LORD SINGULARITY. But thy tears seems as if they were produced from some passion.

AFFECTIONATA. Indeed they are produced from passions and appetites, for passions are the rayes of the mind, and appetites the vapour of the senses, and the rayes of my mind hath drawn up the vapour of my senses into thick moist clouds, which falls in showering tears.

LORD SINGULARITY. Tell me thy griefs, and thy desires, that I may help the one, and ease the other.

AFFECTIONATA. Alas, my Lord, I cannot, for they lye in the conceptions, and conceptions ariseth like mysts, and my thoughts like clouds, lyes one above another.

LORD SINGULARITY. Come, come, let reason the Sun of the soul verifie {rarify} those misty conceptions, and disperse this dull humour, that the mind may be clear, and the thoughts serene.

AFFECTIONATA. I will strive to bring in the light of mirth.

Exeunt.

Scene 35

Enter the Lady WAGTAIL, *the Lady* AMOROUS, *and Sir* HUMPHRY BOLD.

LADY WAGTAIL. Good Sir *Humphry Bold,* carry us to the Court of *Judicature,* to hear the great Tryal, which is said to be to day.

SIR HUMPHRY BOLD. You would go to hear the condemnation of an old man, and his old wife.

LADY WAGTAIL. No, we would go to hear the confessions, as whether they have murthered the young Lady that is missing, or not.

SIR HUMPHRY BOLD. Why, that you may hear from other relations, as well as from their own mouths, and so save you so much pains and trouble, as you will have to get a place, and to stand so long a time, as the examining, accusing, confessing, freeing, or condemning, which will require so long a time, as Ladies will find great inconveniencies, and be put mightily to it.

LADY WAGTAIL. But I long to hear and see the manner of it.

SIR HUMPHRY BOLD. I will wait upon you, but you will be very much crouded.

LADY AMOROUS. I had rather see them hanged, if they be guilty, than hear them judged and condemned.

SIR HUMPHRY BOLD. Why, a condemning Judge is the chief Hang-man, for he hangs with his word, as the other with a cord.

LADY WAGTAIL. Will the Lord *Singularity* be there?

SIR HUMPHRY BOLD. Yes certainly, for he is the man that doth accuse them.

LADY AMOROUS. And will his Son be there?

SIR HUMPHRY BOLD. I know not that.

Exeunt.

Scene 36

Enter the Judges and Jury-men, as in a Court of JUDICATURE; *the Lord* SIN-GULARITY, FOSTER TRUSTY, *and Nurse* FONDLY, *and many others to hear them.*

JUDGES. Who accuses these persons of murther?

LORD SINGULARITY. I, my Lord.

FOSTER TRUSTY. We beseech your Honours, not to condemn us before you have found us guilty.

LORD SINGULARITY. It is a proof sufficient, my Lord, they cannot clear themselves, or produce the party that was delivered to their trust and care.

JUDGES. Jurie, do you find them guilty or not?

JURIES. Guilty, my Lord.

JUDGES. Then from the Jurie, we can—

Enter AFFECTIONATA, *drest very fine in her own Sexes habit, and stops the Judges sentence.*

AFFECTIONATA. Hold, condemn not these innocent persons for their fidelity, constancy and love; I am that maid they are accused to murther, and by good circumstances can prove it.

*All the Assembly, Judges and Jurie, seems as in a maze at her beauty, and stares on
her. The Lord* SINGULARITY,* *as soon as he seeth her, starts back, then goeth
towards her, his eyes all the time fixt on her; speaking as to himself.*

LORD SINGULARITY. Sure it is that face. *He takes her by the Hand, and turns her
to the light;* are not you my *Affectionata,* whom I adopted my Son.

AFFECTIONATA. Shame stops my breath, and chokes the words I should utter.

LORD SINGULARITY. For Heaven sake speak quickly, release my fears, or crown
my joyes.

AFFECTIONATA. My Lord, pray pardon loves follies, and condemn not my
modesty for dissembling my Sex; for my designs were harmless, as only to
follow you as a servant: For by Heaven, my Lord? my only desire was, that
my eyes, and my eares might be fed with the sight of your person, and sound
of your voice, which made me travel to hear, and to see you: But since I am
discovered, I will otherwise conceal my self, and live as an *Anchoret*† from
the view of the World.

LORD SINGULARITY. Pray let me live with you.

AFFECTIONATA. That may not be, for an *Anchoret* is to live alone.

LORD SINGULARITY. If you will accept of me for your husband, we shall be as
one.

AFFECTIONATA. You have declared against marriage, my Lord.

LORD SINGULARITY. I am converted, and shall become so pious a devote, a
I shall offer at Alter but *Hymens,*‡ and since I am your Convert, refuse
me not.

AFFECTIONATA. I love too well to refuse you.

He kneels down on one knee, and kisses her hand.

LORD SINGULARITY. Here on my knee I do receive you as a blessing, and a gift
from the Gods.

He riseth.

AFFECTIONATA. Most Reverend Judges, and Grave Jury, sentence me not with
censure, nor condemn me to scandals, for waiting as a Man, and serving as a
Page; For though I dissembled in my outward habit and behaviour, yet I was
alwaies chaste and modest in my nature.

Exeunt.

---

* Misspelled as "Singulariry" in the original.

† *Anchoret*] Holy hermit, usually living "anchored" to a sanctuary; a woman would normally
be called an anchoress.

‡ *Hymens*] Hymen was the Roman god of marriage.

Scene 37

Enter the Lady WAGTAIL, *and Lady* AMOROUS.

LADY WAGTAIL. Now Lady *Amorous,* is your mind a Mirtel-grove, and your thoughts *Nightingals* to entertain the *Idea* of your *Adonas.*

LADY AMOROUS. Her discovery hath proved the boar that kill'd him; but I desire much to be at my *Adonas* Funeral, which is the Lady *Orphants* wedding.

LADY WAGTAIL. I am acquainted with some of the Lord *Singularity*'s Captains and Officers, and I will speak to some of them to speak to the Lord *Singularity* to invite us.

LADY AMOROUS. I pray do, for since my *Adonas* is dead, I will strive to inamour *Mars,** which is the Lord *Singularity* himself.

LADY WAGTAIL. Faith, that is unfriendly done, for I have laid my designs for himself.

LADY AMOROUS. I fear both of our designs may come to nothing, he is so inamoured with his own She-Page, or female Son.

Exeunt.

Scene 38

Enter Nurse FONDLY, *and* FOSTER TRUSTY.

NURSE FONDLY. O Husband! This is the joyfullest day that ever I had in my whole life, except at mine own wedding.

FOSTER TRUSTY. Indeed, this day is a day of *Jubile.*†

NURSE FONDLY. Of *Juno,*‡ say you; but Husband, have you provided good cheer, and enough; for here are a world of Guests come, more than was invited, and you being Master Steward, will be thought too blame, if there be anything wanting.

FOSTER TRUSTY. If you be as carefull to dress the Brides Chamber, as I do provide for the bridal Guest, you nor I shall be in a fault.

NURSE FONDLY. I faith, if you have done your part, as I have done my part, we shall deserve praise.

FOSTER TRUSTY. I faith, we are almost so old, that we are almost past praise.

NURSE FONDLY. None can merit praise, but those in years; for all Worthy,

---

* *Mars*] Roman god of war.

† *Jubile*] Jubilee, a day of rejoicing and forgiveness; in Hebrew history, a day when slaves were set free.

‡ *Juno*] Roman queen of the gods, associated with jealousy and sometimes with childbirth.

Noble and Heroik Acts requires time to do them, and who was ever wise, that was young?

FOSTER TRUSTY. And few are praised that are old, for as fame divulgeth merits, so time wears out praise, for time hath more power than fame, striving to destroy what fame desires to keep. The truth is, time is a Glutton, for he doth not only strive to destroy what fame divulgeth, but what himself begets and produceth.

Exeunt.

Scene 39

Enter the Lord SINGULARITY, *and the Lady* ORPHANT, *as Bride and Bride-groom, and a company of Bridal-guests.*
Enter Musitians, and meets them.

MUSITIONERS. We desire your Excellence will give us leave to present you with a Song written by my Lord *Marquiss* of *New-Castle*.

LORD SINGULARITY. Your present could have never been less acceptable, by reason it will retard my marriage.

LADY ORPHANT. Pray, my Lord, hear them.

LORD SINGULARITY. Come, come, dispatch, dispatch.

He seems not to listen to them. All the time his eyes fixt on the Bride.

SONG

Love in thy younger age,
Thou then turn'd Page;
When love then stronger grew,
The bright sword drew.
Then Love it was thy fate
To advise in State.
My Love adopted me
His childe to be.
Then offered was my hap
A Cardinals Cap.
Loves juglings thus doth make
the Worlds mistake.

LORD SINGULARITY. By Heaven, Musitioners, you are all so dillotarie with your damnable and harsh prologue of tuning before you play; as the next Parlia-

ment will make it felony in Fidlers, if not treason, when your Great Royal
Eares; begin with a Pox to you.

MUSITIANS. Why, my Noble Lord, we have done.

LORD SINGULARITY. By Heaven, there spake *Apollo!** Give them ten Pieces.

MUSITIANS. Madam, an *Eppilanian!*† we have more to express our further joy,
and then we will pray for blessings on you both.

LORD SINGULARITY. O! It will be my funeral song, you rogues, know all delays
doth kill me; and at this time you best Musick sounds harsh, and out of tune.

LADY ORPHANT. Pray let them sing that one song more; so ends your trouble of
them.

LORD SINGULARITY. Begin, quick, quick.

SONG

> *O Love, some says thou art a Boy!*
> *But now turn'd Girl, thy Masters joy.*
> *Now cease all thy fierce alarms,*
> *In circles of your loving arms.*
> *Who can express the joys to night,*
> *'Twil charm your senses with delight.*
> *Nay, all those pleasures you'l controul,*
> *With joyning your each soul to soul.*
> *Thus in Loves raptures live, till you*
> *Melting, dissolve into a dew;*
> *And then your aery journey take,*
> *So both one constellation make.*

The Song done, the Musick playes, as the Bride and Bridegroom goeth.

Finis

---

* *Apollo*] Greek and Roman sun god, also god of music and poetry.

† *Eppilanian*] epithalamion, a marriage song that celebrates the sexuality of the marriage bed.
This is so variant a spelling that it is probably Cavendish's own.

The First Part of *Bell in Campo*

THE LORD GENERAL

SEIGNEUR VALEROSO

MONSIEUR LA HARDY

MONSIEUR COMERADE

MONSIEUR LA GRAVITY

CAPTAIN RUFFELL

CAPTAIN WHIFFELL, AND SEVERAL
   OTHER GENTLEMEN

DOCTOR EDUCATURE

DOCTOR COMFORT

STEWARDS, MESSENGERS, AND
   SERVANTS

LADY VICTORIA

MADAM JANTIL

MADAM PASSIONATE

MADAM RUFFELL

MADAM WHIFFELL

DOLL PACIFY, MADAM
   PASSIONATES MAID

NELL CARELESS, MADAM
   JANTILS MAID, OTHER SER-
   VANTS AND HEROICKESSES

ACT I

Scene 1

Enter two Gentlemen.

1ST GENT. You hear how this Kingdome of Reformation is preparing for War against the Kingdome of Faction.

2ND GENT. Yea, for I hear the Kingdome of Faction resolves to War with this Kingdome of Reformation.

1ST GENT. 'Tis true, for there are great preparations of either side, men are raised of all sorts and ages fit to bear Arms, and of all degrees to command and obey, and there is one of the gallantest and noblest persons in this Kingdome, which is made General to command in chief; for he is a man that is both valiant and well experienced in Wars, temperate and just in Peace, wise and politick in publick affairs, carefull and prudent in his own Family, and a most generous person.

2ND GENT. Indeed I have heard that he is a most excellent Souldier.

1ST GENT. He is so, for he is not one that sets forth to the Wars with great resolutions and hopes, and returns with maskerd* fears, and despairs; neither is he like those that take more care, and are more industrious to get gay Clothes, and fine Feathers, to flant† in the Field, and vapour‡ in their march, than to get the usefull and necessary provision; but before he will march, he will have all things ready, and proper for use, as to fit himself with well-tempered Arms, which are light to be worn, yet musket proof; for he means not to run away, nor to yield his life upon easy terms unto his Enemy; for he desires to Conquer, and not vain-gloriously to shew his courage by a careless neglect or a vain carelessness; also he chooses such horses as are usefull in War, such as have been made subject to the hand and heel, that have been taught to Trot on the Hanches,§ to change, to Gallop, to stop, and such Horses as have spirit and strength, yet quiet and sober Natures; he regards more the goodness of the Horses than the Colours or marks, and more the fitness of his Saddles than the Imbrodery; also he takes more care that his Waggons should be easy to follow, and light in their carriage, than to have them painted and gilded; and he takes greater care that his Tents should be made, so as to be suddenly put up, and as quickly pull'd down, than for the setting and Imbrodering his Arms thereupon; also he takes more care to have usefull Servants than numerous Servants; and as he is industrious and carefull for his particular affairs, so he is for the general affairs.

2ND GENT. A good Souldier makes good preparations, and a good General doth both for himself and Army; and as the General hath showed himself a good Souldier by the preparations he had made to march, so he hath showen himself a wise man by the settlement he hath made, in what he hath to leave behind him; for I hear he hath setled and ordered his House and Family.

1ST GENT. He hath so, and he hath a fair young and virtuous Lady that he must leave behind him, which cannot choose but trouble him.

2ND GENT. The wisest man that is, cannot order or have all things to his own contentment.

Exeunt.

Scene 2

Enter the Lord GENERAL, *and the Lady* VICTORIA *his Wife.*

GENERAL. My dear heart, you know I am commanded to the Wars, and had I

---

  * maskerd] confused.
  † flant] obsolete form of *flaunt*.
  ‡ vapour] swagger.
  § Hanches] obsolete spelling of *haunches*.

not such Wife as you are, I should have thought Fortune had done me a favour to imploy my life in Heroical Actions for the service of my Country, or to give me a honourable Death, but to leave you is such a Cross as my Nature sinks under; but wheresoever you are there will be my life, I shall only carry a Body which may fight, but my Soul and all the powers thereof will remain with thee.

LADY VICTORIA. Husband, I shall take this expression of love but for feigning words, if you leave me; for 'tis against Nature to part with that we love best, unless it be for the beloveds preservation, which cannot be mine, for my life lives in yours, and the comfort of that life in your Company.

LORD GENERAL. I know you love me so well, as you had rather part with my life than I should part from my honour.

LADY VICTORIA. 'Tis true, my love perswades me so to do, knowing fame is a double life, as infamy is a double death; nay I should perswade you to those actions, were they never so dangerous, were you unwilling therunto, or could they create a world of honour, fully inhabited with praises; but I would not willingly part with your life for an imaginary or supposed honour, which dies in the womb before it is Born; thus I love you the best, preferring the best of what is yours; but I am but in the second place in your affections, for you prefer your honour before me; 'tis true, it is the better choice, but it shows that I am not the best beloved, which makes you follow and glue to that and leave me.

LORD GENERAL. Certainly Wife my honour is your honour, and your honour will be buried in my disgrace, which Heaven avert; for I prefer yours before my own, insomuch as I would have your honour to be the Crown of my glory.

LADY VICTORIA. Then I must partake of your actions, and go along with you.

LORD GENERAL. What to the Wars?

LADY VICTORIA. To any place where you are.

LORD GENERAL. But Wife you consider not, as that long marches, ill lodgings, much watching, cold nights, scorching dayes, hunger and danger are ill Companions for Ladyes, their acquaintance displeases; their conversation is rough and rude, being too boisterous for Ladyes; their tender and strengthless constitutions cannot encounter nor grapell therewith.

LADY VICTORIA. 'Tis said, that Love overcomes all things: in your Company long marches will be but as a breathing walk, the hard ground feel as a Feather-bed, and the starry sky a spangled Canopy, hot dayes a Stove to cure cold Agues, hunger as fasting dayes or an eve to devotion, and danger is honours triumphant Chariot.

LORD GENERAL. But Nature hath made women like China, or Purselyn,* they
must be used gently, and kept warily, or they will break and fall on Death's
head; besides, the inconveniencies in an Army are so many, as put patience
her self out of humour; besides, there is such inconveniences as modesty
cannot allow of.

LADY VICTORIA. There is no immodesty in natural effects, but in unnatural
abuses; but contrive it as well as you can, for go I must, or either I shall dye,
or dishonour you; for if I stay behind you, the very imaginations of your
danger will torture me, sad Dreams will affright me, every little noise will
sound as your passing Bell, and my fearfull mind will transform every object
like as your pale Ghost, untill I am smothered in my Sighs, shrouded in my
Tears, and buried in my Griefs; for whatsoever is joyned with true love, will
dye absented, or else their love will dye, for love and life are joyned together;
as for the honour of constancy, or constant fidelity, or the dishonour of
inconstancy, the lovingest and best wife in all story that is recorded to be, the
most perfectest and constantest wife in her Husbands absence was Penelope,† Ulysses wife, yet she did not Barricado her Ears from Loves soft
Alarums; but parled‡ and received Amorous Treaties, and made a Truce
until she and her Lovers could agree and conclude upon conditions, and
questionless there were Amorous Glances shot from loving eyes of either
party; and though the Siege of her chastity held out, yet her Husbands
Wealth and Estate was impoverished, and great Riots committed both in his
Family and Kingdome, and her Suters had absolute power therof; thus
though she kept the fort of her Chastity, she lost the Kingdom, which was
her Husbands Estate and Government, which was a dishonour both to her
and her Husband; so if you let me stay behind you, it will be a thousand to
one but either you will lose me in Death, or your honour in Life, where if
you let me go you will save both; for if you will consider and reckon all the
married women you have heard or read of, that were absented from their
Husbands, although upon just and necessary occasions, but had some Ink of
aspersions flung upon them, although their wives were old, illfavoured,
decrepid and diseased women, or were they as pure as light, or as innocent as
Heaven; and wheresoever this Ink of aspersion is thrown, it sticks so fast,
that the spots are never rubb'd out, should it fall on Saints, they must wear

---

* Purselyn] porcelain.

† Penelope] see the *Odyssey*. In her husband's absence Penelope held off suitors by agreeing to
marry one of them once she had completed a shroud for her father-in-law. She wove the shroud by
day and unraveled it by night.

‡ parled] spoke.

the marks as a Badge of misfortunes, and what man had not better be thought or called an uxorious Husband, than to be despised and laughed at, as being but thought a Cuckhold? the first only expresses a tender and noble Nature, the second sounds as a base, cowardly, poor, dejected, forsaken Creature; and as for the immodesty you mentioned, there is none, for there can be no breach of modesty, but in unlawfull actions, or at least unnecessary ones; but what Law can warrant, and necessity doth inforce, is allowable amongst men, pure before Angels, Religious before Gods, when unchosing* persons, improper places, unfit times, condemn those actions that are good in themselves, make them appear base to men, hatefull to Angels, and wicked to Gods, and what is more lawfull, fitting, and proper, than for a man and wife to be inseparable together?

LORD GENERAL. Well, you have used so much Rhetorick to perswade, as you have left me none to deny you, wherefore I am resolved you shall try what your tender Sex can endure; but I believe when you hear the Bullets fly about you, you will wish your self at home, and repent your rash adventure.

LADY VICTORIA. I must prove false first, for love doth give me courage.

LORD GENERAL. Then come along, I shall your courage try.

LADY VICTORIA. Ile follow you, though in Deaths Arms I ly.

Exeunt.

Scene 3

Enter the two former Gentlemen.

1ST GENT. Well met, for I was going to thy lodging to call thee to make up the Company of good fellows, which hath appointed a meeting.

2ND GENT. Faith you must go with the odd number, or get another in my room, for I am gong about some affairs which the Lord *General* hath imployed me in.

1ST GENT. I perceive by thee that publick imployments spoil private meetings.

2ND GENT. You say right, for if everyone had good imployment, vice would be out of fashion.

1ST GENT. What do you call vice?

2ND GENT. Drinking, Wenching, and Gaming.

1ST GENT. As for two of them, as Drinking and Wenching, especially Wenching, no imployment can abolish them, no, not the most severest, devotest, or dangerest; for the States-man Divines, and Souldiers, which are the most and greatest imployed, will leave all other affairs to kiss a Mistriss.

---

* unchosing] unchosen; Calvinist term for one who can do no right.

2ND GENT. But you would have me go to a Tavern and not to a Mistriss.

1ST GENT. Why, you may have a Mistriss in a Tavern if you please.

2ND GENT. Well, if my other affairs will give me any leisure, I will come to you. *Exeunt.*

Scene 4

Enter four or five other Gentlemen.

1ST GENT. The Lord *General* was accounted a discreet and wise man, but he shows little wisdom in this action of carrying his wife along with him to the Wars, to be a Clog at his heels, a Chain to his hands, an Incumberance in his march, obstruction in his way; for she will be always puling* and sick, and whining, and crying, and tir'd, and froward,† and if her Dog should be left in any place, as being forgotten, all the whole Army must make a halt whilst the Dog is fetcht, and Trooper after Trooper must be sent to bring intelligence of the Dogs coming, but if there were such a misfortune that the Dog could not be found, the whole Army must be dispersed for the search of it, and if it should be lost, then there must seem to be more lamentation for it than if the Enemy had given us an intire defeat, of else we shall have frowns instead of preferments.‡

2ND GENT. The truth is, I wonder the General will trouble himself with his wife, when it is the only time a married man hath to enjoy a Mistriss without jealousy, a spritely sound wench, that may go along without trouble, with bag and baggage, to wash his linnen, and make his field Bed, and attend to his call, when a wife requires more attendance than Centries to watch the Enemy.

3RD GENT. For my part I wonder that any man should be so fond of his wife as to carry her with him; for I am only glad of the Wars, because I have good pretense to leave my wife behind me; besides an Army is a quiet, solitary place, and yields a man a peaceable life compared to that at home: for what with the faction and mutiny among his Servants, and the noise the women make, for their tongues like as an Alarum beat up qua[r]ters§ in every Corner of the House, that a man can take no rest; besides every day he hath a set Battel with his wife, and from the Army of her angry thoughts, she sends

---

* pueling] puling, whimpering.

† froward] contrary.

‡ preferments] promotions. This speech may refer to a story about Queen Henrietta Maria's search for her lost dog, though legend has it that she endangered herself in searching, not that she "dispersed" soldiers (Grant, *Margaret the First*, 54).

§ beat up qua[r]ters] intrude upon and upset everyone.

forth such vollies of words with her Gunpowder anger, and the fire of her fury, as breaks all the ranks and files of content, and puts happiness to an utter rout, so as for my part I am forced to run away in discontent, although some Husbands will stay, and fight for the Victory.

4 GENT. Gentlemen, Gentlemen, pray condemn not a man for taking his lawfull delight, or for ordering his private affairs to his own humour, every man is free to himself, and to what is his, as long as he disturbs not his Neighbours, nor breaks the Peace of the Kingdome, nor disorders the Commonwealth, but submits to the Laws, and obeys the Magistrates without dispute; besides Gentlemen, 'tis no crime nor wonder, for a man to let his wife go along with him when he goeth to the Wars, for there hath been examples; for *Pompey* had a wife with him, and so had *Germanicus,** and so had many great and worthy Heroicks,† and as for *Alexander* the great‡ he had a wife or two with him; besides, in many Nations men are not only desired, but commanded by the Chiefs to let their wives go with them, and it hath been a practice by long Custome, for women to be spectators in their Battels, to encourage their fights, and so give fire to their Spirits; also to attend them in their Sicknesses, to clense their wounds, to dress their meat; and who fitter than a wife? what other woman will be so lovingly carefull, and industriously helpfull as a wife? and if the *Greeks* had not left their wives behind them, but had carried them along to the *Trojan* Wars,§ they would not have found such disorders as they did at their return, nor had such bad welcome home, as witness *Agamemnons;*‖ besides, there have been many women that have not only been Spectators, but Actors, leading Armies, and directing Battels with good success, and there have been so many of these Heroicks, as it would be tedious at this time to recount; besides the examples of womens courage in Death, as also their wise conduct, and valiant actions in Wars are many, and pray give me to speak without your being offended thereat, it is not Noble, nor the part of a Gentleman, to censure, condemn, or dispraise another mans private actions, which nothing concerns him, especially when there is

---

* *Pompey . . . Germanicus*] Pompey (A.D. 106–48) and Germanicus (15 B.C.–A.D.19) were Roman generals.

† Heroicks] heroes.

‡ *Alexander* the great] king of Macedonia and conqueror of Persia (356–323 B.C.).

§ *Trojan* Wars] The Greeks invaded Troy when Paris, a Trojan prince, abducted Helen, the wife of a Greek king.

‖ *Agamemnons*] Agamemnon was leader of the Greek army, killed by his wife Clytemnestra upon his return from Troy because, before setting out, he had sacrificed their daughter Iphegenia to propitiate the gods.

so gallant a subject to discourse of as the discipline and actions of these Wars we are entring into.

1ST GENT. Introth Sir, you have instructed us so well, and have chid us so handsomely, as we are sorry for our errour, and ask pardon for our fault, and our repentance shall be known by that we will never censure so again.

Exeunt.

ACT II

Scene 5

Enter Captain WHIFFELL *and Madam* WHIFFELL *his Wife.*

CAPTAIN WHIFFELL. I have heard our Generals Lady goeth with the General her Husband to the Wars, wherefore I think it fit for the rest of the Commanders, if it were only for policy, to let our General see that we approve of his actions so well, as to imitate him in ours, carrying our Wives along with us, besides the Generals Lady cannot chose but take it kindly to have our Wives wait upon her, wherefore Wife it is fit you should go.

MADAM WHIFFELL. Alas Husband I am so tender, that I am apt to catch cold if the least puff of wind do but blow upon me; wherefore to ly in the open Fields will kill me the first Night, if not, the very journey will shatter my small bones to peeces.

CAPTAIN WHIFFELL. Why, our Generals Lady is a very fine young Lady, and she ventures to go.

MADAM WHIFFELL. There let her venture, for you must excuse me, for I will stay at home, go you where you please.

CAPTAIN WHIFFELL. Well Wife consider it.

Exeunt.

Scene 6

Enter Captain RUFFELL, *and his Wife Madam* RUFFELL.

CAPTAIN RUFFELL. Wife prepare your self to follow the Army, for 'tis now the fashion for Wives to march, wherefore pack up and away.

MADAM RUFFELL. What with a Knapsack behind me as your Trull? not I, for I will not disquiet my rest with inconveniences, nor divert my pleasures with troubles, nor be affrighted with the roring Cannons, nor indanger my life with every Potgun, nor be frozen up with Cold, nor stew'd to a gelly with heat, nor be powdered up with dust, untill I come to be as dry as a Neats-tongue;* besides, I will not venture my Complexion to the wroth of the Sun, which will tan me like a Sheeps skin.

CAPTAIN RUFFELL. Faith Wife, if you will not go, I will have a Landery-Maid to ride in my Waggon, and ly in my Tent.

MADAM RUFFELL. Prethee Husband take thy Kitching Maid along too, for she may have as much Grease about her as will serve to make Sope to wash your Linnen with, and while you ride with your Landery-Maid in your Waggon, I will ride with my gentleman-Usher in my Coach.

CAPTAIN RUFFELL. Why Wife, it is out of love that I would have thee go.

MADAM RUFFELL. And 'tis out of love that I will stay at home; besides, do you think I mean to follow your Generals Lady as a common Trooper doth a Commander, to feed upon her reversions,† to wait for her favour, to watch for a smile; no, no, I will be *Generalissimo* my self at home, and distribute my Colours to be carried in the Hats of those that will fight in my quarrel, to keep or gain the Victory of my favour and love.

CAPTAIN RUFFELL. So I may chance to be a Cuckhold before I return home.

MADAM RUFFELL. You must trust to Fortune for that, and so I wish you a good Journey.

Exeunt.

Scene 7

Enter Seigneur VALEROSO *and his friend Monsieur la* HARDY, *to take their leaves of their Wives, Madam* JANTIL, *and Madam* PASSIONATE, *Madam* JANTIL *young and beautifull, Madam* PASSIONATE *in years.*

MADAM JANTIL. I cannot chuse but take it unkindly that you will go without me, do you mistrust my affection? as that I have not as much love for you as the General's Lady hath for her Husband; or do you desire to leave me? because you would take a Mistriss along with you, one that perchance hath more Beauty than you think me to have; with whom you may securely, and freely sit in your Tent, and gaze upon; or one that hath more wit than I, whose sweet, smooth, and flattering words may charm your thoughts, and draw your Soul out of your ears to sit upon her Lips, or dancing with delight upon her Tongue.

SEIGNEUR VALEROSO. Prethee Wife be not jealous, I vow to Heaven no other Beauty can attract my eyes but thine, nor any sound can please my brain, but what thy charming Tongue sends in; besides, I prise not what thy Body is,

---

* Neats-tongue] ox tongue.
† reversions] leftovers.

but how thy Soul's adorn'd, thy virtue would make me think thee fair, although thou wert deformed, and wittier far than *Mercury,** hadst thou *Midas's* ears,† but thou hast all that man can wish of women kind, and that is the reason I will leave thee safe at home; for I am loth to venture all my wealth and happiness in Fortunes unconstant Bark, suffering thy tender youth and Sex to float on the rough waves of chance, where dangers like to Northern winds blow high, and who can know but that fatal gusts may come, and overwhelm thee, and drown all my joys? wherefore for my sake keep thyself safe at home.

MADAM JANTIL. I shall obey you, but yet I think it not well I should be a long time from you, and at a great distance.

SEIGNEUR VALEROSO. I will promise you, if I perceive the War is like to be prolonged, and that there be Garrison-Towns so safe as you may securely live in, I will send for you, placing you so where sometimes I may visit you.

MADAM JANTIL. Pray do not forget me so much as to cancell your promise.

SEIGNEUR VALEROSO. Forget thee‡ sweet? I should sooner forget life, and if I do whilst I have memory, Heaven forget me.

MADAM JANTIL. I must ask you a question, which is to know why you will take an under command, being so nobly Born, and bearing a high Title of Honour your self, and being Master of a great Estate.

SEIGNEUR VALEROSO. To let the World see my Courage is above my Birth, Wealth, or Pride, and that I prefer inward worth before outward Title, and I had rather give my life to the Enemy on honourable terms, than basely to stay at home in time of general Wars, out of an ambitious discontent; for valour had rather have dangers to fight with, than Offices to command in.

Seigneur VALEROSO *and his Lady whispers, while the other two Monsieur la* HARDY *and his Lady speaks.*

MADAM PASSIONATE. Why should you go to the Wars now you are in years, and not fit for action as those that are young, and have their strengths about them? besides, we have lived a married pair above these thirty years, and never parted, and shall we now be seperated when we are old?

She weeps.

MONSIEUR LA HARDY. Alas Wife, what would you have me do? when I am commanded out I must obey; besides, I would not have my Country fight a

---

* *Mercury*] messenger to the gods; god of thieves and traders.
† *Midas's* ears] asses' ears received by King Midas in answer to a foolish wish.
‡ This read "the" in the original.

Battel whilst I live, and I not make one, for all the World, for when I cannot fight, my Body shall serve to stop a breach; wherefore leave your crying Wife, and fall to praying for our safe return, and here my noble friend is desirous you should stay with his Lady to comfort one another, and to divert Melancholy and the longing hours of our return.

MADAM PASSIONATE. Farewell, I fear I shall never see you again, for your absence will soon kill me.

She cryes. Exeunt.

Scene 8

Enter two Gentlemen.

1ST GENT. O you are welcome from the Army, what news?

2ND GENT. Why our Army march'd untill they came unto the frontiers of the Kingdome, where they found the Army of the Enemy ready to encounter them, the Lord *General* seeing they must of necessity fight a Battel, thought best to call a Council of War, that there might be nothing of ill conduct laid to his chardge, but that all might be ordered by a wise and experienced Council, whereupon he made an election of Counsellors, joyning together three sorts, as grave, wise, and prudent men, subtill and politick men, and valiant, skillfull, martiall men, that the cold temper of the prudent, might allay the hot temper of the valiant, and that the politick might be as ingenious {Engines} to serve them together by subtill devises, and to make traps of Stragems to catch in the Enemy, and at this Council many debates there were, but at last they did conclude a Battel must be fought; but first they did decree that all women should be sent into one of their Garrison Towns, some two dayes journey from the Army, the reasons were, that if they should be overcome by their Enemyes, the women might be taken by their Enemyes, and made Slaves, using or abusing them as they pleased; but when the women were sent away, they did not shed tears of sorrow, but sent such vollies of angry words, as wounded many mens hearts; but when they were almost at the Town that was to be their aboad, the Generals Lady, was so extremely incensed against the Counsellers, by reason they decreed her departure with the others, as she strove to raise up the Spirits of the rest of her Sex to the height of her own; but what the issue will be I know not.

1ST GENT. Have you been with the King?

2ND GENT. Yes, I was sent to give him an account of the Army.

Exeunt.

Scene 9

Enter the Lady VICTORIA *and a number of women of all sorts with her, she takes her stand upon a heap of green Turfs, as being in the Fields before the Garrison Town, and then speaks to those women.*

LADY VICTORIA. Most Heroical Spirits of most chast and loving Wives, Mistrisses, Sisters, Children or Friends, I know you came not from your several Houses and homes into this Army meerly to enjoy your Husbands, Lovers, Parents and Friends in their safe and secure Garrisons, or only to share of their troublesome and tedious marches, but to venture also in their dangerous and cruel Battels, to run their Fortunes, and to force Destiny to joyn you to their Periods; but the Masculine Sex hath separated us, and cast us out of their Companyes, either out of their loving care and desire of preserving our lives and liberties, lest we might be distroyed in their confusions, or taken Prisoners in their loss, or else it must be out of jealousy we should Eclipse the fame of their valours with the splendour of our constancy; and if it be Love, let us never give the preheminence, for then we should lose that Prerogative that belongs to the Crown of our Sex; and if it be thorough Jealous mistrust of their Fame, it were poor for us to submit and quit that unto men, that men will not unto us, for Fame makes us like the Gods, to live for ever; besides, those women that have staid at home will laugh at us in our return, and their effeminate Lovers and Carpet Knights, that Cowardly and Luxuriously Coin excuses to keep and stay them from the Wars, will make Lampons* of us for them to sing of our disgrace, saying, our Husbands, Lovers, and Friends were so weary of us, as they were forced to take that pretense of affectionate love to be rid of our Companyes; wherefore if you will take my advise, let us return, and force those that sent us away to consent that we shall be partakers with them, and either win them by perswasions, or lose our selves by breaking their decrees; for it were better we should dy by their angry frowns, than by the Tongue of Infamy.

All the women call to her.

ALL THE WOMEN. Let us return, let us return.

Lady VICTORIA *waves her hand for them to keep silence.*

LADY VICTORIA. Noble Heroickesses, I am glad to hear you speak all as with one voice and Tongue, which shows your minds are joyned together, as in one piece, without seam or rent; but let us not return unfit to do them service, so we may cause their ruin by obstruction, which will wound us

---

* Lampons] lampoons, satires.

more than can their anger; wherefore let us strive by our industry to render our selves usefull to their service.

ALL THE WOMEN. Propound the way, and set the Rules, and we will walk in the one, and keep strictly to the other.

LADY VICTORIA. Then thus, we have a body of about five or six thousand women, which came along with some thirty thousand men, but since we came, we are not only thought unusefull, but troublesome, which is the reason we were sent away, for the Masculine Sex is of an opinion we are only fit to breed and bring forth Children, but otherwise a trouble in a Common-wealth, for though we encrease the Common-wealth by our breed, we encomber it by our weakness, as they think, as by our incapacities, as having no ingenuity for Inventions, nor subtill wit for Politicians; nor prudence for direction, nor industry for execution; nor patience for opportunity, nor judgment for Counsellers, nor secrecy for trust; nor method to keep peace, nor courage to make War, nor strength to defend our selves or Country, or to assault an Enemy; also that we have not the wisdome to govern a Common-wealth, and that we are too partial to sit in the Seat of Justice, and too pittifull to execute rigorous Authority when it is needfull, and the reason of these erronious opinions of the Masculine Sex to the Effeminate,* is, that our Bodyes seem weak, being delicate and beautifull, and our minds seem fearfull, being compassionate and gentle natured, but if we were both weak and fearfull, as they imagine us to be, yet custome which is a second Nature will encourage the one and strengthen the other, and had our educations been answerable to theirs, we might have proved as good Souldiers and Privy Counsellers, Rulers and Commanders, Navigators and Architectors, and as learned Scholars† both in Arts and Sciences, as men are; for Time and Custome is the Father and Mother of Strength and Knowledge, they make all things easy and facil, clear and prospitious; they bring acquaintance, and make friendship of every thing; they make Courage and Fear, Strength and Weakness, Difficulty and Facility, Dangers and Securities, Labours and Recreations, Life and Death, all to take and shake as it were hands together; wherefore if we would but accustome our selves we may do such actions, as may gain us such a reputation, as men might change their opinions, insomuch as to believe we are fit to be Copartners in their Governments, and to help to rule the World, where

---

* Emended to "female" or "femal" in the copy of *Plays* (1662) in the Taylor Collection at Princeton University. This emendation appears twice more in *Bell in Campo*, ten times in the whole Taylor copy, always in reference to women; in reference to unmasculine behavior in men, "effeminate" is retained.

† This read "Sholars" in the original.

now we are kept as Slaves forced to obey; wherefore let us make our selves free, either by force, merit, or love, and in order, let us practice and endeavor, and take that which Fortune shall profer unto us, let us practice I say, and make these Fields as Schools of Martial Arts and Sciences, so shall we become learned in their disciplines of War, and if you please to make me your Tutoress, and so your Generalless, I shall take the power and command from your election and Authority, otherwise I shall most willingly, humbly, and obediently submit to those whom you shall choose.

ALL THE WOMEN. You shall be our Generalless, our Instructeress, Ruler and Commanderess, and we will every one in particular, swear to obey all your Commands, to submit and yield to your punishments, to strive and endeavor to merit your rewards.

LADY VICTORIA. Then worthy Heroickesses, give me leave to set the Laws and Rules I would have you keep and observe, in a brass Tablet.

ALL THE WOMEN. We agree and consent to whatsoever you please.

Exeunt.

Scene 10

Enter the Lady JANTIL *alone.*

MADAM JANTIL. How painfull is true love absented from what is loved, 'tis strange that that which pleaseth most should be the greatest torment.

Enter Madam PASSIONATE.

MADAM PASSIONATE. What, all times walking by your self alone? when your Lord returns I will complain, and tell him what dull Company you are.

MADAM JANTIL. I hope I shall not be from him so long, for he promised to send for me.

MADAM PASSIONATE. Nay faith, when you go, as old as I am, I will travell with you to see my Husband too.

MADAM JANTIL. You will be so much the more welcome, by how much you were unexpected.

MADAM PASSIONATE. You look pale in the sudden, are not you well?

MADAM JANTIL. Yes, onely on a sudden I had a chill of cold that seized on my Spirits.

MADAM PASSIONATE. Beshrew me,* their coldness hath nipt the blood out of your Cheeks and Lips.

MADAM JANTIL. If they had been painted, they would have kept their Colour.

Exeunt.

---

* Beshrew me] Oath meaning "Corrupt me."

ACT III

Scene 11

Enter the Lady VICTORIA *with a great Company of Women, after a Table of Brass carried before her, she stands upon the heap of Turfs, and another Woman that carried the Table, wherein the Laws and Rules are inscribed; she bids her read them.*

READER. Noble Heroicks, these are the Laws our Generaless hath caused to be inscribed and read for every one to observe and keep.

First, Be it known, observed and practised, that no woman that is able to bear Arms, shall go unarmed, having Arms to wear, but shall wear them at all times, but when they put them off to change their linnen; they shall Sleep, Eat and Rest, and march with them on their Bodies.

LADY VICTORIA. Give me leave, Noble Heroicks to declare the reason of this Law or Command, as to wear an Iron or Steel Habit, and to be so constantly worn, is, that your Arms should not feel heavy, or be troublesome or painfull for want of use, as they will be when you shall have an occasion to put them on; and certainly, for want of practice, more Masculine Souldiers are overcome by their Arms, than by their Enemies, for the unaccustomedness makes them so unwieldy, as they can neither defend themselves, nor assault their Foes, whereas Custome will make them feel as light, as their Skins on their Flesh, or their Flesh on their Bones, nay Custome hath that force, as they will feel as if their Bodies were Naked, when as their Arms are off, and as Custome makes the Cold and peircing Ayr to have no power over the naked Bodyes of men, for in cold Countreys as well as hot, men have been accustomed to go naked, and have felt no more harm, nor so much, by the cold, than those that are warmly Cloathed, so Custome will make your Arms seem as light as if you had none on, when for want of use their waight will seem heavy, their several pieces troublesome and incombersome, as their Gorgets* will seem to press down on their Shoulders, their Back and Breastplates and the rest of the several pieces to cut their waste, to pinch their Body, to bind their Thighes, to ty their Arms, and their Headpiece to hinder their breath, to darken their sight, and to stop their hearing, and all for want of use and Custome; but enough of this, read on.

READER. Secondly, Be it known, observed and practised, that every Company must watch by turns, whether they have Enemyes neer or no, and at all

---

* Gorgets] armor to protect the throat.

times, and whosoever Drinks any thing but Water, or Eats any thing but Bread, all the time they are on the watch shall be punished with fasting.

LADY VICTORIA. Give me leave to declare the reason of this Law, the reason is, that strong Drinks, and nourishing Meats send many vapours to the Brain, which vapours are like several Keys, which lock up the Senses so fast, as neither loud noises, bright lights, nor strong sents can enter either at the Ears, Eyes, or Nostrils, insomuch as many times their Enemies send Death to break them asunder.

READER. Thirdly, Be it known, observed and practiced, that none of the Troopers march over Corn Fields if it can be avoided, unless the Enemy should be behind, and then the more spoil the better.

LADY VICTORIA. The reason is of this, that it were a great imprudence to destroy through a careless march of Horse and Foot, that which would serve to feed and nourish us in the Winter time, and in our Winter quarters, when it is laid in the Barns and Granaries, by the labour and the industry of the Farmers.

READER. Fourthly, Be it known, observed and practised, that none shall plunder those things which are waighty of carriage, unless it be for safety or necessity.

LADY VICTORIA. The reason of this is, that all that is heavy in the carriage is a hindrance in our march.

READER. Fiftly, Be it known, observed and practised, that no Souldiers shall play as any Game for money or drink, but only for meat to eat.

LADY VICTORIA. The reason of this is, that those that play for drink, the winners will be drunk, and those that are drunk are unfit for service; besides, many disorders are caused by drunkenness; and to play for money, the losers grow Cholerick* and quarrels proceed therefrom, which quarrels many times cause great mutinies through their side taking, and factious parties, besides, having lost their money and not their Appetites, they become weak and faint for want of that nourishing food, their money should get them, having nothing left to buy them victuals withall; besides, it forces them to forrage further about, where by straggling far from the body of the Army, they are subject to be catch'd by the Enemy, but when they play for meat their winnings nourish their Bodies, making them strong and vigorous, and when their Appetites are satisfied, and their Stomacks are fill'd, their hu-

---

* Cholerick] angry. According to the theory of humors, choler is caused by an excess of yellow bile in the body, melancholy by an excess of black bile, sloth by an excess of phlegm, and foolish cheer by an excess of blood.

mours are pleasant, and their minds couragious; besides, it is the Nature of most Creatures, either to distribute or at least to leave the remaining pieces to the next takers, so that the losers may have a share with the winners, and part of what was their own again.

READER. Sixtly, Be it known, observed and practised, that no Captains or Collonels, shall advance beyond their Company, Troop, Regiment or Brigade, but keep in the middle of the first rank, and the Lieutenant or Lieutenant Collonel to come behind in the last rank.

LADY VICTORIA. The reason of this is, that Collonels and Captains going aspace before their Troops, Companies or Regiments, for to encourage and lead on their Souldiers, do ill to set themselves as marks for the Enemy to shoot at, and if the Chief Commanders should be kill'd, the Common Souldiers would have but faint hearts to fight, but for the most part they will run away, as being affraid and ashamed to see the Enemy, when their Chief Commander is kill'd, and if they have no Officer or Commander behind them, the Common Souldiers will be apt to run away, having no worthy witnesses or Judges, to view and condemn their base Cowardly actions, which otherwise they are ashamed of, chusing rather to fight their Enemies than to make known their fears.

READER. Seventhly, Be it known, observed and practised, that none of the Army ly in Garrison Towns, but be always intrenched abroad.

LADY VICTORIA. The reason of this is, that Towns breed or beget a tenderness of Bodies and laziness of limbs, luxurious Appetites, and soften the natural dispositions, which tenderness, luxury, effeminacy, and laziness, corrupts and spoils martial discipline, whereas the open Fields, and casting up trenches makes Souldiers more hardy, laborious and carefull, as being more watchfull.

READER.* Eightly, Be it known, observed and practised, that none unless visibly sick to be idle, but imployed in some Masculine action, as when not imployed against an Enemy, and that they are not imployed about the works, forts or trenches, but have spare time to imploy themselves, in throwing the Bar, Tripping {Pitching},† Wrastling, Running, Vaulting, Riding, and the like exercise.

READER. Ninthly, Be it known, observed and practised, that every Commander when free from the Enemies surprizals, shall train their men thrice a week at

---

* "Reader" inserted by this editor.

† Tripping] running an obstacle course. This term is crossed out and not replaced in the Princeton copy of *Playes* (1662); in the Harvard copy it is emended to "pitching."

least, nay every day, if they can spare so much time, as putting their Souldiers into several ranks, files and figures, in several Bodies apart, changing into several places, and the like.

LADY VICTORIA. The reason of this is, that the Souldiers may be expert and ready, and not be ignorant when they encounter their Enemies, for many a Battel is lost more through the ignorance of the Souldiers, not being well and carefully train'd by their Commanders, or having such Commanders that know not how to train or draw them up, there are more Battels I say lost thus, than for want of men or courage.

READER. Tenthly, Be it known, observed and practised, that every Morning when Incamp'd, that every Commander shall make and offer in the midst of his Souldiers a Prayer to *Mars,* another to *Pallas,** a third to *Fortune,* and a fourth to *Fame;* these Prayers to be presented to these Gods and Goddesses with great Ceremony, both from the Commander and Common Souldiers.

LADY VICTORIA. The reason of this is, that Ceremony strikes a reverence and respect into every breast, raising up a devotion in every heart, and devotion makes obedience, and obedience keeps order, and order is the strength and life to an Army, State, or Common-wealth; and as for the Prayers presented to these particular Gods and Goddesses, is, that *Mars* would give us courage and strength, *Pallas* give us prudent conduct, *Fortune* give us Victory, and *Fame* give us Glory and Renown.

READER. Eleventhly, Be it known, observed and practiced, that the most experienced, practiz'd, and ingenioust Commanders shall preach twice a week of Martial Discipline, also those errors that have been committed in former Wars, and what advantages have been taken, to be cited in their Sermons, as also what was gain'd or lost by meer Fortune.

READER. Twelfthly, Be it known, observed and practised, that when the Army marches, that the Souldiers shall sing in their march the heroical actions done in former times by heroical women.

LADY VICTORIA. The reason of this is, that the remembrance of the actions of gallant persons inflames the Spirit to the like, and begets a courage to a like action, and the reason of singing of heroical actions only of women, is that we are women our selves.

READER. Thirteenthly, Be it known, observed and submitted to, that no Council shall be call'd, but that all affairs be ordered and judged by the Generaless her self.

---

* *Mars . . . Pallas*] Mars was the Roman god of war, and Pallas, the Greek and Roman goddess of war and wisdom.

LADY VICTORIA. The reason of this is, that all great Councils, as of many persons, confounds judgments, for most being of several opinions, and holding strongly and stifly, nay obstinately thereunto, as every one thinking themselves wisest, cause a division, and wheresoever a division is there can be no final conclusion.

READER. Fourteenthly, Be it known, observed and practised, that none of this Effeminate Army admits of the Company of men, whilst they are in Arms or Warlike actions, not so much as to exchange words, without the Generaless her leave or privilege thereto.

LADY VICTORIA. The reason of this is, that men are apt to corrupt the noble minds of women, and to alter their gallant, worthy, and wise resolutions, with their flattering words, and pleasing and subtil insinuations, and if they have any Authority over them, as Husbands, Fathers, Brothers, or the like, they are apt to fright them with their threats into a slavish obedience; yet there shall be chosen some of the most inferiour of this Female Army, to go into the Masculine Army, to learn their designs, and give us intelligence of their removals, that we may order our incampings and removings according as we shall think best; but these women shall neither be of the Body of our Army, nor keep amongst the Army, nor come within the Trenches, but ly without the works in Huts, which shall be set up for that purpose.

READER. Lastly, Whosoever shall break any of these Laws or Orders, shall be put to Death, and those that do not keep them strictly, shall be severely punished.

LADY VICTORIA. But I am to advise you Noble Heroicks, that though I would not have a general Council call'd to trouble our designs in War with tedious disputes, and unnecessary objections, and over cautious doubts, yet in case of life and death, there shall be a Jury chosen to sit and judge their Causes, and the whole Army shall give their votes, and the most voices shall either condemn, or reprieve, or save them, lest I should hereafter be only call'd in question, and not the rest, as being not accessary thereunto; and now you have heard these Laws or Orders, you may assent or dissent therefrom as you please, if you assent, declare it by setting your hands thereto, if you dissent, declare it by word of mouth, and the Tables shall be broken.

ALL THE WOMEN. We assent, and will set our hands thereto.

Exeunt.

Scene 12

Enter Doctor EDUCATURE *the Lady* JANTILS *Chaplain, and* NELL CARELESS *her Maid.*

DOCTOR EDUCATURE. *Nell,* how doth your good Lady?

NELL CARELESS. Faith she seems neither sick nor well, for though her Body seems in health, her Mind seems to be full of trouble, for she will rise in the midst of the Night, and walk about her Chamber only with her Mantle about her.

DOCTOR EDUCATURE. Why doth she so?

NELL CARELESS. I ask'd her why she broke her sleep so as to walk about, and she answered me, that it was frightfull Dreams that broke her sleep, and would not let her rest in quiet.

DOCTOR EDUCATURE. Alas she is Melancholick in the absence of my Lord.
Exeunt.

Scene 13

Enter the Lady VICTORIA *and a number of other Women.*

LADY VICTORIA. Now we are resolved to put our selves into a Warlike body, our greatest difficulty will be to get Arms; but if you will take my advise we may be furnished with those necessaries, as thus, the Garrison we are to enter is full of Arms and Amunition, and few men to guard them, for not only most of the Souldiers are drawn out to strengthen the Generals Army, and to fight in the battel, but as many of the Townsmen as are fit to bear Arms; wherefore it must of necessity be very slenderly guarded, and when we are in the Town, we will all agree in one Night, when they shall think themselves most secure, to rise and surprize those few men that are left, and not only disarm them and possess our selves of the Town and all the Arms and Ammunition, but we will put those men out of the Town or in safe places, untill such time as we can carry away whatsoever is usefull or needfull for us, and then to go forth and intrench, untill such time as we have made our selves ready to march, and being once Master or Mistriss of the Field we shall easily Master the Pesants, who are for the most part naked and defenceless, having not Arms to guard them, by which means we may plunder all their Horses, and victual our selves out of their Granaries; besides, I make no question but our Army will increase numerously by those women that will adhere to our party, either out of private and home discontents, or for honour and fame, or for the love of change, as it were a now course of life; wherefore let us march to the Town and also to our design, but first I must have you all swear secrecy.

ALL THE WOMEN. We are all ready to swear to what you will have us.
Exeunt.

Scene 14

Enter Madam JANTIL *alone as rising out of her Bed, her Mantle wrapt about her, and in her night linnen.*

MADAM JANTIL. I saw his Face pale as a Lilly white,

His wounds fresh bleeding blood like rubies bright;

His Eyes were looking steadfastly on me,

Smiling as joying in my Company;

He mov'd his lips as willing was to speak,

But had no voice, and all his Spirits weak;

He shak'd his hand as if he bid farewell,

That brought the message which his tongue would tell;

He's dead, he's dead, a sunder break my heart,

Let's meet in Death, though Wars our lives did part.

After she had walkt silently a turn or two about her Chamber her eyes being fixt in the ground, she return'd as to her Bed. Exit.

Scene 15

Enter a gentleman, and another meets him as in great haste.

1ST GENT. What news? what news?

2ND GENT. Sad news, for there hath been a Battel fought betwixt the two Armies, and our Army is beaten, and many of our gallant men slain.

1ST GENT. I am sorry for that.

The second gentleman goeth out. Enter a third gentleman.

1ST GENT. Sir I suppose you are come newly from the Army, pray report the Battel?

3RD GENT. Truly I came not now from the Army, but from the Town the Generals heroical Lady and the rest of the heroicks did surprize, seise and plunder.

1ST GENT. What the Garrison Town they were sent to for safety?

3RD GENT. Yes.

1ST GENT. And doth their number encrease?

3RD GENT. O very much, for after the surprisal of the Town the women in that Town did so approve of their gallant actions, as every one desired to be inlisted in the roul, and number of the *Amazonian** Army, but in the mean time of the forming of their Army, intelligence was brought of the Battel

---

* *Amazonian*] After Amazons, women warriors in Greek myth.

which was fought, and that there was such loss of both sides as each Army
retir'd back, being both so weak as neither was able to keep the Field, but
that the loss was greater on the reformed Army, by reason there was so many
of their gallant men slain, but this news made many a sad heart and weeping
eyes in the Female Army; for some have lost their Husbands, some their
Fathers, others their Brothers, Lovers and Friends.

1ST GENT. Certainly this will fright them out of the Field of War, and cause
them to lay by their Heroick designs.

3RD GENT. I know not what they will do, for they are very secret to their designs,
which is strange, being all women.

Exeunt.

ACT IV

Scene 16

Enter two women like AMAZONS.

1ST WOMAN. Our Generaless seems to be troubled, perceiving how heavily this
Female Army takes their losses.

2ND WOMAN. She hath reason, for it may hinder or at least obstruct her high
designs.

Exeunt.

Scene 17

Enter the Lady VICTORIA *and her* AMAZONS, *she takes her stand and speaks to
them.*

LADY VICTORIA. Noble Heroicks, I perceive a mourning veil over the face of
this Female Army, and it becomes it well; for 'tis both natural and human to
grieve for the Death of our friends; but consider constant Heroicks, tears nor
lamentations cannot call them out of the grave, no petitions can perswade
Death to restore them, nor threats to let them go, and since you cannot have
them alive being Dead, study and be industrious to revenge their quarrels on
their Enemies lives, let your justice give them Death for Death, offer upon
the Tombs of your Friends the lives of their Foes, and instead of weeping
eyes, let us make them weep through their Veins; wherefore take courage,
cast off your black Veil of Sorrow, and take up the Firematch of Rage, that
you may shoot Revenge into the hearts of their Enemies, to which I hope
Fortune will favour us; for I hear that as soon as the Masculine Army have
recovered strength there will be another Battel fought, which may be a

means to prove our loves to our Friends, our hate to our Enemies, and an aspiring to our honour and renown; wherefore let us imploy our care to fit our selves for our march.

ALL THE WOMEN. We shall follow and obey you, where, and when, and how you please.

Exeunt.

Scene 18

Enter Doctor EDUCATURE, *and* NELL CARELESS; *the Doctor weeps.*

DOCTOR EDUCATURE. Doth my lady hear of my Lords Death?

NELL CARELESS. The Messenger or Intelligencer of my Lords Death is now with her.

Exeunt.

Scene 19

Enter Madam JANTIL, *and a gentleman Intelligencer; the Lady seems not disturb'd, but appears as usually.*

MADAM JANTIL. How died my Lord?

GENTLEMAN. Madam, he fought with so much courage, as his actions will never dye, and his valour will keep alive the memory of this War: for though he died, his Death was Crown'd with Victory, he digg'd his Grave out of his Enemies sides, and built his Pyramid with heaps of their Bodies; the groans of those he slew did ring his dying Knell.

MADAM JANTIL. What became of his body?

GENTLEMAN. He gave order before the Armies joined to fight, that if he were kill'd, his body should be sought out, and delivered to you: for he said it was yours whilst he lived, and he desired it might be disposed of by you when he was dead; his desires and commands were obeyed, and his body is coming in a Litter lapt in Searcloth.*

MADAM JANTIL. Worthy Sir, I give you many thanks for your noble relation, assuring my self it is true because you report it, and it is my Husband that is the subject and ground of that honourable relation, whom I always did believe would out-act all words.

GENTLEMAN. He hath so Madam.

MADAM JANTIL. Sir, if I can at any time honourably serve you, I shall be ready whensoever you will command me.

GENTLEMAN. Your Servant Madam.

* Searcloth] cerecloth; shroud.

(He was going forth and returns)

If your Ladyship hath not heard of Monsieur la *Hardy*'s Death, give me leave to tell you he is slain.

MADAM JANTIL. I am sorry, and for his Lady, for she loved him most passionably.

The gentleman goes out. Enter as running and calling out DOLL PACIFY, *Madam* PASSIONATE*'s Maid.*

DOLL PACIFY. Help, help, my Lady is dead, my Lady is fallen into a swound at the report of my Masters being kill'd.

The Lady goeth out and the Maid, then they enter straight again with two or three Servants more, bringing in the Lady PASSIONATE *as in a swound.*

MADAM JANTIL. Alas poor Lady, her Spirits are drown'd in Sorrow, and Grief hath stopt her breath; loosen her Garments, for she is swell'd with troubled Thoughts, her Passions lie on heaps, and so oppress life, it cannot stir, but makes her senceless.

Upon the loosing of her garments she revives, and cryes out.

MADAM PASSIONATE. O my Husband, my Husband!

She swounds again.

MADAM JANTIL. Bow her forward, bow her forward.

Madam PASSIONATE *revives again.*

MADAM PASSIONATE. O let me dye, let me dye, and bury, bury me with him.

Swounds again.

MADAM JANTIL. Alas poor Lady, put her to Bed, for her life will find most ease there.

The servants go out with Madam PASSIONATE. *Madam* JANTIL *alone.*

MADAM JANTIL. O life what art thou? and Death where doest thou lead us, or what dissolv'st thou us into?

Exeunt.

Scene 20

Enter two Gentlemen.

1ST GENT. I wonder there is no news or Messenger come from the Army yet, when there usually comes one every day.

Enter a Messenger.

2ND GENT. O sir, what news?

MESSENGER. Faith there hath been nothing acted since the last Battel, but it is said there will be another Battel very suddenly, for the Enemy provokes our men to fight, by reason our Lord General lies sick of his wounds, having had a Feavour, caused by the anguish of his hurts, and by his Sickness the Enemies hope to gain an advantage of his absence, but he hath put a Deputy in his place to command in chief until he recovers.

1ST GENT. What is become of the Female Army?

MESSENGER. I hear they are marched towards the Masculine Army, but upon what design I cannot understand.

Exeunt.

Scene 21

Enter Madam JANTIL, *and her Maid* NELL CARELESS.

MADAM JANTIL. Call my Steward.

The Maid goes out. The Lady walks in a musing posture, her eyes fixt on the ground. Enter the Steward weeping.

STEWARD. O Madam, that I should live to hear this cursed news of my dear Lord and Masters Death.

MADAM JANTIL. Life is a curse, and there's none happy but those that dye in the womb before their birth, because they have the least share of misery; and since you cannot weep out life, bear it with patience; but thy tears have almost washt out the memory of what I was to say, but this it is, that I would have you sell all my Jewels, Plate, and Houshold Furniture to the best advantage, and to turn off all my Servants, but just those to attend my person, but to reward all of them with something more than their wages, and those Servants that are old, and have spent their youth with my Lords Predecessors and in his service, but especially those he favoured most, give them so much during their lives as may keep them from the miseries of necessity, and vexations of poverty. Thirdly, I would have you hire the best and curioust* Carvers or Cutters of Stones to make a Tomb after my direction; as First I will have a marble piece raised from the ground about half a mans height or somthing more, and somthing longer than my Husbands dead body, and then my Husbands Image Carved out of Marble to be laid thereupon, his Image to be Carved with his Armor on, and half a Head-piece in the Head, that the face might be seen, which face I would have to the life as much as Art can make it; also let there be two Statues, one for *Mercury,* and another for *Pallas,* these two Statues to stand at his head, and the hands of these Statues to join and to be laid under as carrying the head of my Husbands figure, or as the head lay thereupon, and their hands as his Pillow; on the right side of

---

* curioust] most curious; most meticulous.

his figure, let there be a Statue for *Mars,* and the hand of *Mars*'s Statue holding the right hand of my Husbands figure, and on the left hand a Statue for *Hymen,** the hand on the place of the heart of my husbands figure, and at the feet of the figure let there be placed a statue for *Fortune* also, about a yard distance from the Tomb at the four Corners therof, let there be four Marble Pillars raised of an indifferent height, and an Arched Marble Cover thereupon, and let all the ground be paved underneath with Marble, and in the midst on the outside of the Marble roof let the statue of *Fame* be placed in a flying posture, and as blowing a Trumpet; then some two yards distance square from those Pillars, let the ground be paved also with Marble, and at the four Corners four other Marble Pillars raised as high as the former, with Capitals at top, and the body of those pillars round, and the Statues of the four Cardinal Virtues placed on those Capitals, sitting as in a weeping posture, and at the feet of those Pillars the Statues of the Graces imbracing each Pillar; as the Statue of Charity, the Pillar whereon the Statue of Justice fits, and the Statue of Patience, the Pillar of Temperance, and the Statue of Hope, the Pillar of Prudence, and the Statue of Faith, the Pillar of Fortitude; then set a grove of Trees all about the out-side of them, as Lawrel, Mirtle, Cipress, and Olive, for in Death is Peace, in which Trees the Birds may sit and sing his Elegy; this Tomb placed in the midst of a piece of ground of some ten or twenty Acres, which I would have incompassed about with a Wall of Brick of a reasonable height, on the inside of the Wall at one end, I would have built a little house divided into three Rooms, as a Gallery, a Bed-chamber, and a Closet, on the outside of the Wall a House for some necessary Servants to live in, to dress my meat, and to be ready at my call, which will be but seldome, and that by the ring of a Bell, but the three Rooms I would have furnished after this manner, my Chamber and Bed therein to be hung with white, to signify the Purity of Chastity, wherein is no Colours made by false lights; the Gallery with several Colours intermixt, to signify the varieties, changes, and incombrances of life; my Closet to be hung with black, to signify the darkness of Death, wherein all things are forgotten and buried in Oblivion; thus will I live a signification, not as a real substance but as a shaddow made betwixt life and death; from this house which shall be my living Tomb, to the Tomb of my dead Husband, I would have a Cloyster built, through which I may walk freely to my Husbands Tomb, from the injuries of the weather, and this Cloyster I would have all the sides therof

---

* *Hymen*] Roman god of marriage.

hung with my Husbands Pictures drawn to the life by the best Painters, and all the several accidents, studies and exercise of his life; thus I will have the story of his life drawn to the life; see this my desire speedily, carefully, and punctually done, and I shall reward your service as a carefull and diligent Steward and Servant.

STEWARD. It shall be done, but why will not your Ladyship have my Lords figure cast in Brass?

MADAM JANTIL. Because the Wars ruin Tombe before Time doth, and metals being usefull therein are often taken away by necessity, and we seldome find any ancient Monuments but what are made of Stone, for covetousness is apt to rob Monuments of metal, committing Sacrileges on the dead, for metals are soonest melted into profit, but Stone is dull and heavy, creeping slowly, bringing but a cold advantage, wherein lies more pains than gains.

STEWARD. But your Ladyship may do all this without selling your Jewels, Plate, and Houshold Furniture.

MADAM JANTIL. It is true, but I would not let so much wealth ly dead in Vanity, when exchanging them for money, I can imploy it to some good use.

STEWARD. Your Ladyship hath forgotten to give orders for blacks.*

MADAM JANTIL. No I have not, but I will give no mourning untill my Husbands body be carried to the Tomb; wherefore I have nothing more to imploy you in at this time, but only to send hither my Chaplain Doctor *Educature.*

The Steward goes out. Enter Doctor EDUCATURE.

MADAM JANTIL. Doctor, although it is not the profession of a Divine to be an Historian, yet you knowing my Husbands life and natural disposition best, being in his Childhood under you Tutorage, and one of his Family ever since, I know none so proper for that work as you; and though you are naturally an eloquent Orator, yet the bare truth of his worthy Virtues and Heroical actions will be sufficient to make the story both profitable, delightfull, and famous; also I must intreat you to choose out a Poet, one that doth not meerly write for gain, or to express his own wit, so much as to endeavor to Pencil with the pen Virtue to the life, which in my Lord was so beautifull as it was beyond all draughts, but the theam will inspire his Muse, and when both of these works are writ, printed and set out, as divulged to the world as a patern for examples, which few will be able to imitate, then I would have these books ly by me as Registers of memory, for next unto the Gods my life shall be spent in Contemplation of him; I know I shall not need to perswade

---

* blacks] black mourning clothes, traditionally worn by a widow for a year.

you to do this, for your affection to his memory is ready of it self; but love and duty binds me to express my desires for his Fame leaving nothing which is for my part thereunto.

DOCTOR EDUCATURE. Madam, all the service I can do towards the memory of my dear Pupil, and noble Lord and Patron, shall be most devoutly observed and followed; for Heaven knows, if I had as many lives to dispose of as I have lived years, I would have Sacrificed them all for to have redeemed his life from Death.

Doctor EDUCATURE *goes out. Madam* JANTIL *alone.*

MADAM JANTIL. When I have interred my Husbands body, and all my desires thereunto be finished, I shall be at some rest, and like an Executrix to my self executing my own will, distributing the Rites and Ceremonies, as Legacies to the dead, thus living gives the dead; but O my Spirits are tired with the heavy burden of Melancholy, and grow faint for want of rest, yet my senses invite me thereunto, yet I cannot rest in my Bed, for frightfull Dreams disturb me; wherefore I will ly down on this floor, and try if I can to get a quiet sleep on the ground, for from Earth I came, and to Earth I would willingly return.

She lays her self down upon the ground, on one side of her Arm bowing, leaning upon her Elbow, her Forehead upon the palm of her hand bowing forwards, her face towards the ground; but her grief elevating her passion, thus speaks.

MADAM JANTIL. Weep cold Earth, through your pores weep,
Or in your bowels my salt tears fast keep;
Inurn my sighs which from my grief is sent,
With my hard groans build up a Monument;
My Tongue like as a pen shall write his name,
My words as letters to divulge his fame;
My life like to an Arch over his Ashes bend,
And my desires to his grave descend;
I warn thee Life keep me not Company,
I am a friend to Death thy Enemy;
For thou art cruell, and every thing torments,
Wounding with pain all that the World presents;
But Death is generous and sets us free,
Breaks off our Chains, and gives us liberty;
Heals up our wounds of trouble with sweet rest,
Draws our corrupted passions from our breast;
Layes us to sleep on Pillows of soft ease,
Rocks us with silence nothing hears nor sees.

She fetches a great sigh.

O that I may here sleep my last.

After a short slumber she wakes.

If it were not for Dreams sleep would be a happiness next unto Death; but I find I cannot sleep a long sleep in Death, I shall not dye so soon as I would.

Love is so strong and pure it cannot dy,
Lives not in sense, but in the Soul doth lye;
Why do I mourn? his love with mine doth dwell,
His love is pleas'd mine entertains it well;
But mine would be like his one imbodied,
Only an Essence or like a Godhead.

Exeunt.

Scene 22

Enter Doctor COMFORT, *and* DOLL PACIFY.

DOCTOR COMFORT. How doth our Lady *Doll?*

DOLL PACIFY. To day she began to sit up, but yet she is very weak and faint.

DOCTOR COMFORT. Heaven help her.

DOLL PACIFY. You that are Heavens Almner,* should distribute Heavens gifts out of the purse of your mouth, and give her single Godly words instead of single silver pence, to buy her some Heavenly food to feed her famisht mind.

DOCTOR COMFORT. Thou are a full-fed wench.

DOLL PACIFY. If I were no better fed than you feed me, which is but once a week, as on Sundayes, I should be starved.

DOCTOR COMFORT. You must fast and pray, fast and pray.

Exeunt.

ACT V

Scene 23

Enter two Gentlemen.

1ST GENT. All the young Gallants in the Town are preparing themselves with fine Cloths and Feathers to go a woing to the two rich Widows, the Lady *Jantil,* and the Lady *Passionate.*

2ND GENT. Riches are the Loadstone of affection, or at least professions.

---

* Heavens Almner] one who gives charity, or alms, in heaven's name.

1ST GENT. The truth is, Riches draw more Suters, than Youth, Beauty, or Virtue. *Exeunt.*

Scene 24

Enter two or three Gentlemen, Monsieur COMERADE, *Monsieur* COMPAGNION, *and Monsieur la* GRAVITY.

MONSIEUR COMERADE. For Heavens sake let us go and address our selves to the two Rich Widows.

MONSIEUR COMPAGNION. For my part I will address my self to none but the young Widow, the Lady *Jantil,* and to her let us go without delay.

MONSIEUR LA GRAVITY. It will be uncivil to go so soon after their Husbands Death, for their Husbands are not yet laid in their Graves.

MONSIEUR COMPAGNION. If they were we should come too late, for I knew a man which was a great friend of mine, who was resolved to settle himself in a married course of life, and so he went a wooing to a Widow, for a Widow he was resolved to marry, and he went a wooing to one whose Husband was but just cold in his grave, but she told him she was promised before, so he wooed another whilst she followed her Husbands Corps, but she told him he came too late, whereat he thought with the third not to be a second in his Sute, and so expressed his desires in her Husbands sickness, she told him she was very sorry that she had past her word before to another, for if she had not, she would have made him her choice, whereat he cursed his imprudence, and wooed the fourth on her wedding day, who gave him a promise after her husband was dead to marry him, and withall she told him, that if she had been married before, it had been ten to one but he had spoke too late, for said she, when we are Maids we are kept from the free conversation of men, by our Parents or Guardians, but on our wedding day we are made free and set at liberty, and like as young Heirs on the day of one and twenty we make promises like bonds for two or three lives; wherefore I fear we shall miss of our hopes, for these two Widows will be promised before we address our Sute.

MONSIEUR LA GRAVITY. No no, for I am confident all do not so, for some love to have the freedoms of their wills, for every promise is a bondage to those that make a Conscience to keep their promise, besides, it is not only variety that pleaseth women, but new Changes; for stale Acquaintance is as unpleasant as want of change, and the only hopes I have to the end of my Sute, is, that I am a Stranger and unknown, for women fancy men beyond what they are when unknown, and prize them less than their merits deserve, when they are acquainted.

MONSIEUR COMERADE. Well, we will not stay, but we will do our indeavour to get admittance.

Exeunt.

Scene 25

Enter Madam PASSIONATE *as very ill, sitting in a Chair groaning, Enter Madam* JANTIL *as to see her.*

MADAM JANTIL. Madam, how do you find your health?

MADAM PASSIONATE. Very bad, for I am very ill, but I wonder at your Fortitude, that you can bear such a Cross as the loss of your Husband so patiently.

MADAM JANTIL. O Madam I am like those that are in a Dropsie, their face seems full and fat, but their liver is consumed, and though my sorrow appears not outwardly, yet my heart is dead within me.

MADAM PASSIONATE. But your young years is a Cordiall to restore it, and a new love will make it as healthfull as ever it was.

Enter DOLL PACIFY *the Lady* PASSIONAT*'s Maid, with a Porrenger of Cawdle.**

DOLL PACIFY. Pray Madam eat somthing, or otherwise you will kill your self with fasting, for you have not eaten any thing since the beginning of your sorrow.

LADY PASSIONATE. O carry that Cawdle away, carry it away, for the very sight doth overcome my Stomack.

DOLL PACIFY. Pray Madam eat but a little.

LADY PASSIONATE. I care not for it, I cannot eat it, nor will not eat it: wherefore carry it away, or I will go away.

Both the Ladies goe out. Enter NELL CARELESS *Madam* JANTILS *Maid.*

NELL CARELESS. Prethee if thy Lady will not eat this Cawdle, give it me, for I have an Appetite to it; but I wonder you will offer your Lady any thing to eat, but rather you should give her somthing to drink, for I have heard sorrow is dry, but never heard it was hungry.

DOLL PACIFY. You are mistaken, for sorrow is sharp, and bites upon the Stomack, which causes an eager Appetite.

NELL CARELESS. I am sure weeping eyes make a dry Throat.

(She eats and talks between each spoonfull.)

DOLL PACIFY. But Melancholy Thoughts make a hungry Stomack; but faith if thou wert a Widow, by thy eating thou wouldst have another Husband quickly.

---

* *Porrenger of Cawdle*] bowl of thin gruel mixed with spiced wine or ale.

NELL CARELESS. Do you think I would marry again?

DOLL PACIFY. Heaven forbid that a young woman should live a Widow.

NELL CARELESS. Why is it a sin for a young woman to live a Widow?

DOLL PACIFY. I know not what it would be to you, but it would be a case of Conscience to me if I were a Widow.

NELL CARELESS. By thy nice Conscience thou seem'st to be a Puritan.

DOLL PACIFY. Well, I can bring many proofs; but were it not a sin, it is a disgrace.

NELL CARELESS. Where lies the disgrace?

DOLL PACIFY. In the opinion of the World, for old Maids and musty Widows are like the plague shun'd of by all men, which affrights young women so much, as by running frow it they catch hold on whatsoever man they meet, without consideration of what or whom they are, by which many times they fall into poverty and create misery.

NELL CARELESS. You teach a Doctrine, that to escape one mischief they fall on another, which is worse than the first; wherefore it were better to live a musty Widow as you call them, than a miserable Wife; besides, a man cannot intimately love a Widow, because he will be a Cuckold, as being made one by her dead Husband, and so live in Adultry, and so she live in sin her self by Cuckolding both her Husbands, having had two.

DOLL PACIFY. I believe if you were a Widow you would be tempted to that sin.

NELL CARELESS. Faith but I should not, for should I commit that sin, I should deserve the Hell of discontent.

DOLL PACIFY. Faith you would marry if you were young, and fair, and rich.

NELL CARELESS. Those you mention would keep me from marrying; for if any would marry me for the love of youth and beauty, they would never love me long, because time ruins both soon; and if any one should marry me meerly for my riches, they would love my riches so well and so much as there would be no love left for me that brought it, and if my Husband be taken Prisoner by my wealth, I shall be made a Slave.

DOLL PACIFY. No, not if you be virtuous.

NELL CARELESS. Faith there is not one in an Age that takes a wife meerly for virtue, nor valews a wife any thing the more for being so; for poor Virtue sits* mourning unregarded and despised, not any one will so much as cast an eye towards her, but all shun her as you say they do old Maids or musty Widows.

---

* This read "Virtune sit" in the original.

DOLL PACIFY. Although you plead excellently well for not marrying, yet I make no question but you would willingly marry if there should come a young Gallant.

NELL CARELESS. What's that, a Fool that spends all his wit and money on his Clothes? or is it a gallant young man which is a man enriched with worth and merit?

DOLL PACIFY. I mean a Gallant both for bravery and merit.

NELL CARELESS. Nay, they seldome go both together.

DOLL PACIFY. Well, I wish to Heaven that *Hymen* would give thee a Husband, and then that *Pluto** would quietly take him away to see whether you would marry again, O I long for that time.

NELL CARELESS. Do not long too earnestly, lest you should miscarry of your desires.

Enter Madam PASSIONATE, *whereat* NELL CARELESS *hearing her come, she runs away.*

MADAM PASSIONATE. Who was it that run away?

DOLL PACIDY. *Nell Careless* Madam *Jantils* Maid.

MADAM PASSIONATE. O that I could contract a bargain for such an indifferent mind as her young Lady hath, or that the pleasures of the World could bury me grief.

DOLL PACIFY. There is no way for that Madam, but to please your self still with the present times, gathering those fruits of life that are ripe, and next to your reach, not to indanger a fall by climing too high, nor to stay for that which is green, nor to let it hang whilst it is rotten with time, nor to murmur for that which is blowen down by chance, nor to curse the weather of accidents for blasting the blossoms, nor the Birds and Worms of Death, which is sickness and pain, for picking and eating the berries, for nature allows them a part as well as you, for there is nothing in the World we can absolutely possess to our selves; for Time, Chance, Fortune and Death, hath a share in all things, life hath the least.

MADAM PASSIONATE. I think so, for I am weary of mine.

The Lady goes out. Enter a Man.

MAN. Mistriss Dorothy, there are two or three Gentlemen that desire to speak with one of the Widows Maids, and you belong to one.

DOLL PACIFY. Well, what is their business?

MAN. I know not, but I suppose they will declare that to your self.

* *Pluto*] Roman god of the underworld; in Greek, *Hades*.

She goeth out, and enters again as meeting the Gentlemen.

DOLL PACIFY. Gentlemen, would you speak with me?

MONSIEUR LA GRAVITY. Yes, for we desire you will help us to the honour of kissing your Ladyes hands, thereon to offer our service.

DOLL PACIFY. Sir, you must excuse me, for the Sign of Widowhood is not as yet hung out, Mourning is not on, nor the Scutcheons are not hung over the Gate, but if you please to come two or three dayes hence I may do you some service, but now it will be to no purpose to tell my Lady, for I am sure she will receive no visits.

Exeunt.

Finis

The Second Part of *Bell in Campo*

THE LORD GENERAL, AND MANY COMMANDERS

MONSIEUR LA GRAVITY

MONSIEUR LE COMPAGNION

MONSIEUR COMERADE

DOCTOR EDUCATURE

DOCTOR COMFORT, AND DIVERS GENTLEMEN, MESSENGERS, SERVANTS,
    OFFICERS AND OTHERS

LADY VICTORIA, AND MANY HEROICKS

LADY JANTIL

LADY PASSIONATE

DOLL PACIFY

NELL CARELESS, CITY WIVES AND OTHERS

ACT I

Scene 1

Enter Doctor COMFORT, *and* DOLL PACIFY.

DOLL PACIFY. Good Master Priest go comfort my old Lady.

DOCTOR COMFORT. If you will Comfort me, I will strive to Comfort her.

DOLL PACIFY. So we shall prove the Crums of Comfort.

DOCTOR COMFORT. But is my Lady so sad still?

DOLL PACIFY. Faith to day she hath been better than I have seen her, for she was
    so patient as to give order for Blacks; but I commend the young Lady
    Madam *Jantil,* who bears out the Siege of Sorrow most Couragiously, and on
    my Conscience I believe will beat grief from the fort of her heart, and
    become victorious over her misfortunes.

DOCTOR COMFORT. Youth is a good Souldier in the Warfare of Life, and like a valiant Cornet or Ensign, keeps the Colours up, and the Flag flying, in despite of the Enemies, and were our Lady as young as Madam *Jantil*, she would grieve less, but to lose an old Friend after the loss of a young Beauty is a double, nay a trible affliction, because there is little or no hopes to get another good Husband, for though an old woman may get a Husband, yet ten thousand to one but he will prove an Enemy, or a Devill.

DOLL PACIFY. It were better for my lady if she would marry again, that her Husband should prove a Devill than a Mortal Enemy, for you can free her from the one though not from the other, for at your words, the great Devil will avoid or vanish, and you can bind the lesser Devils in Chains, and whip them with holy Rods untill they rore again.

DOCTOR COMFORT. Nay, we are strong enough for the Devil at all times, and in all places, neither can he deceive us in any shape, unless it be in the shape of a young Beauty, and then I confess he overcomes us, and torments our hearts in the fire of love, beyond all expression.

DOLL PACIFY. If I were a Devil I would be sure to take a most beautifull shape to torment you, but my Lady will torment me if I stay any longer here.

Exeunt.

Scene 2

Enter two Gentlemen.

1ST GENT. Sir, you being newly come from the Army, pray what news?

2ND GENT. I suppose you have heard how our Army was forced to fight by the Enemies provocations, hearing the Lord General lay sick, whereupon the Generals Lady the Lady *Victoria*, caused her *Amazonians* to march toward the Masculine Army, and to entrench some half a mile distance therefrom, which when the Masculine Army heard thereof, they were very much troubled thereat, and sent a command for them to retreat back, fearing they might be a disturbance, so a destruction unto them by, doing some untimely or unnecessary action; but the Female Army returned the Masculine Army an Answer, that they would not retreat unless they were beaten back, which they did believe the Masculine Sex would not, having more honour than to fight with the Female Sex; but if the men were so base, they were resolved to stand upon their own defence; but if they would let them alone, they would promise them upon the honour of their words not to advance any nearer unto the Masculine Army, as long as the Masculine Army could assault their Enemies, or defend themselves, and in this posture I left them.

Exeunt.

Scene 3

Enter the Lady VICTORIA, *and her Heroickesses.*

LADY VICTORIA. Noble Heroickesses, I have intelligence that the Army of Reformations begins to flag, wherefore now or never is the time to prove the courage of our Sex, to get liberty and freedome from the Female Slavery, and to make our selves equal with men; for shall Men only sit in Honours chair, and Women stand as waiters by? shall only Men in Triumphant Chariots ride, and Women run as Captives by? shall only men be Conquerors, and women Slaves? shall only men live by Fame, and women dy in Oblivion? no, no, gallant Heroicks raise your Spirits to a noble pitch, to a deaticall* height, to get an everlasting Renown, and infinite praises, by honourable, but unusual actions; for honourable Fame is not got only by contemplating thoughts which lie lasily in the Womb of the Mind, and prove Abortive, if not brought forth in living deeds; but worthy Heroickesses, at this time Fortune desires to be the Midwife, and if the Gods and Goddesses did not intend to favour our proceedings with a safe deliverance, they would not have offered us so fair and fit an opportunity to be the Mothers of glorious Actions, and everlasting Fame, which if you be so unnatural to strangle in the Birth by fearfull Cowardize, may you be blasted with Infamy, which is worse than to dye and be forgotten; may you be whipt with the torturing tongues of our own Sex we left behind us, and may be scorned and neglected by the Masculine Sex, whilst other women are preferr'd and beloved, and may you walk unregarded untill you become a Plague to your selves; but if you Arm with Courage and fight valiantly, may men bow down and worship you, birds taught to sing your praises, Kings offer up their Crowns unto you, and honour inthrone you in a mighty power.

> *May time and destiny attend your will,*
> *Fame be your Scribe to write your actions still;*
> *And may the Gods each act with praises fill.*

ALL THE WOMEN. Fear us not, Fear us not, we dare and will follow you wheresoever and to what you dare or will lead us, be it through the jawes of Death.

---

* deaticall] like a goddess.

THE PRAYER

LADY VICTORIA. *Great* Mars *thou God of War, grant that our Squadrons may like unbroaken Clouds move with intire Bodyes, let Courage be the wind to drive us on, and let our thick swell'd Army darken their Sun of hope with black despair, let us powre down showers of their blood, to quench the firy flames of our revenge.*

> And where those showers fall, their Deaths as seeds
> Sown in times memory sprout up our deeds;
> And may our Acts Triumphant garlands make,
> Which Fame may wear for our Heroicks sake.

Exeunt.

Scene 4

Enter Doctor COMFORT *and* DOLL PACIFY.

DOCTOR COMFORT. Doll, how doth our Lady since the burying of my Patron?

DOLL PACIFY. Faith she begins now to have regard to her health, for she take Jackalato every Morning in her Bed fasting, and then she hath a mess of Gelly broath for her Breakfast, and drinks a Cup of Sack before Dinner, and eats a Whitewine Cawdle every afternoon, and for her Supper she hath new laid Eggs, and when she goes to Bed, she drinks a hearty draught of Muskadine* to make her sleep well; besides, if she chances to wake in the Night, she takes comfortable Spirits, as *Angelica, Aniseeds, Besor, aquamirabilis,*† and the like hot waters, to comfort her heart, and to drive away all Melancholy thoughts.

DOCTOR COMFORT. Those things will do it if it be to be done, but I am sorry that my Lady hath sold all my Patrons Horses, Saddles, Arms, Cloaths, and such like things at the Drums head, and by out-cryes, to get a little the more money for them, I fear the World will condemn her, as believing her to be covetous.

DOLL PACIFY. O that's nothing, for what she loses by being thought covetous, she will regain by being thought rich, for the World esteems and respects nothing so much as riches.

Exeunt.

---

* Jackalato . . . Muskadine] jackalato, chocolate; sack, sherry wine; muskadine, a sweet wine.

† *Angelica . . . aquamirabilis*] angelica, an herb used for both medicine and candy; aniseeds, licorice-flavored seeds; besor, a tonic; aquamirabilis, highly spiced wine.

ACT II

Scene 5

Enter two Gentlemen.

1ST GENT. Pray Sir what news from the Army? you are newly come from thence.

2ND GENT. I suppose you have heard how the Effeminate Army was some half a mile from the Masculine Armies; but the Masculine Army being very earnest to fight, not only to get Victory and power, but to revenge each others losses, as their Friends slain in the former Battel, which thoughts of revenge did so fire their minds and inflame their Spirits, that if their Eyes had been as much illuminated as their flaming Spirits were, there might have been seen two blazing Armies thus joining their Forces against each other; at last began a cruell fight, where both the Armies fought with such equal Courages and active Limbs, as for a long time neither side could get the better, but at the last the Army of Faction broak the Ranks and Files of the Army of Reformation, whereupon every Squadron began to fall into a Confusion, no order was kept, no chardge was heard, no command obey'd, terror and fear ran maskerd about, which helpt to rout our Army, whereupon the Enemy kill'd many of our men, and wounded many more, and took numbers of Prisoners; but upon this defeat came in the Female Army, in the time that some of the Enemy was busy gathering up the Conquered spoils, others in pursute of the remainders of our men, others were binding up the Prisoners, others driving them to their Quarters like a Company of Sheep to a Market there to be sold; but when as some of the Commanders perceived a fresh Army coming towards them, their General commanded the Trumpets to sound a Retreat to gather them together, and also made haste to order and settle his men in Battel Array, and desirous their General was to have all the Prisoners slain; but the Female Army came up so fast and so close to prevent that mischief, as they had not time to execute that design; but their General encouraged his Souldiers, and bid them not to be disheartened, perswading them not to lose what they had got from an Army of men to an Army of boys, for said he they seem to be no other by the appearance of their shapes and statures; but when the Female Army came to encounter them, they found their charge so hot and furious as made them give place, which advantage they took with that prudence and dexterity, as they did not only rout this Army of Faction, killing and wounding many, and set their own Countrymen at liberty, and recovered their losses, and gained many spoils, and took numbers of Prisoners of their Enemies with Bag and Baggage, but they pursued those that fled into their Trenches, and beat them out of their works, and took possession thereof, where they found much riches; these Trenches being taken, the Lady *Victoria* took possession, and made them her Quarters, calling all her Female Souldiers to enter therein by the sound of Flutes, which they always used instead of Trumpets, and their Drums were Kettel-Drums; but upon this Victory the Masculine Sex of the Army of Reformation was much out of Countenance, being doubly or trebly over-come, twice by their Enemy, and then by the gallant actions of the Females which out-did them, yet they thought it best to take advantage whilst the Victory was fresh and flourishing, and their Enemies weak and fearfull, to lay siege to the next Towns in the Enemies Country; whereupon the Lady *Victoria* and her Female Souldiers hearing of the Army of Reformations designs, for they had sent the men to their own Quarters as soon as the Battel was won and Victory got; Also the Masculine Prisoners they sent to the mens Quarters, not intermixing themselves with men, but as I said they hearing the design they had to besiege the Towns were much inraged for not making them of their Councils, whereupon they sent a Messenger like as an Embas-sadour to tell the Masculine Army they did wonder at their ingratitude, that they should forget so much their relievers as to go upon any Warlike design without making them acquainted therewith, striving as it were to steal the Victory out of their hands, but said they, since we are become victorious over our Enemies, and Masters, and Mistresses of the Field, by our own valiant actions and prudent conducts, we will maintain our power by our own strengths, for our Army is now become numerous, full and flourishing, formed, and comfortable by our Discipline, skillfull by our practice, valiant by our resolutions, powerfull by our victory, terrible to our Enemies, hon-ourable to our Friends, and a subject of Envy to the Masculine Sex; but your Army is weak and decrepid, fitter for an Hospital than for a Field of War, your power is lost, your courage is cold, your discipline disorderous, and your command sleighted, despised by your Enemies, pittied by your Friends, forsaken of good Fortune, and made subject unto our Effeminate Sex, which we will use by our power like Slaves. But when our Lord General who was recovered out of his sickness, and all his Commanders about him heard this message, which was delivered in a full assembly, according as the Lady *Victoria* had commanded the message should be, the men could not chose but smile at the womens high and mighty words, knowing that they had all sweet and gentle dispositions and complying Natures, yet they were at a stand which to be pleased at most, as in hearing them disparage their Mas-

culine Sex, or in advancing their own Female Sex by their self Commendations, but howsoever so well pleased the men were with the womens gallant
actions, that every man was proud that had but a Female acquaintance in the
Female Army; but our Lord General was mightily taken with their bra-
vadoes, and much mirth amongst the Commanders was about it; but when
they were to advise what to do in the affairs of War, and the warring women,
the General told them he made no question but that most men knew by
experience that women were won by gentle perswasions and fair promises,
and not by rigid actions or angry frowns, besides said he, all noble natures
strive to assist the weakest in all lawfull actions, and that he was no gallant
man that submits not to a woman in all things that are honourable, and
when he doth dissent it must be in a Courtly manner, and a Complemental
behaviour and expression, for that women were Creatures made by nature,
for men to love and admire, to protect and defend, to cherish and maintain,
to seek and to sue to, and especially such women which have out-done all
their Sex, which nature ever made before them; wherefore said he, 'tis fit to
these women above all others we should yield our selves Prisoners, not only
in love but in Arms; wherefore let us treat fairly with them, and give them
their own conditions. But in the mean time the Lady *Victoria* thought it best
not to lose any opportunity with talking out the time, wherefore she besieged a considerable Fort, a place which was as it were the Key that unlockt
the passage into the heart of the Enemies Kingdome, and at this siege they
were when I came away, but the General and his Council had sent a Messenger unto them, but what his message was I cannot give you an account.
Exeunt.

Scene 6

Enter two men in Mourning.

1ST MAN. Now my Lord is Intombed, our Lady will enanchor her self by his
Ashes.

2ND MAN. 'Tis strange so young and beautifull a Lady should bury her self from
the World, and quit all the pleasures thereof, to live with dead Ashes.

1ST MAN. A grieved Mind, Melancholy Thoughts, and an Oppressed Heart,
considers not the Body, nor the World.

2ND MAN. But yet I think 'tis an example that few of her Sex will imitate.

1ST MAN. Because few of the Female Sex can truly Grieve or be Melancholy.

2ND MAN. No, it is that few of the Female Sex can truly and constantly Love.

Exeunt.

Scene 7

The Tomb being thrust on the Stage, enter Madam JANTIL *and a Company of Mourners, but the Lady* JANTIL *was attired in a Garment of rich Cloth of gold girt loosly about her, and a Mantle of Crimson Velvet lined with powdered Ermins over that, her woman bearing up the Train therof being long, her Hair all unbound hung loose upon her Shoulders and Back, upon her Head a rich Crown of Jewels, as also Pendant Jewels in her Ears, and on her Wrists costly Bracelets; when she came in she goeth towards the Tomb, and bows with great respect and devotion thereto, then speaks, directing her speech to every several Figure.*

These following Verses or Speeches were written by my Lord Marquiss of Newcastle.*

LADY JANTIL. *Pallas* and *Mercury* at thy Death mourned,
  So as to marble Statues here th'are turned;
  Mars sheaths his Sword, and begs of thee a room,
  To bury all his courage in thy Tomb;
  Hymen amazed stands, and is in doubt,
  Thy Death his holy fier hath put out;
  What various shapes of Fortune thou didst meet,
  Thou scorn'st her frowns and kicks her with thy feet,
  Now found aloud the Trumpet of good Fame,
  And blow abroad his everlasting name.
After this she directs her speech to the outward figures about the Tomb.
  The Cardinal Virtues Pillars of thy fame,
  Weep to see now each but an empty name
  Only for Painters and for Carvers be,
  When thy life sustain'd them more than they Thee;
  Each Capital a sadder Virtue bears,
  But for the Graces would be drowned in tears;
  Faith strengthens Fortitude lest she should faint,
  Hope comforts Prudence as her only Saint;
  And Charity to Justice doth advance
  To Counsel her, as Patience Temperance;
  But wofull Counsellors they are each one,
  Since grief for thy Death turn'd them all to stone.

---

* Newcastle is credited with his contributions on printed strips pasted into the texts of both *Playes* (1662) and *Plays, Never Before Printed* (1668).

Then putting off her rich Garments and Ornaments before mentioned, as she was undressing she spake thus.

> Now I depose my self, and here lay down,
> Titles, not Honour, with my richer Crown;
> This Crimson Velvet Mantle I throw by,
> There ease and plenty in rich Ermins lie;
> Off with this glittring Gown which once did bear
> Ambition and fond pride ly you all there;
> Bracelets and Pendants which I now do wear,
> Here I devest my Arms and so each Ear;
> Cut off these dangling Tresses once a crime,
> Urging my Glass to look away my time;
> Thus all these Worldly vanities I wave,
> And bury them all in my Husbands grave.

After this she calls for her other Garments, which was a pure white light silk loose Garment, girt about her with a white silk Cord, and then puts on a thin black Veil over it, and then takes a Book in her hand, but speaks as they were a putting on those latter Garments.

More of my Lord Marquesses, are these.

LADY JANTIL. Put on that pure and spotless garment white,
> To shew my chaster thoughts, my Souls delight;
> Cord of Humility about my waste,
> A Veil of obscure Mourning about me cast;
> Here by this sadder Tomb shall be my Station,
> And in this Book my holy Contemplation.

She turns her self to her Servants.

> Farewell my Servants, farewell every one,
> As you all love me pray leave me alone.

They all go forth weeping. When they were all gone and she alone, she turns her self to the Tomb.

> No dust shall on thy marble ever stay,
> But with my sadder sighs ile blow't away;
> And the least spot that any Pillar bears,
> Ile wash it clean with grief of dropping tears;
> Sun fly this Hemisphær, and feast my Eyes,
> With Melancholy night, and never rise,
> Nor by reflection, for all light I hate,
> Therefore no Planet do illuminate;

The twinkling Stars that in cold nights are seen,
Clouds muster up and hide them as a Screen,
The Centrick fire raise vapours from the Earth,
Get and be Midwife for those fogs their birth;
Then chilling colds freeze up thy pores without,
That trembling Earth-quakes no where may get out;
And that our Mother Earth may nothing wear,
But Snow and Icicles to curl her hair;
And so Dame Nature Barren nothing bring,
Wishing a Chaos, since despairs a Spring;
Since all my joys are gone, what shall I do,
But wish the whole World ruined with me too?

Here ends my Lord Marquesses Verses.

Exeunt.

ACT III

Scene 8

Enter the Lady VICTORIA, *and many of her* AMAZONS, *then enters a Messenger from the Masculine Army.*

MESSENGER. May it please your Excellence, our Lord General and the rest of the Commanders have sent you and your Heroicks a Letter, desiring it may be read in full Assembly.

LADY VICTORIA. One of you take the Letter and read it.

One of the women takes the Letter and reads it to all the Company.

THE LETTER

To the most Excellent of her Sex, and her most
worthy Heroickesses.

You Goddesses on Earth, who have power and dominion over men, 'tis you we worship and adore, we pray and implore your better opinions of us, than to believe we are so unjust as to take the Victory out of your fair hands, or so vain-glorious as to attribute it to our selves, or so ungratefull as not to acknowledge our lives and liberties from your valours, wisdoms, and good fortune, or so imprudent as to neglect your power, or so ill-bred as to pass by you without making our addresses, or so foolish as to go about any action without your knowledge, or so unmannerly as to do any thing without your leave; wherefore we entreat you and pray you to believe that we have so much honour in us, as to admire your beauties, to be attentive to your discourses, to dote on your persons, to honour your virtues, to divulge your sweet graces, to praise your behaviours, to wait your commands, to obey your directions, to be proud of your favours, and we wear our lives only for your service, and believe we are not only taken Captives by your Beauties, but that we acknowledge we are bound as your Slaves by your valours; wherefore we all pray that you may not misinterpret our affections and care to your persons, in believing we sent you away because we were weary of you, which if so, it had been a sin unpardonable, but we sent you away for your safety, for Heaven knows your departure was our Hell, and your Absence our Torments; but we confess our errors, and do humbly beg our pardons, for if you had accompanied us in our Battels, you had kept us safe, for had we fought in your presence, our Enemies had never overcome us, since we take courage from your Eyes, life from your smiles, and victory from your good wishes, and had become Conquerors by your incourage-ments, and so we might have triumpht in your favours, but hereafter your rules shall be our methods, by which we will govern all our actions, attending only wholy your directions, yet give us leave humbly to offer our advise as Subjects to their Princess if you think fit, we think it best to follow close the victory, lest that our Enemies recruit their forces, with a sufficient strength to beat us out of what we have gained, or at least to hinder and oppose our entrance, and hopes of Conquer-ing them, where if you will give us leave we will besiege and enter their Towns, and rase their Walls down to the ground, which harbour their disorders, offending their Neighbours Kingdoms; yet we are not so ambitious as to desire to be Commanders, but to join our forces to yours, and to be your assistants, and as your Common Souldiers; but leaving all these affairs of War to your direction, offering our selves to your service,

We kiss your hands; and take our
leaves for this time.

All the women fall into a great laughter, ha, ha, ha, ha.

LADY VICTORIA. Noble heroickesses, by your valours, and constant, and reso-lute proceedings, you have brought your Tyrants to be your Slaves; those that Commanded your absence, now humbly sue your presence, those that thought you a hindrance have felt your assistance, the time is well altered since we were sent to retreat back from the Masculine Army; and now nothing to be done in that Army without our advise, with an humble desire they may join their forces with ours; but gallant Heroickesses, by this you may perceive we were as ignorant of our selves as men were of us, thinking our selves shiftless, weak, and unprofitable Creatures, but by our actions of War we have proved our selves to be every way equal with men; for what we want of strength, we have supplied by industry, and had we not done what we have done, we should have lived in ignorance and slavery.

ALL THE FEMALE COMMANDERS. All the knowledge of our selves, the honour of renown, the freedome from slavery, and the submission of men, we acknowledge from you; for you advised us, counselled us, instructed us, and encouraged us to those actions of War; wherefore to you we owe our thanks, and to you we give our thanks.

LADY VICTORIA. What answer will you return to the Masculine Army?

ALL THE COMMANDERS. What answer you will think best.

LADY VICTORIA. We shall not need to write back an answer, for this Messenger may deliver it by word of mouth; Wherefore Sir pray remember us to your General and his Commanders, and tell them, that we are willing upon their submissions to be friends, and that we have not neglected our good Fortune, for we have laid siege to so considerable a Fort, which if taken, may give an easy passage into the Kingdome, which Fort we will deliver to their forces when they come, that they may have the honour of taking it; for tell them, we have got honour enough in the Battel we fought, and victory we did win.

Exeunt.

Scene 9

Enter Monsieur la GRAVITY, *Monsieur* COMPAGNION, *and Monsieur* COMERADE.

MONSIEUR COMPAGNION. We are bound to curse you Monsieur *Gravity,* for retarding our visits to the Widows, for I told you we should come too late if we did not go before their Husbands were buried.

MONSIEUR LA GRAVITY. But I do not hear they have made a promise to marry any as yet.

MONSIEUR COMPAGNION. That's all one unto us, but the noblest, youngest, richest, and fairest Widow is gone; for though she is not promised or married, yet she is incloistered, and that is worse that marriage; for if she had been married there might have been some hopes her Husband would have died, or been kill'd, or some wayes or other Death would have found to have taken him away.

MONSIEUR COMERADE. Let us comfort our selves with hopes, that it is but a Ladies humour, which she will be soon weary of, for when her Melancholy fit is over, she will come forth of her Cloister, and be fonder to marry than if she had never gone in.

MONSIEUR LA GRAVITY. Well, since she is gone, let us assault the other.

MONSIEUR COMPAGNION. What, the old woman that hath never a Tooth in her head?

MONSIEUR COMERADE. Why, she is rich, and she will kiss softer for having no Bones in her mouth.

MONSIEUR COMPAGNION. The Devill shall kiss her before I will; besides, an old woman is thought a Witch.

MONSIEUR LA GRAVITY. Pish, that is because they are grown ill-favoured with Age, and all young people think whatsoever is ill-favoured belongs to the Devill.

MONSIEUR COMPAGNION. An ancient man is a comely sight, being grave and wise by experience, and what he hath lost in his person, he hath gained in his understanding; besides, beauty in men looks as unhandsome as age in women, as being effeminate; but an old woman looks like the picture of Envy, with hollow Eyes, fallen Cheeks, lank Sides, black pale Complexion, and more Wrinkles than time hath Minutes.

MONSIEUR COMERADE. Nay by your favour, some old women look like the full Moon, with a red, swell'd, great, broad face, and their Bodies like as a spungy Cloud, thick and gross, like our fat Hostess.

MONSIEUR LA GRAVITY. Gentlemen, why do you rail against ancient women so much, since those that are wise will never marry such Boyes as you?

MONSIEUR COMPAGNION. It is to be observed, that always old Girls match themselves with young Boyes.

MONSIEUR LA GRAVITY. None but Fools will do so.

MONSIEUR COMPAGNION. Why did you or any man else ever know a wise old woman, or a chaste young woman in their lives? for one dotes with Age, the other is corrupted with Flattery, which is a Bawd* to self-conceit.

MONSIEUR LA GRAVITY. Grant it be so, yet it is better to marry an old doting Fool, than a wanton young Fille.

MONSIEUR COMPAGNION. For my part, I think now it is the best way to marry none, since Madam *Jantil* is gone, but to live like the *Lacedemonians*,† all in Common.

MONSIEUR LA GRAVITY. I am of another opinion, wherefore if you will go along with me to the old Widow Madam *Passionate,* and help to Countenance my Sute, I shall take it as an act of Friendship.

MONSIEUR COMERADE. Come, we will be thy Pillars to support thee.

Exeunt.

* Bawd] pimp.
† *Lacedemonians*] Spartans.

Scene 10

Enter NELL CARELESS, *and* DOLL PACIFY.

DOLL PACIFY. What, doth thy Lady resolve to live an Anchoret?*

NELL CARELESS. I think so.

DOLL PACIFY. How doth she pass away her time in her solitary Sell?

NELL CARELESS. Why, as soon as she rises she goeth to my Lords Tomb, and says her Prayers, then she returns and eats some little Breakfast, as a Crust of Bread and a Draught of Water, then she goeth to her Gallery and walks and Contemplates all the Forenoon, then about twelve a Clock at Noon she goeth to the Tomb again and sayes more Prayers, then returns and eats a small Dinner of some Spoon-meats, and most of the Afternoon she sits by the Tomb and reads, or walks in the Cloyster, and views the Pictures of my Lord that are placed upon the Walls, then in the Evening she sayes her Evening Prayers at the Tomb, and eats some light Supper, and then prayes at the Tomb before she goeth to Bed, and at Midnight she rises and takes a white waxen Torch lighted in her hand, and goeth to the Tomb to pray, and then returns to Bed.

DOLL PACIFY. Faith she prayes often enough in the day, she shall not need to pray at Midnight; but why doth she rise just at Midnight?

NELL CARELESS. I know not, unless she is of that opinion which some have been of, which is, that the Souls or Spirits of the dead rise at that hour out of their Graves and Tombs, to visit the face of the Earth, and perhaps my Lady watches or hopes to converse by that means with my Lords Ghost; for since she cannot converse with him living, she desires to converse with him dead, or otherwise she would not spend most of her time at this Tomb as she doth; but how doth thy Lady spend her time now?

DOLL PACIFY. Faith as a Lady should do, with nourishing her Body with good hearty meats and drink. And though my Lady doth not pray at Midnight, yet she converses with Spirits at that time of Night.

NELL CARELESS. What Spirits?

DOLL PACIFY. Marry Spirits distilled from Wine and other Cordials, which she drinks when she wakes, which is at Midnight; but do you watch fast and pray as thy Lady doth?

NELL CARELESS. No truly, for I feed with the rest of my Ladies Servants, which live within the House without the Cloyster, and they eat and drink more liberally.

Exeunt.

---

* Anchoret] Holy hermit, usually living "anchored" to a sanctuary.

Scene 11

Enter Monsieur la GRAVITY, *Monsieur* COMPAGNION, *and Monsieur* COM-
ERADE, *as to Madam* PASSIONATE's *House; enter Madam* PASSIONATE's *gentleman Usher.*

MONSIEUR LA GRAVITY. Sir, we are come to kiss the hands of the Lady *Passionate,* if you please to inform your Lady of us.

GENTLEMAN USHER. I shall, if't please you to enter into another Room.
Exeunt.

Scene 12

Enter DOLL PACIFY, *as to her Lady* PASSIONATE *in her Chamber where her
Cabinets were.*

DOLL PACIFY. Madam, there are three Gentlemen come to visit you, desiring
you would give them leave to kiss your hands.

MADAM PASSIONATE. Shut down the lid of the Seller of Strong-waters, and rid
away the loose things that lie about, that my Chamber may appear in some
order.

*The Maid sets things in order, whilst the old Lady is trimming her self in the
Looking-glass.*

MADAM PASSIONATE. Bring in those Gentlemen?

*The Maid goes out, then enters with the Gentlemen; the two young men speak to
each other the time that Monsieur la* GRAVITY *is saluting.*

MONSIEUR COMPAGNION. I marry Sir, here is a comfortable smell indeed.

MONSIEUR COMERADE. Faith the smell of these Spirits overcomes my Spirits,
for I am ready to swound.

Then they go and salute the Lady.

MADAM PASSIONATE. Pray Gentlemen sit down.

They sit.

Truly I have had so great a wind in my Stomack as it hath troubled me very
much.

COMPAGNION *speaks softly to* COMERADE.

MONSIEUR COMPAGNION. Which to express the better, she rasps at every word
to make a full stop.

MONSIEUR LA GRAVITY. Perchance Madam you have eaten some meat that
digests not well.

Speaks aside.

MONSIEUR COMPAGNION. A Toad.

LADY PASSIONATE. No, truly I cannot gess what should cause it, unless it be an old piping* and that is accounted a great restorative.

She fetches a great sigh.

But I believe it is the drugs of my sorrow which stick in my Stomack; for I have grieved mightily for my dead Husband rest his Soul; he was a good Man, and as kind a Husband as ever woman had.

MONSIEUR LA GRAVITY. But the destinies Madam are not to be controuled, Death seizes on all, be it early or late; wherefore every one is to make their life as happy as they can, since life is so short; and in order to that, you should chuse a new Companion to live withall; wherefore you must marry again.

LADY PASSIONATE. 'Tis true, the Destinies are not to be controuled as you say, wherefore if my Destiny be to marry, I shall marry, or else I shall dye a Widow.

Monsieur COMPAGNION *aside softly, as in the ear of Monsieur* COMERADE.

MONSIEUR COMPAGNION. She will lay the fault of her second Marriage on Destiny, as many the like foolish actions are laid to Destinies charge, which she was never guilty of.

MONSIEUR LA GRAVITY. If I should guess at your destiny, I should judge you will marry again, by the quickness of your eyes which are fair and lovely.

She simpers.

LADY PASSIONATE. O Sir you flatter me.

MONSIEUR COMPAGNION. Ile be sworn that he doth. *Aside.*

LADY PASSIONATE. But my Eyes were good, as I have been told, both by my Glass and Friends, when I was young, but now my face is in the Autumnal.

Softly to COMERADE *aside.*

MONSIEUR COMPAGNION. Nay faith, it is in the midst of Winter.

LADY PASSIONATE. But now you talk of Eyes, that young Gentlemans Eyes *(points to Compagnion)* do resemble my Husbands as I can scarce look off from them, they have a good Aspect.

MONSIEUR COMPAGNION. I am glad they have an influence upon your Ladiship.

She speaks softly to her self.

LADY PASSIONATE. By my faith wittily answered, I dare say he is a notable youth. Sir, for resemblance of him which is dead, I shall desire your continued Acquaintance.

COMPAGNION *softly to* COMERADE.

MONSIEUR COMPAGNION. She wooes me with her Husbands dead skull.

---

* piping] pippen; apple.

I shall render my Service to your Ladyship.

She bowes him thanks with simpring and smiling Countenance, and a bridled head. Monsieur la GRAVITY *softly to himself.*

MONSIEUR LA GRAVITY. Those young youths I perceive will be my ruin if not prevented. Madam, will your Ladyship honor me so much as to give me the private hearing of a few words.

LADY PASSIONATE. Yes Sir.

She removes with him a little space.

MONSIEUR LA GRAVITY. Madam, although I am not such a one as I could wish my self for your sake, yet I am a Gentleman, and what I want in person or estate, my affection, respect, and tender regard to your person, worth, and merit shall make good; besides Madam, my years suiting to your Ladyship will make the better agreement in marriage.

LADY PASSIONATE. Sir you must excuse me; for though you merit a better wife than I, yet I cannot answer your affections; wherefore I desire you will desist in your Sute, for I am resolved, if I do marry, to please my fancy.

MONSIEUR LA GRAVITY. If your Ladyship cannot love me, Heaven forbid I should marry you; wherefore I wish your Ladyship such a Husband as you can fancy best, and love most.

They return to the two other Gentlemen, they all take their leaves.

Madam your most humble Servant.

They go through the Stage, and come upon it again, as it were at the Street Door.

MONSIEUR LA GRAVITY. Where is our Coach?

Enter a Footman.

Call the Coach to the Door?

Enter DOLL PACIFY *as from her Lady to Monsieur* COMPAGNION.

DOLL PACIFY. Sir, pray give me leave to speak a word or two with you.

MONSIEUR COMPAGNION. As many as you please.

DOLL PACIFY. Sir, my Lady desires your Company to morrow to Dinner, but she desires you will come alone.

MONSIEUR COMPAGNION. Pray give your Lady thanks for her favours, and tell her if I can possibly I will wait on her Ladyship.

DOLL PACIFY *goes out.*

MONSIEUR COMERADE. Now what encouragement have you from the old Lady?

MONSIEUR COMPAGNION. Faith so much as I am ashamed of it, for she invites me to come alone.

MONSIEUR COMERADE. On my life if thou wilt not woo her, she will woo thee.

MONSIEUR COMPAGNION. Like enough; for there is nothing so impudent as an old woman, they will put a young man be he never so deboist* out of Countenance.

MONSIEUR COMERADE. But faith consider of it, for she is rich.

MONSIEUR COMPAGNION. So is the Devil, as Poets say, *Pluto* the God of riches.

MONSIEUR COMERADE. I grant it, and is he not best served? for every one bows with respect, nay worships and adores riches, and they have reason so to do, since all are miserable that have it not, for Poverty is a torment beyond all sufferance, which causes many to hang themselves, either in the Chain of Infamy, or in a Hempen rope, or to do acts against the strict Laws of a Commonwealth which is to commit self-murther; besides, Poverty is the Slave and druge,† the scorn and reproach of the World, & it makes all younger Brothers Sherks,‡ and meer Cheats, whereas this old Ladies riches will not only give you an honest mind, and create noble thoughts, but will give you an honourable reputation in the World; for every one will think you Wise although you were a Fool, Valiant although you were a Coward, and you shall have the first offers of all Offices, and all Officers will be at your devotion, they will attend you as Slaves, the Lawyers will plead on your side, and Judges will give sentence according as you desire, Courtiers will flatter you, and Divines will pray for you in their Pulpits, and if your old Lady dy, and leave you her wealth, you shall have all the young beautifull Virgins in the Kingdome gather to that City, Town, or Village where you live, omitting no Art that may prefer them to your affection.

MONSIEUR COMPAGNION. You say well, and I could approve of your Counsel, if she would dy soon after I had married her.

MONSIEUR COMERADE. Why, put the case she should live a great while, as the truth is old women are tough, and indure long, yet you will have her Estate to please yourself withall, which Estate will buy you fine Horses, great Coaches, maintain Servants and great Retinues to follow you.

MONSIEUR COMPAGNION. But she is so devillish old.

MONSIEUR COMERADE. Why, let her keep her Age to her self, whilst you keep a young Mistress to your self, and it is better to have an old Wife that will look after your Family, and be carefull and watchfull therein, and a young Mistriss, than a young Wife, which will be a Tyrannical Mistriss, which will look after nothing but Vanities, and love Servants, whilst you poor wretch look

---

* deboist] debauched.

† druge] drudge.

‡ Sherks] those who shirk.

like a contented Cuckold, and so out of Countenance as you dare not shew your face, whilst she spends your Estate running about with every vain idle fellow to Playes, Masks, Balls, Exchanges, Taverns, or meets at a private Friends private Lodging, also making great Feasts and Entertainments, where after Dinner and Supper, there must be gaming at Cards and Dice; where for her honour, or at least seeming so, to lose five hundred or a thousand pounds away, and when they rise with or from their losses, singing with a feigned voice, as if it were a trifle not to be considered or considerable, thus if you marry an old and rich Lady you may live and spend her Estate, but if you marry for youth and beauty, your wife will live and spend your Estate; besides, the Husband of an old Lady lives like the great Turk, having a Seraglio, but marrying a young wife you live like a Prisoner never durst show your head.

MONSIEUR LA GRAVITY. He gives you good Counsel, and let me advise you to go to this Lady as she hath invited you, for I perceive she hath a young Tooth in her old head by refusing me, and there is none so fit to pull it out as you are, wherefore go.

MONSIEUR COMPAGNION. Well Gentlemen, I will try if my Reason and your Counsel can prevail in my choice.

Exeunt.

ACT IV

Scene 13

Enter Madam JANTIL in her habit with a white Taper lighted in her hand, the Tomb being thrust upon the Stage she goeth to the Tomb, then kneels down and seems as praying, after that she rises, holding out the Torch with the other hand speaks as follow.

These Verses being writ by my Lord, the Marquess of NEWCASTLE.

MADAM JANTIL. Welcome sad thoughts that's heapt up without measure,
  They're joys to me and wealthy Sons of treasure;
  Were all my breath turn'd into sighs 'twould ease me,
  And showrs of tears to bath my griefs would please me;
  Then every groan so kind to take my part,
  To vent some sorrows still thus from my heart;
  But there's no Vacuum, O my heart is full,

As it vents sorrows new griefs in doth pull;
Is there no comfort left upon the Earth?
Let me consider Vegitable birth;
The new born virgin Lilly of the day,
In a few hours dyes, withers away;
And all the odoriferous flow'rs that's sweet,
Breath but a while, and then with Death do meet;
The stouter Oak at last doth yield, and must
Cast his rough skin and crumble all to dust;
But what do Sensitives? alas they be,
Beasts, Birds and flesh to dy as well as we;
And harder minerals though longer stay
Here for a time, yet at the last decay,
And dye as all things else that's in this World,
For into Death's Arms every thing is hurll'd;
Alas poor man thou'rt in the worst Estate,
Thou diest as these, yet an unhappier fate;
Thy life's but trouble still of numerous passions,
Torments thy self in many various fashions;
Condemn'd thou art to vexing thoughts within;
When Beasts both live and dye without a sin;
O happy Beasts than grasing look no higher,
Or are tormented with thoughts flaming fire;
Thus by thy self and others still annoid,
And made a purpose but to be destroyed
Poor Man.

Here ends my Lord Marquesses Verses.

*Muses some short time, then kneels to the Tomb again and prayes as to her self,
then rises and bows to the Tomb, so Exit.*

Scene 14

Enter two Gentlemen.

1ST GENT. What news Sir of our Armies abroad?

2ND GENT. Why Sir thus, in the time of our Masculine Armies recruiting, the
Female Army had taken the Fort they besieged, where upon the taking of
that Fort, many considerable Towns and strong holds surrendered, and
submitted to the Female Army; whereupon the Lady *Victoria* sent to her

Husband to bring his Army, when the General and all the Masculine Army came to the Female Army, much mirth and jesting there was betwixt the Heroicks and Heroickesses, and so well they did agree, as the Female Army feasted the Masculine Army, and then gave the possession of the surrendred Towns to the Lord General, and the Lady *Victoria,* and all her Army kept themselves in and about the Fort, laying all their victorious spoils therein, and whilst the Masculine Army is gone to Conquer the Kingdome of Faction, they stay there upon the Frontiers, passing their time in Heroick sports, as hunting the Stags, wild Boars, and the like, and those that have the good Fortune to kill the Chase,* is brought to the Fort and Trenches in Triumph, and is Queen until another Chase is kill'd; but we hear the Masculine Army goeth on with victorious success.

1ST GENT. I am very glad to hear it.

Exeunt.

Scene 15

Enter DOLL PACIFY *and* NELL CARELESS.

NELL CARELESS. O *Doll,* I hear thy Lady is married, and not only married, but she hath married a very young man, one that might be her Grand-Son, or Son at least.

DOLL PACIFY. Yes, yes, my Lady doth not intend to live with the dead as your Lady doth, but to have the Company and pleasure of that which hath most life, which is a young man.

NELL CARELESS. Her marriage was very sudden.

DOLL PACIFY. So are all inconsidered marriages, but happy is the wooing that is not long a doing.

NELL CARELESS. If I had been your Lady, I would have prolonged the time of my wooing, for the wooing time is the happiest time.

DOLL PACIFY. Yes, if she had been as young as you or your Lady, but time bids my Lady make haste.

Exeunt.

Scene 16

Enter two Gentlemen.

1ST GENT. Do you hear the news?

2ND GENT. What news?

---

* Chase] quarry.

1ST GENT. Why the news is that all the Kingdome of Faction hath submitted to the Kingdom of Reformation, and that the Armies are returning home.

2ND GENT. I am glad of it.

Exeunt.

Scene 17

Enter Madam PASSIONATE *alone.*

MADAM PASSIONATE. O unfortunate woman that I am, I was rich, and lived in plenty, none to control me, I was Mistriss of my self, Estate and Family, all my Servants obeyed me, none durst contradict me, but all flattered me, filling my Ears with praises, my Eyes with their humble bows and respectfull behaviours, devising delightfull sports to entertain my time, making delicious meats to please my palat, sought out the most comfortable drinks to strengthen and encrease my Spirits, thus did I live luxuriously, but now I am made a Slave, and in my old Age which requires rest and peace, which now Heaven knows I have but little of, for the minstrels keep me waking, which play whilst my Husband and his Whores dance, and he is not only contented to live riotously with my Estate, but sits amongst his Wenches and rails on me, or else comes and scoffs at me to my face; besides, all my Servants slight and neglect me, following those that command the purse, for this idle young fellow which I have married first seized on all my goods, then let Leases for many lives out of my Lands, for which he had great fines, and now he cuts down all my Woods, and sells all my Lands of Inheritance, which I foolishly and fondly delivered by deed of gift, the first day I married, devesting my self of all power, which power had I kept in my own hands I might have been used better, whereas now when he comes home drunk, he swears and storms, and kiks me out of my warm Bed, and makes me sit shivering and shaking in the Cold, whilst my Maid takes my place; but I find I cannot live long, for age and disorders bring weakness and sickness, and weakness and sickness bring Death, wherefore my marriage Bed is like to prove my grave, whilst my Husbands Curses are my passing Bell, hay ho.

Exit.

Scene 18

Enter two Gentlemen.

1ST GENT. I hear the Army is returning home.

2ND GENT. Yes, for they are returned as far back as to the Effeminate Army, and all the Masculine Commanders have presented the Female Commanders with their spoils got in the Kingdome of Faction, as a tribute to their heroical acts, and due for their assistance, and safety of their lives and Country.

1ST GENT. And do you not hear what privileges and honours the King and his Counsel hath resolved and agreed upon to be given to the Female Army, and the honours particularly given to the Lady *Victoria?*

2ND GENT. No.

1ST GENT. Why then I will tell you some, the Lady *Victoria* shall be brought through the City in triumph, which is a great honour, for never any one makes triumphs in Monarchy but the King himself; then that there shall be a blank for the Female Army to write their desires and demands; also there is an Armour of gold and a Sword a making, the hilt being set with Diamonds, and a Chariot all gilt and imbrodered to be presented to the Lady *Victoria,* and the City is making great preparation against her arrival.

2ND GENT. Certainly she is a Lady that deserves as much as can be given either from Kings, States, or Poets.

Exeunt.

Scene 19

Enter the Lady JANTIL *as being sick brought by two men in a Chair, and set by the Tomb of her dead Lord, and many Servants and Friends about her weeping.*

MADAM JANTIL. Where is my Secretary?

SECRETARY. Here Madam.

MADAM JANTIL. Read the Will I caus'd you to write down.

THE WILL READ

I Jantil *the widow of* Seigneur Valeroso, *do here make a free gift of all these following.*

Item, All my Husbands Horses and Saddels and whatsoever belongs to those Horses, with all his Arms, Pikes, Guns, Drums, Trumpets, Colours, Waggons, Coaches, Tents, and all he had belonging to the War, to be distributed amongst his Officers of War, according to each degree, I freely give.

Item, All his Library of Books I give to that College he was a Pupill in when he was at the University.

Item, To all his Servants I give the sum of their yearly wages to be yearly paid them during their lives.

Item, I give two hundred pounds a year pension to his Chaplin Doctor Educature *during his life.*

Item, I give a hundred pound a year pension to his Steward during his life.

Item, I give fifty pound a year pension to his Secretary during his life.

Item, I give a hundred pound per annum, *for the use and repair of this Tomb of my dead Husbands.*

Item, I give a thousand pounds a year to maintain ten religious persons to live in this place or House by this Tomb.

Item, I give three thousand pounds to enlarge the House, and three thousand pounds more to build a Chapell by my Husbands Tomb.

Item, Two hundred pounds a year I give for the use and repair of the House and Chapell.

Item, I give my maid Nell Careless *a thousand pound to live a single life.*

Item, I give the rest of my Estate which was left me by my Husband Seigneur Valeroso *to the next of his name.*

These following Speeches and Songs of hers, my Lord the Marquess of Newcastle *writ.*

JANTIL. So 'tis well
    O Death hath shakt me kindly by the hand,
    To bid me welcome to the silent grave;
    'Tis dead and num sweet Death how thou doest court me,
    O let me clap thy fallen Cheeks with joy,
    And kiss the Emblem of what once was lips,
    Thy hollow Eyes I am in love withall,
    And thy ball'd head beyond youth's best curl'd hair,
    Prethee imbrace me in thy colder Arms,
    And hug me there to fit me for thy Mansion;
    Then bid our Neighbour worms to feast with us,
    Thus to rejoyce upon my holy day;
    But thou art slow, I prethee hasten Death,
    And linger not my hopes thus with thy stay,
    'Tis not thy fault thou sayest, but fearfull nature
    That hinders thus Deaths progress in his way;
    Oh foolish nature thinks thou canst withstand,
    Deaths Conquering and inevitable hand;
    Let me have Musick for divertisment,
    This is my Mask, Deaths Ball, my Soul to dance

Out of her frail and fleshly prison here;
Oh could I now dissolve and melt, I long
To free my Soul in Slumbers with a Song;
In soft and quiet sleep here as I ly,
Steal gently out O Soul, and let me dy.
Lies as a sleep.

SONG

O You Gods pure Angels send her,
Here about her to attend her;
Let them wait and here condoul,
Till receive her spotless Soul;
So Serene it is and fair,
It will sweeten all the Air;
You this holy wonder hears,
With the Musick of the spheres;
Her Souls journey in a trice,
You'l bring safe to Paradice;
And rejoice the Saints that say,
She makes Heavens Holy-day.
The Song ended she opens her Eyes, then speaks.
Death hath not finish'd yet his work, h'is slow,
But he is sure, for he will do't at last;
Turn me to my dear Lord, that I may breath
My last words unto him, my dear,
Our marriage join'd our flesh and bone,
Contracted by those holy words made one;
But by our Loves we join'd each others heart,
And vow'd that death should never us depart;
Now death doth marry us, since now we must,
Ashes to ashes be mingling our dust,
And our joy'd Souls in Heaven married then,
When our frail bodyes rise, wee'l wed again;
And now I am joy'd to lie by thy lov'd side,
My Soul with thy Soul shall in Heaven reside.
For that is all my

In this last word she dies, which when her Servants saw, they cryed out she is dead, she is dead.

Here ends my Lord Marquesses writing.

Doctor EDUCATURE *sayes thus.*
DOCTOR EDUCATURE. She is dead, she is dead, the body hence convey.
    And to our Mistriss our last rights wee'l pay.
So they laid her by her Husband upon the Tomb, and drawing off the Tomb goe out.
Exeunt.

ACT V

Scene 20

Enter Citizens Wives and their Apprentices.
1ST CITIZENS WIFE. Where shall we stand to see this triumphing?
2ND CITIZENS WIFE. I think Neighbour this is the best place.
3RD CITIZENS WIFE. We shall be mightily crouded there.
2ND CITIZENS WIFE. For my part I will stand here, and my Apprentice *Nathaniel* shall stand by me, and keep off the croud from crouding me.
NATHANIEL. Truly Mistress that is more than I am able to do.
3RD CITIZENS WIFE. Well Neighbour if you be resolved to stand here, we will keep you Company. *Timothy* stand by me.
TIMOTHY. If you stand here Mistriss the Squibs* will run under your Clothes.
3RD CITIZENS WIFE. No matter *Timothy,* let them run where they will.
They take their stand.
1ST CITIZENS WIFE. I hope Neighbour none will stand before us, for I would not but see this Lady *Victoria* for any thing, for they say she hath brought Articles for all women to have as many Husbands as they will, and all Tradesmens Wives shall have as many Apprentices as they will.
2ND CITIZENS WIFE. The Gods bless her for it.
Enter a Croud of people.
She is coming, she is coming.
Officers come.
Stand up close, make way.
Enter many Prisoners which march by two and two, then enter many that carry

---

* Squibs] firecrackers; Cavendish may be making a pun on worthless fellows.

the Conquered spoils, then enters the Lady VICTORIA *in a gilt Chariot drawn with eight white Horses, four on a breast, the Horses covered with Cloth of gold, and great plumes of feathers on their heads.*

The Lady VICTORIA *was adorned after this manner; she had a Coat on all imbroidered with silver and gold, which Coat reach'd no further than the Calfs of her leggs, and on her leggs and feet she had Buskins and Sandals imbroidered suitable to her Coat; on her head she had a Wreath or Garland of Lawrel, and her hair curl'd and loosely flowing; in her hand a Crystall Bolt headed with gold at each end, and after the Chariot marched all her Female Officers with Lawrel Branches in their hands, and after them the inferiour she Souldiers, then going through the Stage, as through the City, and so entring again, where on the midst of the Stage as if it were the midst of the City, the Magistrates meet her, so her Chariot makes a Stand, and one as the Recorder speaks a Speech to her.*

RECORDER. Victorious Lady, you have brought Peace, Safety, Conquest to this Kingdome by your prudent conduct and valiant actions, which never any of your Sex in this Kingdome did before you. Wherefore our Gracious King is pleased to give you that which was never granted nor given to any before, which is to make you Triumphant, for no triumph is ever made in Monarchies, but by the Kings thereof; besides our Gracious King hath caused an act to be made and granted to all your Sex, which Act I have order to declare, as

First, That all women shall hereafter in this Kingdome be Mistriss on their own Houses and Families.

Secondly, They shall sit at the upper end of the Table above their Husbands.

Thirdly, That they shall keep the purse.

Fourthly, They shall order their Servants, turning from, or taking into their service what number they will, placing them how they will, and ordering them how they will, and giving them what wages they will or think fit.

Fiftly, They shall buy in what Provisions they will.

Sixtly, All the Jewels, Plate, and Household Furniture they shall claim as their own, and order them as they think good.

Seventhly, they shall wear what fashioned Clothes they will.

Eightly, They shall go abroad when they will, without controul, or giving of any account thereof.

Ninthly, They shall eat when they will, and of what they will, and as much as they will, and as often as they will.

Tenthly, They shall go to Playes, Masks, Balls, Churchings, Christenings, Preachings, whensoever they will, and as fine and bravely attired as they will.

Lastly, That they shall be of their Husbands Counsel.

When those were read, all the women cryed out, God save the King, God save the King, and Heaven reward the Lady VICTORIA.

Then an act was read concerning the Lady *Victoria*.

As for you most gallant Lady, the King hath caused to be enacted, that

First, All Poets shall strive to set forth your praise.

Secondly, That all your gallant acts shall be recorded in story, and put in the chief Library of the Kingdome.

Thirdly, That your Arms you fought in, shall be set in the Kings Armory.

Fourthly, That you shall always wear a Lawrel Garland.

Fifthly, You shall have place next to the Kings Children.

Sixthly, That all those women that have committed such faults as is a dishonour to the Female Sex, shall be more severely punished than heretofore, in not following your exemplary virtues, and all those that have followed your example shall have respective honour done to them by the State.

Seventhly and lastly, Your figure shall be cast in Brass, and then set in the midst of the City armed as it was in the day of Battel.

The Lady VICTORIA *rises up in her Chariot, and then bowes her self to the Magistrates.*

LADY VICTORIA. Worthy Sir, the honour and privileges my Gracious King and Sovreign hath bestowed upon me, is beyond my merit.

Then was read the Acts concerning the rest of the Female Army.

Our gracious king hath caused to be enacted, as

First, All the Chief Female Commanders shall have place, as every Lords wife shall take place of an Earls Wife that hath not been a Souldier in the Army; Every Knights Wife before a Barons Wife that hath not been a Souldier in the Army; an Esquires Wife before a Knights Wife; a Doctors Wife before an Esquires Wife that hath not been Souldiers in the Army; a Citizens Wife before a Doctors Wife; a Yeomans Wife before a Citizens Wife that hath not been a Souldier in the Army; and all Trades-mens Wives that have been Souldiers in the Army shall be free in all the Corporations in this Kingdome, these Acts during their lives, and all the Chief Commanders shall be presented according to their quality and merit.

ALL THE FEMALE SOULDIERS *cryed out*, God save the King, God save the King.

After this the Lady VICTORIA *is drawn on her Chariot, and the rest walk after all. Exeunt.*

Scene 21

Enter DOLL PACIFY, *and* NELL CARELESS.

DOLL PACIFY. O *Nell*, I hear thy Lady is dead, and hath left thee a thousand pound.

NELL *Weeps.*

NELL CARELESS.{*blot out* Nell Careless} What doest thou weep for joy of thy thousand pound, or for grief of thy Ladies Death?

NELL CARELESS. I wish my Lady had liv'd, although I had begg'd all my life.

DOLL PACIFY. I am not of your mind, I had rather live well my self, as to live in plenty, than to live poor for the life of any body, and if upon that condition my Lady would leave me a thousand pound, I care not if she died to morrow; but my young Master hath robbed me of all; but *Nell,* for all thou art left a thousand pound, it is upon such a condition, as for my part had it been to me, I should not thank the giver, for they say it is given thee upon condition to live a single life.

NELL CARELESS. Truly I have seen so much sorrow in my Lady, and so much folly in your Lady concerning Husbands, that had not my Lady injoyned me to live a single life, I would never have married; wherefore my Ladies generosity did not only provide for my bodily life, and for my plentifull living, but provided for the tranquillity of my mind, for which I am trebly obliged to reverence her memory.

Exeunt.

Scene 22

Enter two Gentlemen.

1ST GENT. The Lady *Victoria* hath been at Court, and hath had a publick Audience.

2ND GENT. Yes, and the Lady *Victoria* and her she Officers and Commanders have distributed all their spoils got in these Wars amongst the Common she Souldiers.

1ST GENT. All the Ladies that went not with the Army look most pittifully out of Countenance.

2ND GENT. Yes, and they are much troubled that the Heroicks shall take place.

1ST GENT. The Lord General seems to be very proud of his Lady, methinks he looks upon her with a most pleased Eye.

2ND GENT. He hath reason, for never man had so gallant and noble a Lady, nor more virtuous and loving a Wife than the Lord General hath.

Exeunt.

Finis

The Bridals

A Comedy

MONSIEUR	TAKE-PLEASURE, ADVISER, FACIL. COURTLY.	BRIDEMEN

MASTER LONGLIFE

MASTER AGED

SIR MERCURY POET, AND THE LADY FANCY HIS BRIDE

SIR WILLIAM SAGE, AND THE LADY VERTUE HIS BRIDE

SIR JOHN AMOROUS, AND THE LADY COY HIS BRIDE

MADAM MEDIATOR. AND OTHER LADIES

MIMICK THE FOOL

JOAN, A COOK-MAID

ACT I

Scene 1

Enter Monsieur TAKE-PLEASURE *and Monsieur* ADVISER, *and meet Monsieur* FACIL.

MONSIEUR ADVISER. Mons. *Facil*, where have you been so early this morning, abroad?

FACIL. I have been at Church, to see a young Virgin and a Batchellor married to day.

TAKE-PLEAS. How do you know she is a Virgin?

FACIL. By her modest Countenance.

TAKE-PLEAS. Faith, Women have more modesty in their countenance, then in their natures; wherefore you may be deceived by her countenance; for Womens countenances, like false glasses, make their minds appear fairer then they are; for a modest countenance may have a wanton mind.

FACIL. But this Brides countenance was so modest, I wish that I had been her Bridegroom.

ADVISER. Would you have married her only for her modest countenance?

FACIL. Yes, for a modest countenance is the greatest Beauty in my eye.

ADVISER. Faith, that Beauty never lasts above a day, nay, an hours acquaintance fadeth it, two hours wither it, and in three hours it is quite vanish'd away.

FACIL. Some Women have modest countenances and natures all their life-time.

ADVISER. Their life must be very short, if it last no longer then their modesty. 'Tis true, Women have feigned modesty, but not real modesty; for they put on modesty as they do paint, the one to make them appear fairer, the other to make them appear chaster then they are.

FACIL. You do not deserve either a modest, or chaste Woman.

ADVISER. Faith, I hate both modesty and chastity in Women; for modesty and chastity are enemies to the Masculine Sex, and worse then a Cloister, as being more restraint.

FACIL. Well, leaving Modesty, Chastity, and Cloisters, will you go to the Bridal-House?

ADVISER. Yes, for I believe there will be liberty and choice.

FACIL. There will be two choice Brides.

TAKE-PLEAS. Why, hath one Man married two Women?

FACIL. No, but two Men have married two Women; for there are two Brides and two Bridegrooms.

ADVISER. It had been better that one Bridegroom had two Brides, for then he might have spar'd one for a Friend.

FACIL. It had not been better for you, unless you had been that Friend to receive that Courtesie.

TAKE-PLEAS. I would have endeavour'd with all the Rhetorick I have, and all the Protestations I could make, and all the Oaths I could swear, to make him believe I was his Friend, that he might be my Friend.

FACIL. Come, come, they would have done thee no service.

ADVISER. But I might have done him service, at least to his spare-Bride; but who are those that are Married?

FACIL. Sir *John Amorous,* to the Lady *Coy;* and Sir *William Sage,* to the Lady *Vertue.*

Exeunt. Enter MR. LONGLIFE, *and* MR. AGED.

AGED. Mr. *Longlife,* I am glad to see you look so well, and that you are strong and lusty.

LONGL. So am I to see you so, good Master *Aged.*

AGED. I thank God, though I am old, I feel no stitches.

LONGL. Beshrew me, I feel some stitches now and then.

AGED. O! that is nothing, for the youngest and strongest Man of them all, will feel stitches sometimes.

LONGL. I rather wish the young Men did feel them, then I, for they are better able to endure them; but what News do you hear Mr. *Aged?*

AGED. Faith, none that is good, or that is worth the hearing.

LONGL. It is a sign the times are bad, the times are bad.

AGED. Men are so evil, Mr. *Longlife,* that the times must needs be so.

LONGL. The times were better when we were young.

AGED. We thought them so, being young; for young Men have not much experience, nor long acquaintance of the World; they endeavour to know, and be acquainted with the Vices in the World, though not the Vertues.

LONGL. Faith, Vertue is rather talked of, then known, at least then practiced.

AGED. Indeed Men preach Vertue, but practice Vice.

LONGL. 'Tis such old Men as we are, that are the Preachers, and young Men the Practitioners.

AGED. Yes, evil young Men say, That old Men preach Vertue, when they are past practicing Vice.

LONGL. Indeed young Men despise old Men's Counsels and Advice, and will believe nothing they say, untill they live to be old themselves, and then they see their past-follies, and think themselves only wise, because they are old.

AGED. Then all Men think themselves wise, if young Men think themselves wiser then old Men, and old Men think themselves wiser then young Men.

LONGL. 'Tis true, they do so; and the same way Men think other Men Fools; for young Men think old Men Fools, and old Men think young Men Fools.

AGED. Nay, old Men do more then think young men Fools, for they know young Men are Fools; for 'tis impossible they can be wise, for wisdom is not born with Men, nor left to Men as Inheritances are.

LONGL. No, By'rlady, they must be bound Apprentices to Time, and serve Time many years, before they can be wise Men.

AGED. Well, let us leave foolish young Men to Time, and let you and I go take the fresh air for Health.

LONGL. With all my heart, let us go.

Exeunt. Enter the Brides and Bridegrooms, and all the Bridal Guests, Sir MER-CURY POET *one of the Bride-Men, and the Lady* FANCY *one of the Bride-Maids, that helps to lead one of the Brides to the Church.*

ADVISER. Gentlemen *Bridegrooms,* we must rifle your Brides of their Bride-Garters.

SIR J. AMOROUS. If it be the custom, I submit.

SAGE. But I will not agree to such an uncivil custom, for no man shall pull off my Wives Garters, unless it be myself.

VERTUE. We have pull'd off our Garters already, and therefore if these Batchellor Gentlemen, will have them, we will send for them.

FACIL. Pray Ladies let us have them, for the Bride-Garters are the young Batchellors fees.

COURTLY. Since we must not rifle for their Garters, let us cast Dice for them.

TAKE-PLEAS. Content.

M. MEDIATOR. The Bridegrooms points being our fees, therefore we must rifle for the points.

SIR W. SAGE. If you please Ladies, we are ready to be rifled.

The Women offer to take off the Points, but Lady VERTUE *hinders them.*

VERTUE. Ladies, pray stay, for it is the custom, not to unpoint the Bridegrooms, until they be ready to go to bed.

SIR W. SAGE. I am ready to go to Bed, if the Ladies please.

ONE OF THE FEMALE GUESTS. No, we will stay till Night.

Exeunt all, only two of the Ladies.

1. LADY. The Lady *Coy* is one of the most modest and bashful Brides that ever I saw; insomuch, as she is ashamed to look upon her Bridegroom.

2. LADY. Some of her modesty ought to be reserved, or else she will have none left for to morrow.

1. LADY. Why, doth Modesty wast like a Watch-candle, in a night?

2. LADY. Yes, faith, it is a light that soon goes out, or rather a shadow that soon vanishes.

1. LADY. Then the Lady *Vertue* has no shadows, for she appears neither bashful, nor bold; but she is both in her Behaviour and Countenance like a Bridal-Guest, rather then a Bride.

Exeunt.

Scene 2

Enter the Brides, Bridegrooms, and all their Bridal-Guests, Men and Women.

SIR JOHN AMOROUS. Pray let us not dance, but go to bed.

M. MEDIATOR. That will be an injury to your Bridal-Guests, to rob them of their Mirth and Musick, by going to bed so soon.

L. VERTUE. No, Ladies, we will dance; Musick, play.

The Musick plays, and they dance; Sir JOHN AMOROUS *kisses his Bride, and courts her with smiles and amorous looks.*

SIR W. SAGE. Gentlemen, and Ladies, for Heavens sake, have mercy upon two languishing Bridegrooms, and leave off dancing for this time.

M. MEDIATOR. Have I found you out, Sir *William Sage!*

SIR W. SAGE. I was never hid, Madam.

M. MEDIATOR. Yes, but you were; for now I perceive you would go to bed with your Bride.

SAGE. I shall not need to obscure my desires, Madam, for it is lawful for any Man to lie with his own wife.

MEDIATOR. You are a Wag, you are a Wag, Sir *William.*

SAGE. No Madam, for to be a Wag, is to be unseasonably wanton, which I am not.

AMOROUS. Faith, this dancing is unseasonable, therefore fair Ladies, attend the fair Brides to bed.

FEMALE GUESTS. Come, Lady *Coy*, we will help to undress you.

COY. No truly, but you shall not, for I will not go to bed.

They seem earnest to have her to bed, and she to stay.

SAGE. What is the matter, Ladies, will not you let our Brides go to bed?

FEMALE GUESTS. We desire to wait on them, and to help to undress them, but the Lady *Coy* will not go to bed.

SAGE. Then pray go with my Bride.

ONE OF THE LADIES. Yes, if she please to go to bed.

SAGE. Wife will not you go to bed?

VERTUE. Yes, if you please to have me.

SAGE. 'Tis my desire.

Exit Lady VERTUE, *and some of the Ladies with her: Sir* JOHN AMOROUS *comes and kisses his Bride.*

AMOROUS. Pray go to Bed.

COY. Pray let me stay here.

ADVISER. Faith, she would be carried to bed; carry your Wife to bed, Sir *John Amorous.*

AMOROUS. Not against her will, although against her consent.

ADVISER. In words you mean.

AMOROUS. Come, Sweet-heart, I will usher you into your Chamber.

Exit Sir JOHN AMOROUS, *leading his Bride, who seems very unwilling to go, all the Company goeth with them, only* ADVISER *and* FACIL *stay;* FACIL *fetches a sigh.*

FACIL. O how happy a man is Sir *John Amorous!* and how unhappy a man am I!

ADVISER. Perchance two days hence, Sir *J. Amorous* will think himself as unhappy, as you think yourself now, for a great surfeit is as bad as a sharp hunger.

Exeunt.

Scene 3

Enter the Lady VERTUE *as in her Chamber, with some other female Guests; she seems to undress herself.*

LADY VERTUE. Pray Ladies help to undress me.

M. MEDIATOR. That we will.

They unpin her Gorget.*

M. MEDIATOR. Shall we fling the Stockins when you and your Bridegroom are a bed?

L. VERTUE. Yes, if you please, Ladies.

M. MEDIATOR. And shall we break the Bride-Cake over your head?

L. VERTUE. I must intreat you to omit that custom, as also setting a Sack-posset† upon the bed; for the crumbs of Cake and drops of Posset, will be very ill bed-fellows; besides, it is not a cleanly Custom; but I have given order that all such Junkets shall be provided for you in another room, to make you merry, when I and my Husband are a bed.

M. MEDIATOR. So I perceive, you will send us away, as soon as you can.

L. VERTUE. I'le leave your staying, or going away, to your own discretion.

Enter a Maid-Servant.

SERVANT. Madam, your Bridegroom hath sent to know, whether you be in Bed.

L. VERTUE. I shall be in a short time, tell him: Come Ladies, let us go into the Bed-chamber.

Exeunt. Enter Sir JOHN AMOROUS, *and his Bride, with the rest of the Female-Guests.*

SIR J. AMOROUS. Ladies, I shall leave my Bride with you, to help her to bed.

Exit Sir J. AMOROUS.

M. MEDIATOR. Come, Lady *Coy,* to morrow you will be Lady *Amorous.*

1. LADY. Why, do Wives never take their Husbands name till the day after Marriage?

M. MEDIATOR. No, for the first day, they neither are called by their own, nor their Husbands name; but are called Brides, as an Interlude between both.

1. LADY. Come, come, undress the Bride.

M. MEDIATOR. That we will soon do.

L. COY. I will not be undrest.

1. LADY. What, Lady, will you lie in your Clothes?

---

* Gorget] neckpiece.
† Sack-posset] drink made of sherry wine and spices.

M. MEDIATOR. If she will lie in her Clothes, it will neither be easie, convenient, nor cleanly; but come, come Lady we will undress you.

They offer to undress her, but she puts them back.

L. COY. I will not be undrest.

M. MEDIATOR. Lady, give me leave to ask you, whether you married your Gown or your Person to your Husband?

L. COY. My Person.

M. MEDIATOR. Then pull off your Gown, and go unclothed to bed.

L. COY. I would undress me, but I am ashamed to lie with a Man.

M. MEDIATOR. That shame is very unnecessary at this time; wherefore cast it off with your Clothes.

L. COY. I am afraid to lie by a Man.

M. MEDIATOR. That fear is an effeminate fear, and will not last long; wherefore undress, undress, for Loves sake.

L. COY. I must go, and say my Prayers first.

M. MEDIATOR. Faith, *Jove* will dispence, with a Bride one night; the truth is, Bridal-Prayers are irreligious.

Enter a Maid in hast.

MAID. Here comes the Bridegroom and all the Gentlemen attending him.

L. COY. O! shut the door, shut the door, for *Jupiters* sake.

The Scene to shut the door, the Men knock.

ADVISER. Open the Door, and let the Bridegroom in.

M. MEDIATOR. He cannot come as yet, the Bride's not a bed.

SIR J. AMOROUS. Let me come in, or I'le break open the door.

L. COY. O keep him out, or I shall die for fear.

1. LADY. You shall not come, until we please.

FACIL. Let us come, or we will enter by force.

1. LADY. You shall not, for we will defend the breach.

COURTLY. With what? with what?

2. LADY. With our Tongues and Armes.

COURTLY. Your Tongues are pointless and edgless, and your Armes are weak defences.

M. MEDIATOR. You shall find them otherwise; but pray Sir *J. Amorous* carry away your unruly Regiment, and we will promise upon our words, and honours, that as soon as the Bride is in Bed, we will come to you and give you notice, then usher you into the Bride-bed, with Epithalamiums.

SIR J. AMOROUS. Upon condition that you will be speedy, I will depart.

LADIES. We will, we will: Come Lady *Coy* to bed, to bed, for shame.

Exeunt.

Scene 4

Enter Sir WILLIAM SAGE, *with all the Gentlemen, his Bridal-Guests, passing over the Stage, and going away again; after them comes Sir* JOHN AMOROUS, *as going to bed in his Night-Gown, Madame* MEDIATOR *and the Ladies usher him, and when he passes, this* EPITHALAMIUM *is sung.*

Written by my Lord Duke.*

EPITHALAMIUM

Now at the Door
You'l stand no more,
But enter the Bridal-bed:
Where you will prove
The Sweets of Love
With God Hymen's *banquet fed.*

Then Noble Knight
Put out the Light,
Her flaming Eyes will guide you;
And in her Armes
Those Circled Charmes
In Wedlock's Islands hide you.

Now all the joyes
Of Girles and Boyes,
Of sweeter pledges send you,
And know no strife
'Twixt Man and Wife,
But all the Blessings send you.

Exeunt. Enter Madame FANCY, *and Sir* MERCURY *Poet, coming out of the Bridal-Chamber together.*

MERCURY. Madame *Fancy* do you not wish to be a Bride, and that this night were your Wedding night?

FANCY. I should be well content to be a Bride, and to have a Wedding day,

---

* The duke's contributions are acknowledged on printed strips pasted into the text in both collections of plays. An exception is Huntington 120157, *Playes* (1662), where the attributions appear to be printed.

conditionally the day would last to the end of my life; but mistake me not, I mean for the length of the day, not shortness of life.

MERCURY. I perceive you would have no sleeping time.

FANCY. You mistake, I would have no Wedding night.

Exeunt.

ACT II

Scene 1

Enter FACIL *and* ADVISER.

ADVISER. But are you seriously in love with the Lady *Coy,* now the Lady *Amorous?*

FACIL. Yes seriously, but I may despair. I shall never compass my desires.

ADVISER. Faith, it is not probable you should obtain them, but yet you had best try.

FACIL. That were but to plunge myself deeper into an unfortunate love.

ADVISER. But a wise Man will omit no industry to compass his desires, neither do the Gods assist idle and cowardly Men.

FACIL. But she is not only new Married, but so guarded with Modesty and Vertue, as unlawful love cannot get audience, much less a favour.

ADVISER. Faith, if I were you, I would try in despite of her Modesty and Vertue.

FACIL. I dare not.

ADVISER. Fie! a Lover and a Coward! when the worst is but to be denied; but yet I would take many denials, before I would desist of my Suit; and if you do not pursue it, you partly deny your self.

FACIL. How should I make my love known unto her?

ADVISER. By some Lady confident, or she-servant Favourite; as also by Complemental Letters, and Love-Verses made in her praise; besides, making Balls and Collations to entertain her.

FACIL. I'le take your Counsel.

Enter MIMICK *in hast.*

ADVISER. But Stay, here comes *Mimick* the Lady *Amorous* Fool, who will be the fittest of all for this Employment; I'le speak to him: Stay, stay, honest friend, and let us speak a word or two.

MIMICK *goes on in hast.*

MIMICK. God be with you, Sir.

ADVISER. But will you not stay, a word or two?

MIMICK. Sir, I have stay'd twice two, that is four; nay by the Mass it was six at least; for you have asked me twice to stay, till you speak a word or two, and a word, and a word, and two and two is six, by my Calculation; and if you speak a word and two more, it will make three times three, that is just nine, the Golden Number, if I be not mistaken.

ADVISER. You are right, friend.

MIMICK. A right friend is a great friend, and a great friend is a good friend; and so God be with you, Sir.

ADVISER. Nay stay and tell me, are not you the Lady *Amorous Mimick?*

MIMICK. No truly, Sir, I am the Lady *Vertue*'s Mimick and the Lady *Amorous* Fool.

ADVISER. What, do you serve both the Ladies?

MIMICK. I am at both the Ladies service, Sir; God help me and give me Grace to please them well.

ADVISER. Thou art an honest fellow.

MIMICK. But an honest fellow cannot serve two Mistresses, the more the pity!

ADVISER. But you may serve this Gentleman, and he will serve thee; for if thou wilt but conveigh Letters, or can any way bring him to the private speech of the Lady *Amorous*, he will reward you bountifully.

MIMICK. I like the reward well; but I do not serve the Lady *Amorous*, but the Lady *Vertue;* but she being my Ladies Friend, and her Maid my Friend, I shall do my endeavor to deserve his gifts.

Exit Mimick.

ADVISER. Faith, I doubt not, but our design will go on well.

FACIL. I wish it may.

Exit FACIL *at one door, and* ADVISER *at another, who meets* TAKE-PLEASURE *as in hast.*

ADVISER. Whether away so fast, *Take-pleasure?*

TAKE-PLEAS. I am going to a Company of Ladies that have sent for me.

ADVISER. Let me go with you; for one Man can never please a company of Ladies; and surely it seems that they are in great distress, otherwise they would not have sent for you in such hast.

TAKE-PLEAS. Not sent for me! why, what do you think of me?

ADVISER. Why, I think you are a good fellow, and love a Mistress well; but I do not think you the Grand Signior.

TAKE-PLEAS. If I were, you should not come near my Seraglio.

ADVISER. But let me go with thee to these Ladies, for they are not in a Seraglio, nor never will be; they love their liberty so well.

TAKE-PLEAS. I am content, upon condition, you do not so much as look upon those Ladies I court.

ADVISER. But how if these Ladies look upon me?

TAKE-PLEAS. Yes, there is the mischief; therefore you shall not go.

ADVISER. But if you let me go, I'le promise you, I'le wink to those Ladies that look on me.

TAKE-PLEAS. Winking is more dangerous then if you should plainly woo them; for winking is a kind of Wooing and will win a Lady as soon as words will do.

ADVISER. Then I will shut both my eyes.

TAKE-PLEAS. That will be worse, for that will put them in mind of going to bed; it will be like sleeping.

ADVISER. Prithee let me go, and order me as you will.

TAKE-PLEAS. Wellcome, and as we go I'le tell you, how you shall behave your-self to those Ladies.

ADVISER. I will be govern'd according to your instructions.

Exeunt.

Scene 2

Enter M. MEDIATOR, and the Female-Guests, the day after the Wedding, to the Lady AMOROUS, who sits in a shaded place, and Curtains drawn about her, a Maid stands by.

M. MEDIATOR. Where is the Lady *Coy*, the now Lady *Amorous*?

MAID. There; my Lady is within those Curtains.

M. MEDIATOR. Why are you so benighted, as to have your Curtains drawn so darkly about you?

L. AMOROUS. I do not love the light.

M. MEDIATOR. Are you faln out with the light?

L. AMOROUS. In truth I am ashamed to see the light.

M. MEDIATOR. Ashamed! let's see your face, whether you blush or not?

The Lady offers to draw the Curtain, the Lady AMOROUS endeavors to hold it, and hideth herself behind it.

L. AMOROUS. O fie! for *Cupid* and *Venus* sake do not look upon me, for if you do, I shall die with blushing.

LADIES. Come, come, we will see you.

L. AMOROUS. I'le rather run away.

She runs away, the Ladies follow her, and meet the Lady VERTUE.

M. MEDIATOR. Madam, we were a going to see how you appear, since you are a Wife.

L. VERTUE. I hope I do not appear worse then I did, when I was a Maid; for I have not been Married so long as to have Children, Cares and Troubles, to decay my Youth and Beauty.

M. MEDIATOR. No, but we did imagine you would have been as most Brides are, shame-faced, and out of Countenance.

L. VERTUE. Why so, since Marriage is lawful, honest, and honourable? for if Marriage had been an act, that deserves a blush, I would not have Married.

1. LADY. But the Lady *Coy,* the now Lady *Amorous,* your fellow-Bride, is so out of Countenance, and doth so blush, as she is asham'd to appear in the light, and is forced to shut her eyes through shame, when her Husband looks upon her.

L. VERTUE. Why, hath she deceived her Husband? was she not a Virgin when she Married, that she is so out of Countenance as not to return her Husbands looks?

1. LADY. No, it is, that she is so extream modest.

L. VERTUE. Modesty is only ashamed of dishonesty, and not of that, which is honest to the Laws of God, Nature, and all civil Nations and People; but to answer for my self, if my Husband approves, likes, and is pleased with me, I have no reason to be out of Countenance; and I hope my Vertue is such, as not to be ashamed of the light: But come Ladies, I have prepared a Banquet, to which I invite you, to join with me in rejoicing at my happy Union.

Exeunt.

Scene 3

Enter Monsieur ADVISER, *and Monsieur* FACIL, *to Monsieur* COURTLY, *who is sitting at the Table, and writing.*

MONSIEUR ADVISER. What! writing!

COURTLY. I am casting up some Accounts.

ADVISER. Faith, I will see what a good Husband you are.

He takes up the Paper.

COURTLY. That Paper is the account of yesterday's expence.

ADVISER. I can judge by a day's expence a week's, and by a week's a year's.

COURTLY. That you cannot, for some days and weeks are more expensive then others.

ADVISER. Faith, at the years end several sums comes to one and the same yearly sum, as so much yearly spent.

COURTLY. Indeed for the most part it doth.

ADVISER. Leave your talking, and let me read your Expences, this is the yesterday's expence; let me see, here is the account of the expence of Ushering four Ladies.

    Imprimis, to a *Sexton,* to place four Ladies in several Pews in *Puritan* Church, to hear a holy Brother preach,   2 *Crowns.*

Item, for Sillibubs in the Park for those Ladies, 20 *s.*

For two little baskets of Cherries, that hold some dozen Cherries a piece, but the first of this year, 15 *s.*

To the Keeper of the Park-gate, *half a Crown.*

Item. for Cheesecakes and Rhennish-Wine in the fine Garden for those Ladies, 20 *s.*

To a Fortune-teller, to tell those Ladies their Fortunes, 40 *s.*

Also to the Door-keeper of the Garden, *half a Crown.*

Item. for a Supper for those Ladies at my Lodgings, 5 *l.*

To the Musick, 3 *l.*

For Torches to light those Ladies home to their Lodgings, 5 *shill.*

The total comes to 13 *l* 15 *s.*

You might have saved the 5 *s.* for Torch-light, by keeping those Ladies all night in your Lodgings.

COURTLY. I should have been a loser by that thrift.

FACIL. But do you spend every day thus much on Ladies?

COURTLY. Not every day, but most days I do.

ADVISER. After one and the same manner, and in the same places, and with the same Ladies?

COURTLY. No, I have variety for my money.

FACIL. Why, that is some comfort to you, and pleasure to the Ladies; but will it hold out?

COURTLY. No, faith, for neither my purse nor person will hold out; wherefore I must leave off to play the Gentleman-usher to Ladies, and go into the Country.

ADVISER. You had better be the fore-horse in a Cart, then first Gentleman-usher in a Coach; ushering is so laborious; besides, the intollerable charge; in so much that you may with less expence maintain a whole Village of Country Wives with their Daughters and Maid-servants, then entertain one Lady; moreover, those Villages will serve you, when as you are forced through civility to serve the Ladies.

COURTLY. You say true; therefore I'le go into the Country.

ADVISER. But will not those Ladies follow you?

COURTLY. I cannot tell.

ADVISER. Let me tell you, That is to be consider'd; and I would not have you go into the Country, for I and the rest of your friends would be sorry to lose your Company.

COURTLY. Faith, the Ladies ingross me so much, as I have no time to say my Prayers, or to think of my self, much less to keep Company with my friends.

FACIL. It seems you do not take the Ladies to be your friends.

COURTLY. If they be, they are very troublesome, and chargeable friends, which Friends, I could be very well content to be quit off, if I could tell how or which way.

ADVISER. There be a hundred ways to shake off those Ladies, if you will.

COURTLY. No, faith, I cannot; for they stick as close as burres, unless I should rudely quarrel with them, and basely raile against them; and if I did, it would be a question still whether I should be quit of them?

ADVISER. Let me advise you, how you may civilly be quit of them.

COURTLY. I shall gladly follow your advice.

ADVISER. Do not visit them, out of some pretence you are not well.

COURTLY. If I do not visit them, they'l visit me.

ADVISER. Then pretend some Law-suit.

COURTLY. Faith, they will follow me, and go to all the Courts of Judicature, to hear my Cause pleaded and judged.

ADVISER. Then go to a Tavern every day, they will not follow you thither.

COURTLY. Yes faith, some of them will, at least to the Tavern door in their Coaches to require my Company; but howsoever, they will send messenger after messenger to hasten me to them, pretending earnest business; and when I come, 'tis either to usher them to a Play, or to Church, or to the Exchange, or to the places of pleasure, or to the Fields, Park, or Garden, or else to some Ball, or particular meeting, or to some Picture-drawer, or to play at Cards, or the like; and to Man them to these places, they will send to me, before I am up or awake; the truth is, they will not let me rest in quiet.

FACIL. But this is a slavish life.

COURTLY. It is so.

ADVISER. But do they never reward thy service, *Courtly?*

COURTLY. Yes, as the Devil doth his Servants.

ADVISER. How is that?

COURTLY. With fire; for they send me hot burning Spirits, which are called Cordials.

ADVISER. It seems they think you want strength.

COURTLY. I must needs, when they tire me off my legs, ushering them from place to place.

FACIL. Do they give thee no Amorous favours?

COURTLY. Yes; but they are better pleased, I should prevent* them, and take favours from them before they are presented.

---

* prevent] come before, make the first move.

FACIL. But that is some recompence for thy time and charge.

COURTLY. The recompence, if you call it so, is the worse; for I had rather give them my Estate, then receive their Rewards; for though they make their favours, as a reward to their Courting-servants; yet their rewards are their chief pleasures, and the rewarded pains, for* their Courting-servants, lose more health by their favours, then they get wealth in their service.

ADVISER. The last advice is, You must be as if you were drunk.

COURTLY. That advice is worst of all; for then they are so busie, and make such puddering about me, to lay me to sleep, as they make me almost mad.

ADVISER. You have said so much, as I perceive your own advice is the best, to go into the Country; and if the Country will not save your body, life and estate, from these Locust-Ladies, you must travel into some other Kingdom.

COURTLY. If I do, they will follow me; for Ladies are as far-travellers in this age, as the Men; and I know some Gentlemen that are followed by Ladies out of one Kingdom into another, so as they do not know whether to go, for the World is not sufficient to hide or obscure them from the Ladies search.

ADVISER. Why, then most of the Men must turn Fryers, for that is to live in this world, as if they liv'd out of it.

COURTLY. That shift will not serve their turn; for if the Cavaliers turn Fryers, the Ladies will turn Nunnes, and then make those Fryers their Confessors.

ADVISER. Then there is no way for Men to escape those Ladies followers.

COURTLY. Yes, there is one way.

ADVISER. What way is that?

COURTLY. You must excuse me, for I will not declare it.

Exeunt. Enter FACIL, *and he speaks to himself.*

FACIL. I wonder *Mimick* stays so long, and doth not bring me an answer yet, from the Lady *Amorous.*

Enter MIMICK.

    But here he is.

FACIL. Monsieur *Mimick!* well met; have you delivered my Letter to the Lady *Amorous?*

MIMICK. Yes, Mr. *Facil,* I did deliver it to her.

FACIL. And how did she receive it?

MIMICK. Faith, she received your Letter, as all Women do Love-Presents.

FACIL. How is that?

MIMICK. With an outward dislike, and an inward affection.

---

* Emended from "of" in a seventeenth-century hand.

FACIL. If she received my Letter, with a displeased countenance, I judg she doth not love me.

MIMICK. Then your judgment is not wise; for love lives not in the countenance, but in the heart.

FACIL. But the Countenance expresses love; for a well pleased Countenance, expresses a well affected heart.

MIMICK. If you ground your belief on a Womans Countenance, you will be deceived; for Womens Countenances for the most part are as false as their faces; the one is glast with smiles, as the other with Pomatum; and dissembling modesty is like *Spanish* Red,* which is soon rub'd off with acquaintance and jealousie; or a peevish humour wipes off their smiles; so that there is no trust in their Countenances; for they change every minute of an hour; wherefore, they are unskilful Men, and unhappy Lovers, that steer the course of their desires, by the Card† of their Mistresses Countenances, which vary almost every moment, or by the Stars of their Mistresses eyes, which are wandring Planets. The truth is, most Lovers have troublesome Voyages in love, by reason all Womens minds are as inconstant as the wind.

FACIL. But I hope, by your favour and industry for me, to the Lady, my Voyage will be easie and free.

MIMICK. Do you believe I have power on your Mistress mind, as the Witches of *Lapland* have on the Winds?

FACIL. Faith, Monkies, Dogs, Parrots, and Fools, are powerful with Women, especially with Ladies.

MIMICK. Then deliver your Love-Letters to the Ladies Monkys, tell your Love-Messages to the Ladies Parrots, and give your Love-Collations to the Ladies Dogs, and your Love-bribes to my Ladies Fool.

FACIL. It is the easiest way; only to employ her Fool, and to encourage you, I give you five Pounds for the present, and more I promise you hereafter, to plead my suit, and to speak in my behalf.

MIMICK. Faith, your case is so bad, as it requires a witty and ingenuous knave to make it seem a good case, and an elegant Orator to make it seem a clear case; for Oratory makes a foul case seem fair, and great fees make an Orator's wit quick, and his tongue smooth.

FACIL. Well, I will trust to your Knavery, wish well to your Oratory, and hope Fortune will favour your Wisdom.

MIMICK. You mistake; for Fortune never favours wise Men, but Fools.

* *Spanish* Red] red ocher; clay and iron oxide used as rouge.
† Card] chart or map.

Exit FACIL.

MIMICK. Well, craft shall serve for wisdom, and the chief part of my craft must be to Fool this Lover, or rather to cozen him; for Lovers are Fools of *Cupid's* making, and they wear Fool's Coats in *Cupid's* Court.

Exeunt. Enter the Lady VERTUE, *and Sir* WILLIAM SAGE.* MIMICK, *who seems to be in a very serious study, not taking any notice of his Master and Lady.*

SIR W. SAGE. Surely *Mimick* has State-matters in his head, he is so studious and serious.

L. VERTUE. *Mimick?*

He doth not answer.

L. VERTUE. Why *Mimick*, are you deaf?

MIMICK. I am somewhat thick of hearing.

SIR W. SAGE. But *Mimick*, let us know what is the cause you are in so serious a study.

MIMICK. I am considering with my self, what profession I shall be of.

L. VERTUE. And what Profession have you chosen to be of?

MIMICK. I have not chosen any as yet, for I waver in my mind amongst many Professions, as an amorous Lover doth amongst many Ladies, not resolving which to address himself to; for though he would enjoy them all, yet he can court but one at a time; and though he resolveth to court all, yet he can but enjoy one at a time.

SIR W. SAGE. But he may court and enjoy them all, one after another.

MIMICK. Faith, that is endless work; for before the last Lady is courted and enjoyed, he will be forced to be of the Profession of a Priest, to preach his own funeral Sermon, or of a Sexton, to dig his own grave: But leaving Priests and amorous Lovers, what Profession shall I be of?

L. VERTUE. What think you of being a Courtier?

MIMICK. There are so many Court-fools, that they never thrive with that Profession; for what they get by flattery, they spend in vanity.

L. VERTUE. What think you of being a Lawyer?

MIMICK. The Law is more of the Knaves then the Fool's side, therefore I shall never thrive in that Profession.

SIR W. SAGE. What think you of being a Merchant?

MIMICK. I could Traffick with Jest, but I am afraid in some of my Ventures I should have my head broke; therefore I will not be of that Profession.

L. VERTUE. What think you of being a States-man?

MIMICK. Faith, I think I am fool enough to be a States-man, but I have not

---

* "Sage" added by this editor.

Formality enough; besides, I shall make such disorders and disturbances in State-affairs, as I may chance to be kill'd in an uproar or seditious Tumult.

SIR W. SAGE. What think you of being a Soldier?

MIMICK. No, for I am more safe from danger in my Fools Coat then they in their Iron-arms; and shall get more by a Fool's Profession, then a Soldiers.

SIR W. SAGE. What think you of being a Scholar?

MIMICK. That I am now; for I learn every day to play the Fool better and better.

L. VERTUE. What think you of being a City-Magistrate?

MIMICK. I like that best; for my Fools Coat will serve for my Magistrates Gown; but yet I am afraid of the Common-people in these seditious times.

SIR W. SAGE. What think you of being a Traveller?

MIMICK. O Lord! so I may travel to my wit's end.

L. VERTUE. What think you of being a Chymist?

MIMICK. Faith, I get more gold by playing the Fool with Lords and Ladies, then Chymists do by playing the Fools with Fire and Furnace.

SIR W. SAGE. Then I think you had best continue your own Profession still, which is to play the Fool.

MIMICK. But my Profession of playing the Fool is a general Profession, and I would fain have a particular Profession; for there are few Men but have some other Profession besides their Natural Profession; Wherefore, I must study some other Profession.

L. VERTUE. What do you think then of being a Vintner?

MIMICK. My Guests will drink up my Wine, and leave me their Scores; lie with my Wife, and give her the Pox; and if I have not a handsom Woman to my Wife, I shall have no Guests.

L. VERTUE. What think you of being a Taylor?

MIMICK. I shall have only my Measures for my pains, and the shreds for my labour.

SIR W. SAGE. What think you of being a Usurer?

MIMICK. So a Fool and his Money would be soon parted, and I shall have bonds for my Money; but a hundred to one if I get my Money by the bonds.

L. VERTUE. What think you of being an Amorous Lover?

MIMICK. I shall woo more Mistresses, then I shall win, and win more Mistresses then I shall use.

L. VERTUE. But you may get a rich Wife, if you Woo well.

MIMICK. If I should woo the best of any Man, I shall sooner get the Pox with a Mistress, then Wealth with a Wife; for Fortune is the only Match-maker.

SIR W. SAGE. But there is a saying, That Fools have Fortune.

MIMICK. Not all fools; for there be more fools then good fortune; the truth is, There are so many Fools, as it is impossible for Fortune to favour them all.

L. VERTUE. But Fortune may favour those that are most foolish.

MIMICK. Then she will not favour me; wherefore I'le reject Fortune, relie upon my own wit.

L. VERTUE. Your Wit is so weak, as it cannot uphold you.

MIMICK. I'le try the strength of it, and when I fall for want of Wit, it is a proper time for Fortune to raise me up to shew her power.

SIR W. SAGE. Well, we will leave you to your study, and when you have chosen a Profession, I suppose you will make us acquainted with it.

MIMICK. No doubt of it; for you must help to put me into practice.

Exeunt. Enter Mr. LONGLIFE, *and Mr.* AGED.

AGED. *Longlife.* How are you since you went abroad.

LONG. Very well, I thank you Mr. *Aged.*

AGED. I am now come to you, to ask you a question, whether you would not think it were wise for us, we having only two Children you a Son and I a Daughter, to match them together, and so we being both rich, we may joyn our Estates together, by joyning our Children together which will make them both flow in plenty.

LONG. I like your proposition, concerning the joyning our riches together, by joyning our Children together: But my Son is a Wit, Mr. *Aged,* and your Daughter I hear is a Wit, and if their wits be joyned together, it may over-power their Wealth; for Wit and Wealth doth never agree together; for wit regards not Wealth, and wealth regards not wit; which is the reason that those, which have most Wit, (which are Poets) are poor; for you shall seldom read, or hear, That natural Poets are rich. And both our Children being Poetical, should we marry them together, would undo them.

AGED. By the Mass, you say true.

LONG. Then we must endeavour to marry our Children to Fooles; you must provide a foolish man for your Daughter, and I a foolish woman for my Son; That the dulness of the Fool, may allay the quickness of the Wit, which will make a good temper, causing them to thrive in wealth, and to increase Posterity; for let me tell you, That great Wits for the most part have few Children, but what their brain produces, which are Ideas, Inventions and Opinions; Ideas are Daughters; Inventions are Sons, and Opinions Hermaphrodites; and the production of these Incorporeal Children, hinders the production of Corporeal Children; and we both desire to have Corporeal Grand-Children to uphold our Families.

AGED. You say wisely, Mr. *Long-life;* and therefore, we must endeavour to marry
our Children to Fools, for the Wealth and Posterities of our Families.
Exeunt.

ACT III

Scene 1

Enter Sir JOHN AMOROUS, *and his* LADY.

LADY. Sir *John,* Sir *John,* I take it very unkindly, that you should go abroad, and
leave my Company?

SIR J. AMOR. Sometimes, Wife, to be absent from each other, is a refreshment,
and Temperance is part of Prudence.

LADY. I love not such Refreshments, Temperance, and Prudence; wherefore,
you must either stay at home and keep me Company, or I shall seek other
Company elsewhere.

Exit LADY. *Sir* J. AMOROUS *Solus.*

SIR J. AMOR. That will be some ease; for I had rather be a Cuckold then be
bound to one Woman, especially my Wife.

Enter his Wife's Maid.

SIR J. AMOR. *Mal,* I'le prefer thee.

MAID. I thank you, Master.

SIR J. AMOR. I'le prefer thee from my Servant, to be my Mistress.

MAID. If you had been unmarried, and would prefer me from being your
Mistress, to be your Wife, I should have taken it for an honour.

SIR J. AMOR. But I am Married, *Mal,* and thou shalt take thy Ladie's place, in thy
Ladie's absence.

MAID. I had rather marry *Tom* your Butler lawfully, then lie with my Master
unlawfully.

SIR J. AMOR. Why, *Mal,* Love is lawful, and to serve your Master is lawful;
wherefore, it is lawful to serve your Master's Love.

MAID. But some kinds of Love are unlawful, and some kinds of Service are
unlawful; for it is unlawful to love Vice, and unlawful to serve the Devil;
wherefore it is unlawful to be my Master's Whore.

SIR J. AMOR. To be your Master's Whore, is to be your Master's Mistress; and to
be the Butler's Wife, is to be the Butler's Slave; but I'le leave you to the
Butler's droppings of his Taps: But howsoever, Consider it well, *Mal,* for you
will be good enough for the Butler afterwards.

Exeunt.

Scene 2

Enter Sir WILLIAM SAGE *and his* LADY.

SIR WILLIAM SAGE. I wonder that *Mimick* is not here! for his company is very delightful, to pass away idle time;* for idle time is only free for Fools Company.

LADY. He is rather a Knave then a Fool; but here he comes.

Enter MIMICK.

SIR W. SAGE. *Mimick,* have you chosen a Profession yet?

MIMICK. Yes, marry have I, for I intend to be an Orator.

SIR W. SAGE. If you be a professed Orator, I suppose you have studied a speech.

MIMICK. Yes, I have studied, as Orators use to do, in making an Oration; for I have rackt my Brain, stretch'd my Wit, strapado'd† my Memory, tortured my thoughts, and kept my Sences awake.

SIR W. SAGE. Certainly, it is a very eloquent and wise Oration, since you have taken so much pains.

MIMICK. Labour and Study is not a certain rule for wise, witty, or eloquent Orations or Speeches; for many studied Speeches are very foolish: But will you hear my Speech?

SIR W. SAGE. I will.

MIMICK. But then Master, you must stand for, signifie, or represent a Multi-tude, or an Assembly.

SIR W. SAGE. That is impossible, being but a single person.

MIMICK. Why doth not a single Figure stand for a Number, as the Figure of Five, Eight or Nine, and joining Ciphers to them, they stand for so many Hundreds, or Thousands: And here be two Joint-Stools, one of which Stools and you Lady shall serve for two Ciphers and my Master for the Figure of Nine, and so you two and the Joint-Stool make Nine hundred.

SIR W. SAGE. But if the Assembly be so big, as to be a Company of Nine hundred they cannot all stand so near, as to hear what you speak, neither can your voice reach to the Circumferent Ears.

MIMICK. The greatest Glory of an Orator is to have Crouds of People follow him, and those that hear the least will praise him the most; and the truth is, That all Orators gain more renown by those that do not hear them, but only see them, then by those that stand so near, as to hear what they speak; for

---

* In the original this read "idle; time."

† strapado'd] form of torture in which the victim is tied by the wrists and repeatedly dropped to just short of the ground.

there is ten to one of those that do not hear them, to those that do hear them;* So that if those that do hear them, should dispraise their Orations, yet those that hear them not, will commend them, and having ten to one of their side, they may say what they will, they shall be applauded, and the most Voices carry them up to Fame's Tower; which considering, I will set another Joint-stool as another Cipher to my Lady, and three Ciphers, with the Figure of Nine, my Master, will make it Nine thousand.

SIR W. SAGE. As many as you please.

MIMICK. But what shall I have for a Pulpit or standing-place? for I must mount above all the Assembly?

LADY. Take another Joint-stool, and stand upon that.

MIMICK. O fie! that will not appear well; besides, I shall stand tottering, ready to fall, and the very fear of falling, will put me out of my Speech.

LADY. But you will appear standing upon a Joint-stool, like as a Statue upon a Pedestal.

MIMICK. I should be well pleased to have a Statue made for me, and set up as an honour and remembrance of me; but I shall not be pleased to stand as a Statue my self.

SIR W. SAGE. Why then get a Tub; and stand in that.

MIMICK. A Tub will not do me any service, unless it be a mounted Tub. But for this time I'le stand upon the Table, without Tub or Case, to speak the naked truth; and thus I ascend.

He ascends upon the Table.

LADY. Begin.

MIMICK. Stay, I must breathe first, hawk, spit, blow my nose, humm, and look gravely round about upon the People, and then speak at first in a low voice, then raise my Voice by degrees, until I come to the highest strain or point.

He Speaks.

Noble, Honourable, and Worthy Auditors, I am come here to speak of a Subject which concerns all Men; which General Subject is *Women;* and I am not only to Treat of *Women,* which is an easie Subject to be Treated of; but of the *Chastity* of *Women,* which is an hard, frozen Subject; and so hard frozen it is, that all the heat Love can bring is not able to thaw it; the truth is, Chastity is a Subject, that lives at a great distance; for though the two names, *Woman* and *Chastity,* are oft-times joined together, yet the several Subjects of those Names, dwell not near each other; for *Chastity* dwells at the Poles, where no *Woman* is; and *Women* dwell or inhabit the Torrid Zone, where no

---

* Misspelled "chem" in the original.

Chastity is: Thus you may perceive that Names are more easily joined, then the things they signifie; but how to bring *Chastity* and *Women* together, is the difficulty, indeed so difficult as it is impossible; and as impossible for hot Hell and cold Heaven to meet, or for gods and devils to be friends: But noble Auditors the Names *Chast Women* being join'd together, are sufficient; for that Conjunction of Names contents, satifies and pleases all Men, as Fathers, Sons, Brothers, and Husbands, that would have their Daughters, Sisters, Mothers and Wives Chast; and as for Amorous Lovers, they are pleased to have the Subjects dwell at distance; so that Art and Nature, Deceit and Verity have agreed together to make all Men happy, so far as concerns *Women*.

LADY. Leave off your Prating, or I'le fling one of these Ciphers at your head.

MIMICK. Will not you let me speak out my Oration?

LADY. No, unless it were better.

MIMICK. If you will let me speak out my Speech, I'le make the two Poles meet in the very forehead of the Torrid Zone of a Man's head.*

LADY. I'le hear no more; wherefore come off from the Table.

MIMICK. Well, I obey, although I am vexed at the heart, that I must not speak out my Speech, as also to be disgraced before an Assembly of Nine thousand.

LADY. You knavish Fool, what cause invited, perswaded, or commanded you to speak an Oration concerning the Chastity of Women?

MIMICK. That which perswaded me to speak an Oration, and not only an Oration, but a factious or malicious Oration was that which perswaded all Orators; first, self-love to shew their Wit; next, their ill Nature to make a division and dissention amongst Mankind.

LADY. Well, since you have express'd the evil Orators of these evil times, such as make Factions and Divisions; I will express such Orators as ought to be; and thus I'le speak to this Assembly.

She Speaks.

Noble, Honourable, and Worthy Auditors, I am come here to contradict a Knavish Fool, that has spoken to the Disgrace of Women; saying, That only the Names of Women and Chastity are joined together, but the Subjects dwell far asunder; which is false; for though some Women, as the scum of the female Sex, be Incontinent, yet all Women are not so; for some Women are Chast by Nature, others by Vertue, and some by Honour; as for Vertue and Honour, they are like to Plants set or planted by Education, and grow up like to tall Cedars or strong Oaks in the Mind, which bear no evil fruits; as Vices and base qualities, or evil and dishonest desires: But worthy Auditors,

* Torrid Zone of a Man's Head] a reference to cuckoldry.

give me leave to tell you, That Women are the unhappiest Creatures which Nature ever made; not only that they are the most shiftless Creatures, but the most abused of any other Creatures, and only by Men; who do not only continually assault them, and endeavor to corrupt and betray them, but they have enslaved them, and do often defame them with slanders and reproaches, vainglorious boasts, and lying brags; the truth is, Men are like Devils to Women, seeking whom they may devour; inticing, alluring, perswading and flattering Women, to the ruin of their Souls, Bodies, Minds, Fortunes, and good Names; but Women are beloved and favoured by the gods, who endue their Bodies with Beauty, and their Minds with Spiritual Grace, their Thoughts with Religious Zeal, and their Lives with Pious Devotions; which keeps their Bodies Chast, their Minds pure, and their Lives Vertuous; But those few Women that are Incontinent, are rather Beasts then Women; but most Women are Angelical; and though Men defame them, yet the Gods glorifie them.

MIMICK. Lady, if you speak any longer of the Female Subject, you will cast them from Heaven into Hell; for you cannot go beyond Heaven, Angels and Gods.

LADY. I am content to speak no more of them at this time, but leave them in bliss.

SIR W. SAGE. Mimick, your Lady will be too hard for you.

MIMICK. Yes, in Foolery, but not in Wit.

Exeunt.

Scene 3

Enter Monsieur ADVISER, *and Monsieur* COURTLY.

MONSIEUR COURTLY. Where were you, that I did not see you all yesterday, nor most part of this day?

ADVISER. Faith, I was all the Morning at a Sermon, and at Noon I went to a Tavern, in the Afternoon I went to a Play, and at night I went to a Commonhouse, and from thence I went to the Gaming-house, and there I stay'd till late in the Morning; and then I went home, and lay and slept so long, as I have but newly dined.

COURTLY. Dined, say you! why it is almost Supper-time.

ADVISER. Not with me.

COURTLY. No; for you turn the Day into Night, and Night into Day.

ADVISER. I did not so yesterday.

COURTLY. Yes, but you did; for you spent all the day in deeds of darkness.

ADVISER. Will you say, that hearing a Sermon is a deed of darkness?

COURTLY. Yes, unless you did profit by it, which I do not perceive you did; the truth is, by your after-actions you seem the worse for it.

ADVISER. I'le confess to you, my friend, that the Sermon made me so dull and melancholy, as I was forced to go to a Tavern, to revive and comfort my Mind with some Spiritual Liquor; and from thence I went to a Play to recreate my Thoughts, and to take them from all sad Contemplations, in seeing and hearing a merry Comedy acted; and the truth is, the Play made me so lively, as I became so wanton, that I was forced to go to a Common-house, and after I had convers'd with the Woman, I was as dull and melancholy as I was after the Sermon; so I went to the Gaming-house for diversion, knowing I should meet store of Company; and being there, I fell to play, where I lost all my Money; for which I was so troubled, as I wish my self dead, having not any Money left to live; and being moneyless, I went home to bed, that I might sleep and forget my loss for a time.

COURTLY. But did not the thoughts of the loss hinder your sleep?

ADVISER. No faith; for my thoughts were so opprest with grief, as they fell fast asleep, and so fast asleep they were, as I did not dream.

COURTLY. But now they are awake, they remember your losses, do they not?

ADVISER. Yes, but I will perswade you to go with me to the Tavern, there to drink out the remembrance.

For when my head is fill'd with Vaporous Wine,
My thoughts for Losses will not then repine.

Enter TAKE-PLEASURE *to* ADVISER *and* COURTLY.

COURTLY. *Tom,* Thou art welcome.

TAKE-PLEAS. Go hang your self, for you are not a Man of your word, for you promis'd to meet me at the Crown-Tavern, where I stay'd for you till twelve a Clock last night, expecting your coming.

COURTLY. And how did you pass away the solitary time?

TAKE-PLEAS. Faith, I call'd for some Tobacco, and a pint of Wine, and then I took a Pipe, then drunk a glass of Wine, and you did not come; then I took another Pipe, and drunk another glass of Wine, and you did not come; so I took Pipe after Pipe, and drunk Glass after Glass, until the Pint-pot was empty; then I call'd for another Pint, and another Pint, and drunk them as the first; and still you stay'd, and still I drunk so long as I was almost drunk, expecting your Company; but at last finding my Stomack full, and my head light, and the night far spent I went home and so to bed.

ADVISER. Without saying your Prayers?

TAKE-PLEAS. Faith, I could not say my Prayers for Cursing of *Courtly;* but at last I fell asleep with a Curse in my mouth, which Curse I found in my mouth when I did awake in the morning.

ADVISER. Did you swallow the Curse down, or spit it out?

TAKE-PLEAS. Faith, it had almost choak'd me; for it stuck so in my Throat, as I could neither get it up, nor down, but at last I spit it out, for it was as bitter as Gall.

COURTLY. You had no reason to curse me, if you were drunk; for the only design of our meeting at the Tavern, was but to be drunk.

TAKE-PLEAS. That is true; but there is no pleasure to be drunk without a Companion.

COURTLY. The truth is, I could not come; for I was forced against my will to Sup with a Lady.

TAKE-PLEAS. Faith, Women spoil all good fellowship; but I had been better Company for her last night, then you were.

COURTLY. Come, come, let us go to the same Tavern, and there end all Quarrels. *Exeunt.*

Scene 4

Enter Monsieur FACIL, *and* MIMICK.

MONSIEUR FACIL. Master *Mimick,* I am come according to your appointment.

MIMICK. Then Mr. *Facil* you may depart according to my appointment.

FACIL. But you assured me, That if I came at this hour, I should have access to your Lady.

MIMICK. But Women change their mind every minute, and are in threescore several minds or humors in an hour; and this minute the Lady is in a very angry humor, which will not agree with you amorous humor.

FACIL. But I'le stay until her angry humor is past.

MIMICK. Then you may stay until you be weary; for she will change out of one angry humor into another, until she hath run out an hour; for there be many several kinds and sorts of angry Humors.

FACIL. But I will stay an hour.

MIMICK. But if you do, it is not likely that the Lady will be in a humor to entertain your Courtly address; for it is probable, as being most usual, that from the last angry humor, she will change into the first degree of a Melancholy humor.

FACIL. Then I will attend two hours, until such time as she will be out of her Melancholy humor.

MIMICK. That will not do you any service; for out of the last Melancholy humor she will change into a pious humor, and so from one pious humor into another, until such time as she comes to weep like a *Mary Magdalen,** and after floods of Tears she will fall fast asleep; her Sences and Spirits being tired with Kneeling, Praying, Sighing, and Weeping, and after she awakes from her devout sleep, she may chance to bestow a Charity upon you.

FACIL. I'le attend in hope of that Charity.

MIMICK. I perceive by you, that Lovers will take no excuses or denials; but yet this last I hope will drive you away, which is, the Lady has the Wind-collock;† wherefore she will not admit of a visit, especially Amorous Suiters this day.

FACIL. By this I find you have fill'd me with hope, to delude me.

MIMICK. Let me tell you, that Love is the greatest Deluder, or Cheater, especially Amorous Love; but to keep you from dispair, I'le promise you (for Promises keep Lovers alive) I will devise some way to corrupt this Lady to your desires, though it requires much labour, study, wit, and time, to corrupt Chastity; and since my Service will be great, my Reward must not be small.

FACIL. Then here I give you Ten pounds to reward your Knavery.

Exit FACIL. MIMICK *solus.*

MIMICK. Why, this is right as it should be, for one Knave to Fee another, that Knavery may thrive.

Exeunt. Enter Sir MERCURY *Poet, and the Lady* FANCY.

MERC. Madam, I take it for a great favour and obligation, that you will receive my visit.

FANCY. It would be an Obligation to my self, to oblige a worthy person, such as I believe you are, but I do not perceive how I can merit thanks in receiving your Visit, for I suppose you can better pass your time, then with my dull Company; and unprofitable Conversation.

MERC. It is a particular favour, because you do not usually receive Visits.

FANCY. The reason why I do not usually receive Visits, is out of a respect to the Visiters, knowing I have not Wit to entertain them, Speech to delight them, nor Learning to profit them; so they would but lose their time in visiting me; and I chuse rather to lose the profit I might gain by hearing wise, witty, and learned Visiters; then they should lose their time by learning nothing them-selves; for Wisdom and Wit desires to advance in Knowledg, and not to

---

* *Mary Magdalen*] The weeping woman of Luke 7 and Mary Magdalene cured of demons in Luke 8 are popularly conflated with each other and with the image of a repentant but susceptible prostitute.

  † Wind-collock] cholic; pain in the colon caused by gas.

stand at a stay; for though prating Fools take pleasure to inform, and formal Fools to reform; yet wise Men delight to be informed and reformed, through a noble ambition to attain to perfection.

MERC. Which Perfection, Madam, you have arrived to.

FANCY. That is impossible, for Nature hath made Women so defective, as they are not capable of Perfection.

MERC. Madam, my Soul is wedded to your Vertue, and my Contemplations to your Fancy, and my Love and Person longs to be wedded to your Beauty and Chastity.

> *And if our Wits agree,*
> *I'm sure you'l favour me.*
> *For Wit the Brain doth move,*
> *And causes Souls to love:*
> *For Fools cannot love well,*
> *Nor reason for Love tell;*
> *They understand not Merit,*
> *Nor a Cœlestial Spirit.*

Enter MR. *Aged.*

AGED. How is that! Merit, Spirit, and I know not what! Daughter, I am come to forbid you the Company of Sir *Mercury Poet*, and that you receive not any of his Visits: And Sir *Mercury Poet*, I do forbid you my Daughters Company.

MERC. Sir, I have not visited your Daughter, without your leave; for you were pleased to invite me to wait on your Daughter.

AGED. 'Tis true, for I did believe, (by reason your Father and I being old acquaintance, and loving friends, and both being rich, and having Children, he a Son, and I a Daughter) it might be proper and fit to have matched you together; but since your Father and I have debated and considered well upon the Case, we find it no ways profitable for either.

MERC. Where is the disadvantage or hinderance?

AGED. Your Wit.

MERC. Is Wit a Crime?

AGED. It ought to be made Criminal; for it is not only unprofitable, but ruinous; not any person thrives that has it; and it makes those that are rich, poor; and those that are poor, uncapable to be rich.

MERC. They that have Wit, need no other wealth, Sir.

Enter LONGLIFE.

AGED. Mr. *Longlife,* I find now your words true, That Wit regards not Wealth; for your Son says, That Wit is Wealth enough of it self.

LONGL. Yes, yes, Mr. *Aged;* but he will find, Wit cannot buy Land, unless he joins Knavery to it.

MERC. True Wit is always just, and honest, it knows no double dealing; and honour is the ground on which it builds a Fame.

LONGL. But if you have no other ground, nor other building, but Honour and Fame, you may beg for your livelihood, or starve for want of bread.

MERC. I had rather die for want of bread, then live without honourable Fame; and Fortune's goods are poor to those that Nature gives.

LONGL. O Mr. *Aged,* I am unhappy, undone; for I perceive my Posterity will be all Beggars: And therefore, if you will not change your Principles soon, I will disinherit you.

MERC. You cannot, Sir; for though you may give away your Land, you cannot give away my Wit (if I have any.)

LONGL. If I cannot, I will marry you to a Fool; so that though you be poor, your Children may be rich.

MERC. If you please, Sir, and Mr. *Aged* consent, I desire I may Marry this Lady.

LONGL. No, no, Son she hath Wit, I know by her silence, otherwise her tongue would have run a race in this time.

FANCY. I can speak, Sir, but I doubt I have not Wit to speak well.

LONGL. Nay, if you talk of Wit, you are not for my Son.

FANCY. Your Son hath so much Wit, that what Woman soever he Marries, cannot continue a Fool long, for she will get Wit from him, and yet he will have no less, for Nature still supplies his store.

LONGL. But my Grand-Children may be Fools, if my Son's Wife be none of Natures witty Daughters.

FANCY. His Children cannot be Fools; for Wit begets Wit, although a Fool should be the breeder.

LONGL. Good Mr. *Aged,* lock up your Daughter, until I have sent my Son to Travel; for otherwise we shall ruin our Posterities.

Exeunt.

ACT IV

Scene 1

Enter Lady AMOROUS, *Lady* VERTUE, *and Madam* MEDIATOR.

LADY AMOROUS. Madam, what makes you so fine to day? and not only your person is finer, but your house is finer trim'd and trickt, then usually it was; have you a Servant to visit you to day?

L. VERTUE. No, but I have a Master that is to come out of the Country to day.

L. AMOR. Who is your Master?

L. VERTUE. My Husband, who comes home to day.

L. AMOR. Do you make your self and your house so fine only for your Husband?

L. VERTUE. Only for my Husband, say you! Why, he is the only Man that I desire to appear fine to; and the only person I desire to please and delight.

M. MEDIAT. But Husbands take no notice of the bravery* of their Wives.

L. VERTUE. Howsoever, it is the part of every good wife to express, on all occasions, their Love and Respect to their Husbands; in their absence to mourn, at their return to rejoice, and in their Company to be best pleased.

M. MEDIAT. Love, Respect, and Duty, are only expressible in Humors, Words, and Service, and not in Habit.†

L. VERTUE. But Joy is expressed in habit, as much as mourning; witness Triumphs and Triumphant Shews; and Triumphs of Joy, and Funerals, are not alike.

M. MEDIAT. All Noble Persons are buried in Triumphs.

L. VERTUE. Indeed they are buried with Ceremony, but it is such Ceremony as expresses Dolor, not Joy; for they are followed with black Mourners, and weeping eyes: But however, I endeavour to appear to my Husband, at his returning home, like a gay and joyful Bride, and not as a sad mourning Widow.

L. AMOR. Let me not live, Lady *Vertue,* if you be not the most simple Woman alive.

L. VERTUE. In what?

L. AMOR. First, That you can take pleasure in the dull Company of a Husband; next, That you do not delight your self with the Gallants of the Times; and thirdly, That you do not only spoile your own Husband, but all other Womens Husbands, with your example; for which folly, you ought to be condemned by all our Sex.

L. VERTUE. If they condemn me for my Vertue, I will despise them for their Vices.

L. AMOR. But Vice is a Vertue in this age; ask Madam *Mediator* else.

L. VERTUE. What say you, Madame *Mediator?*

M. MEDIAT. I say, that Vice was never so confident as it is now, nor never so glorified as it is now, nor never so beloved as it is now, nor never so practiced as it is now.

---

* bravery] dressing in fine clothes, living in high style.
† Habit] costume.

L. AMOR. Well, since Vice is so beloved, and Vertue despised, I will go to a merry Meeting. Come, Madam *Mediator,* you'l make one, although Lady *Vertue* will not.

Exeunt.

Scene 2

Enter Monsieur FACIL, *and* MIMICK.

MIMICK. Monsieur *Facil,* I have tired my Legs, and worn out the Soles of my Shooes to find you out, to give you a Letter from the Lady *Amorous.*

FACIL. I am sorry you have taken such pains.

MIMICK. You may requite my pains when you please; but here is the Letter.

He receives the Letter.

FACIL. Faithful *Mimick!* happy *Facil!* divine Lady! delicious Letter!

He kisses the Letter.

MIMICK. What delicious pleasure do you receive in that Kiss, Monsieur *Facil?*

FACIL. As much pleasure as Joy can give me.

He opens the Letter.

What is this, a plain sheet of Paper! you Rogue, do you abuse and cozen me?

MIMICK. Did you not give me Ten pound to reward my Knavery? for which I should be ungrateful, should I not be a Knave to you; but yet you have no reason to be angry for this unletter'd Paper, which is the royall'st Kindness, and most generous Present, the Lady could send you; for she has sent you a blank to write down your own desires, demands, or condition of agreement, love and friendship.

FACIL. If it be so, I ask you Pardon, and will requite your fidelity with Gold.

MIMICK. I'le take your requital.

FACIL. Pray go with me to my Lodgings, and there I'le write in this white Paper, that came from the whiter hands of my Mistress, my love and affections, and you shall guide it unto her.

MIMICK. You must ballace* the Letter with Gold, or otherwise it will be drown'd in the returning-Voyage.

FACIL. I will.

Scene 3

Enter Lady AMOROUS, *and two or three other Ladies.*

FIRST LADY. Lady *Amorous,* Marriage has made you a boon Companion.

---

* ballace] ballast; give steadiness to.

L. AMOR. I was a Novice before I married; but now I find that there is no pleasure, like Liberty, Mirth and good Company.

1. LADY. You say true, Lady, for a Stoical life is the worst life in the World.

2. LADY. But the Lady *Vertue,* and Sir *W. Sage* live the life of Stoicks.*

L. AMOR. The more Fools they; but my Husband and I, live the life of Libertines; for he takes his pleasure, and I take mine: have you sent for Mr. *Courtly?*

2. LADY. Yes, there are at least half a score Messengers sent one after another to invite him hither.

Enter Monsieur COURTLY.

L. AMOR. O Sir! you're welcome, we were even now wishing for you to go abroad with us.

COURT. I account my self happy, Ladies, that I am come according to your wishes, as also to do you service.

1. LADY. We did send a dozen Messengers for you.

COURTLY. I did happily meet them, Madam.

1. LADY. But whether shall we go?

COURTLY. Where you please, Lady; for I am ready at your service.

2. LADY. Let us go to the Great Park.

L. AMOR. No, let us go to the Fruit-Garden.

2. LADY. No faith, upon better Consideration, let us stay and play at Cards.

L. AMOR. That is dull; rather let us send for Fidlers, and Dance.

1. LADY. We have not Men enough to dance, and Mr. *Courtly* cannot dance with us all.

COURTLY. I'le do my endeavor, Ladies.

2. LADY. No, let us hire a Barge, and row upon the Water.

L. AMOR. No, let us go and sup at the Tavern at the Bridg-foot; what say you, Mr. *Courtly,* will you entertain us?

COURTLY. Yes, Lady, as well as I can.

1. LADY. Let us go.

2. LADY. No, let us first draw lots, and let Fortune decide the place of our Recreations.

L. AMOR. Content; but which lot shall carry it?

1 LADY. The long lot.

2 LADY. The short lot.

1 LADY. I say the long lot.

L. AMOR. Let the most voices carry it.

COURTLY. Ladies, if I might perswade you, it should be at the Tavern at the

---

* Stoicks] Greek philosophers (c. 300 B.C.) known for austerity and restraint.

Bridg-foot, and there you shall have the best Meat, Wine and Musick, that place affords.

ALL. Content, content.

Exeunt.

Scene 4

Enter Monsieur FACIL *and Monsieur* ADVISER.

MONSIEUR ADVISER. *Facil,* how do you prosper in Loves Adventure?

FACIL. More happily then I could imagine, for she receives my Letters, and returns me Answers.

ADVISER. Then you shall not need to despair, since you have such encouragement.

FACIL. No faith, for now I fear she will be kinder then I would have her; for she has consented to a private meeting.

Enter TAKE-PLEASURE *as in hast.*

ADVISER. Whether away in such hast, *Tom?*

TAKE-PLEAS. Faith, *Courtly,* hath sent his Footman to me in such hast, as the poor fellow is almost melted with the heat he has with running, to bring me a note from his Master, who writes to me, that of all love and friendship I should speedily come to him, and to bring half a dozen other Gentlemen with me to the Tavern, to help him to entertain a Company of Ladies, otherwise he shall die in their service; wherefore prithee *Adviser,* and *Facil,* go with me thither.

FACIL. Faith, we cannot, for we have other business.

TAKE-PLEAS. The same answer I have had from a dozen other Gentlemen, and cannot perswade any one to go; wherefore I fear my friend *Courtly* will be overpower'd by those many Ladies.

ADVISER. Why would *Courtly* engage him self to so many Women?

TAKE-PLEAS. Alas, he could not help it; for they sent so many Messengers to desire him to come to them, as he was almost smother'd in the croud, so that he was forced as it were, to go out in his own defence; but he finds that the Company of Ladies is worse then the number of Messengers, for he hath leaped out of the Frying-pan into the fire.

ADVISER. I confess Men can hardly avoid the Females, and are more tormented with them then Beggars are with Lice, or a Horse with Flies; for since the Wars,* numbers of Women do swarm about one Man, as Bees about a honey-pot.

---

* the Wars] probably the English Civil War of 1640–49.

TAKE-PLEAS. I confess it, and I fear my Friend *Courtly* will be devoured;
wherefore, for Charity, go with me, and help him in distress, and I'le engage
that he and I will do the like for either, or both of you.

ADVISER. Upon that condition we are content; then let us go with all speed.

Exeunt. Enter Sir MERCURY POET *to the Lady* FANCY, *whom He finds Weeping.*

MERC. Sweet Mistress! let not our Parents folly
    Be a cause to make us Melancholy:
    For Natures, Fates, and mighty gods above
    Did make, Decree, and cause our Souls to love;
    Then do not mourn, or cloud your Eyes with Tears,
    But banish from your Mind all Griefs and Fears;
    For still our Loving Souls will constant be,
    Cœlestial powers have joyn'd in that Decree.

L. FANCY. But at full Moon, the winds blow high,
    And in the wain they silent lie.
    So doth a Lover's full griev'd Mind
    Cause storms of Passions, like as Wind,
    Beating the Thoughts, like Clouds about,
    Which being prest, Tears streameth out.

MERC. But when that Grief is in the wain
    The Mind is smooth, and calm again;
    Thoughts are serene, Joy shineth clear;
    The Eyes are fair, no Tears appear:
    But if that you with me consent,
    Our Parents follies we'l prevent
    With holy Ceremony, bind so sure
    In Sacred Marriage, shall for life endure.

L. FANCY. I do consent to be your Wife.
    For without you, I have no Life.

Exeunt.

Scene 5

Enter Sir WILLIAM SAGE, *Lady* VERTUE, *and* MIMICK.

SIR WILLIAM SAGE. What are you studying your Play?

MIMICK. Yes faith, I am getting some speeches by heart.

SIR W. SAGE. Let us hear some of them.

MIMICK. I cannot speak like a Woman in Breeches and Doublet, unless I have a
    Petticoat.

Enter the Cook-maid.

MAID. Madame, I come to know what shall be drest for Supper?

MIMICK. My Lady will fast and pray to night; wherefore, lend me one of thy Petticoats.

MAID. What will you do with it?

MIMICK. I'le not eat thy Petticoat, though it would fry in its own grease, but I would use it another way.

MAID. What other way?

MIMICK. Why, I will wear thy Petticoat over my Breeches.

MAID. No, by my Faith, but you shall not; for then my Petticoat and your Breeches may commit Fornication.

MIMICK. It were better our Clothes should commit Fornication, then our Persons; but in my Conscience our Clothes will be honest; but it is probable, that the Fleas in your Petticoat, and the Fleas in my Breeches may commit Fornication; and so our Clothes, or rather our selves will be guilty of another such like Vertue, as Fornication; which is, I shall be a Pimp, and you a Bawd for Adulterous Fleas; but howsoever I must borrow thy Petticoat.

MAID. Would you have me lend you my Petticoat and stand my self naked?

MIMICK. If you should, it would seem a deed of Charity, to give thy Petticoat from off thee, to those that want it; besides, you will appear like the Picture of *Eve* in her state of Innocence; and when I have done acting my part, of seeming a Woman, I will be like *Adam;* and so we shall be both like our first Parents.

MAID. I'le see you hang'd in an Apple-tree, before I lend you my Petticoat.

MIMICK. Then I shall not need it, unless it be for a shroud to lap me in; but rather then you will see me hang'd, you will cut the cord or halter, although you were sure to damn your Soul for the deed; but if thou wilt lend me thy Petticoat, I will promise hereafter to be thy Champion Knight, armed with thy Kitchin-Vessels; thy Spit shall be my long Sword or Tuck, and thy Dripping-pan my Target, thy Porridg-pot my Head-piece, one of thy Pie-plates shall serve for a breast-plate, and a Buff-coat made of the smuddy skins of Gammons of Bacon.

MAID. Upon that condition, to see you so armed, I will lend you my upper-Petticoat, if my Master and Lady will give me leave.

MIMICK. Thou hast their leave; for I must act my part for them to see me; and I had rather wear thy upper-Coat, then thy under-Petticoat.

She pulls off her Petticoat.

L. VERTUE. *Joan,* help him to put it on.

MIMICK. No, I will put it on my self, for she will put it over my head, and I will put it under my feet, for I had rather my feet should go thorough her Petticoat, then my nose should be in her tayl, which will be, if I put her Petticoat over my head.

She snatches her Petticoat away.

Maid. You jeering Fool, you shall not have my Petticoat to play the Fool with.

MIMICK. You Slut, take your Coat again, for the smell makes me sick, and suffocates my breath.

MAID. You are a lying fellow, for saying my Petticoat stinks.

MIMICK. Prithee *Joan,* be pacified; for I confess my smell is a foolish, nice, sickly smell; but for thy comfort, many right Honorable, and right noble Persons love the *haut-goust** of such Petticoats; but the perfume of thy Petticoat, has spoiled the part of my Play; for it hath put me quite out of the Amorous Speeches, I should have rehears'd.

SIR W. SAGE. But it is not so proper for a Woman to speak Amorous Speeches, as for a Man; wherefore, speak some Amorous Speeches to *Joan,* as a Man in your own Garments.

MIMICK. But my Speech was to be spoken in the absence of my Lover; complaining to the gods, and imploring their favours to assist me to the sight of my Love.

SIR W. SAGE. That would have been rather as a Prayer, then an Amorous Speech.

MIMICK. No, no, I would have order'd my Speech so as it should have been Amorous.

L. VERTUE. Then I perceive we shall hear none of your Play at this time.

MIMICK. I have parts to act as a Man; which is to address myself in a Courtly manner to some fine, fair, sweet, young Lady.

L. VERTUE. Imagine *Joan* such a Lady.

MIMICK. My imagination is not so powerful, as to Metamorphose *Joan* in my Thoughts to such a Lady; besides, *Joan* cannot answer a Man as she should.

MAID. You lie, you Rogue, for I have answer'd better men then thou art, or ever wilt be.

MIMICK. But can you talk Court-talks?

MAID. I know not what Court-talk is, but I can talk.

MIMICK. Stand forth here, and I will court thee as a Gallant doth his Mistress: Lady, your Beauty shines.

---

* *haut-goust*] high flavor.

MAID. That is, because I wash'd it with some of the Beef-broth, and wiped it with a greasie clout, I use to wipe the dishes; otherwise, the great hot shining fire i'th'Kitchin would burn and parch it so dry, as it would be scurvy, or scabby.

MIMICK. Setting aside your basted, rosted face, I must tell you, it is not the Courtly manner to interrupt a Man in his speech; you must be silent until the end of the Speech, and then speak; but you spoke when I had not said above four words: hold your peace, and I'le begin again.

Lady, your Beauty shineth like a blazing-Star, whereon Men gaze, and in their Minds do wonder at the sight; but the effects are not alike; your Beauty strikes them not with fear, but Love; your frowns and smiles are Destiny and Fate, either to kill or cure.

MAID. What language is this, *French* or *Dutch*, or *Welch*, or *Irish*, or *Scotch!*

MIMICK. No, it is *Greek* and *Hebrew*.

MAID. Speak to me so, as I may understand you; otherwise, I cannot answer you.

MIMICK. *Joan*, thy face shines like a Sea-coal fire.

MAID. Why, doth it look red?

MIMICK. Faith, thy Nose appears like a burning coal, rak'd over with black ashes, but all thy face else appears like the outside of a roasted Pig.

MAID. You are a roasted Ass, for saying my face appears like the outside of a roasted Pig; my face is a face of God's own making, and not a Pig's face.

MIMICK. No, I know your face is a Sow's face; but I say the colour of your face is like the Coat of a roasted Pig.

MAID. My face is as good a face as your own, without any dispraise to the party.

MIMICK. Which party? the Fools party, or the Sluts party?

MAID. Well, for saying my face is like a Pig's Coat, i'faith when I roast a Pig again, you shall not have any part of it; and let me give you warning, you come not into the Kitchin; for if you do, I will fling a Ladle full of Drippings upon your Fools Coat.

Exit Maid.

MIMICK. O wo is me! I shall lose many a hot bit; but Master and Lady, this is your fault to make *Joan* and I fall out.

L. VERTUE. We did not make you fall out.

MIMICK. You commanded me to Court *Joan,* and she doth not understand Courtships in words; for *Joan* is used to be kiss'd, and not wooed; but I will go and promise *Joan* a kiss, although I never pay it her; for the more hungry she is, the better she'l feed me.

Exeunt.

ACT V

Scene 1

Enter Monsieur FACIL, *Monsieur* ADVISER, *and Monsieur* TAKE-PLEASURE.

MONSIEUR TAKE-PLEASURE. *Facil,* I am come to fetch thee to the Horn-Tavern, for there be a number of Good-fellows that want thy Company.

FACIL. Stay, stay; I must go and make a Cuckold first.

TAKE-PLEAS. Thou hast made a Hundred in thy time.

FACIL. But I must go and make one to day; for I am going to meet a young beautiful Wife in private.

TAKE-PLEAS. Put off thy Meeting until another time.

FACIL. That I cannot, I am so engaged; besides, she is a Lady of Honour.

ADVISER. Of Title, you mean; for Ladies of Honour, or Honorable Ladies, do not use to have private Meetings with such wild deboist* Men as thou art; and if she be a Wife, as you say she is, it will be no great honour for her Husband.

FACIL. You speak as if you were a Married Man, and were sensible of a Husbands disgrace.

ADVISER. The truth is, I find I have a Commiseration and Compassion for Married Men.

FACIL. But not when you are to lie with any of their Wives.

ADVISER. I seldom make love to Married Wives; for they are not worth the trouble and danger which a Man must pass through before they can be enjoyed; besides, a Man loses a great deal of time in Wooing them, not but that they are as yielding, nay, more yielding then Maids; but they are more fearful to venture, lest their Husbands should know it.

FACIL. Faith, Maids are more troublesome and chargable then Wives; for they are apt to claim Marriage, or to sue for maintenance at least; besides, their lying in, and Christening, breeding and bringing up of their Children, is an intollerable Charge; which charge is sav'd with Married Wives; and for their Husbands, they are content to wink, not willing to see their disgraces, at least not to divulge them.

ADVISER. Not all; for some will look with more eyes then their own, setting spies to watch them.

FACIL. Those are old-fashioned Husbands, and not Mode-Husbands.

ADVISER. Indeed, I observe, that Mode-Husbands do not love their Wives,

---

* deboist] debauched.

unless other Men Court them; and if your Mistress's Husband is such a one, you shall not need to meet in private.

FACIL. I think my Mistress's Husband is not so much in the *French* fashion, although my Mistress is *Frenchified.*

TAKE-PLEAS. What, has she the *French* Pox?*

FACIL. I hope not; for Ladies of her Quality have not that foul infectious Disease; but I mean my Mistress is in the *French* Fashion, not in the *French* Disease: but farwell, for I must be gone; otherwise I shall slip my time.

TAKE-PLEAS. Prithee go along with me.

FACIL. I'le leave you, my friend here; for my self I must go, otherwise I should prove myself a Fool, to lose the time I have spent in Wooing, the Money I have given in bribing, the Sleeps I have mist with watching, the Protestations and Vows I have made in swearing, and my word that is past in promising, if I should not meet her and enjoy her; but when I am parted from her, I will come to you.

TAKE-PLEAS. Well, I am content to spare thee so long; for I would not have thee a loser, although my faith tells me, you will not gain much: but remember the meeting at the Horn-Tavern.

FACIL. I shall not forget that sign of any sign; wherefore, doubt not of my company.

Exeunt.

Scene 2

Enter Lady VERTUE *and* MIMICK.

LADY VERTUE. *Mimick,* to my sight you appear dull, since you are Married!

MIMICK. Faith, I do not find my self so lively as I was before I Married; for a Wife is a clog to a Man's heels, and a cloud in a Man's mind; but your Ladyship seems more lively since you were Married, then you did before.

LADY. The reason is, That a good Husband is a light to a Woman's life, a friend to a Woman's Vertue, and a Crown to a Woman's honour.

MIMICK. And an ill Wife is a Horn to a Man's head, a Plague to a Man's life, and a death to a Man's wit.

LADY. Indeed your *Mimick*-Wit seems dead since you Married; but yet my Maid *Nan,* whom you Married, is a good Wife.

MIMICK. Yes, when she is in a good humor.

LADY. Let me advise you to return to your *Mimick*-humour, or I will tell your Wife, that you repent your Marriage.

---

* the *French* Pox] syphilis.

MIMICK. She may perceive that by my cold kindness; howsoever, I'le live like a Batchellor, although I am a Married Man.

LADY. How can you do so?

MIMICK. Why, I will live Chast.

LADY. That will be well for Nan.

Enter Sir WILLIAM SAGE.

SIR W. SAGE. Wife; I have invited some Strangers to dine with me tomorrow; wherefore, I would have you dress your self fine to entertain them.

LADY. If you like me in plain Garments as well as in rich, I care not how Strangers like me.

SIR W. SAGE. I would have my Wife appear so handsome to Strangers, as they may approve of my Choice.

LADY. Some Men would be afraid if their Wives should be seen by Strangers, least they might like so well their Choice, as to chuse them for their Mistresses.

SIR W. SAGE. But my Wife's Vertue makes me fearless of Strangers.

LADY. But Vertue is not proved, until it be tryed.

SIR W. SAGE. True love is never inconstant.

LADY. But true love is not known until it be tryed.

SIR W. SAGE. I fear not a trial.

LADY. But a trial of Chastity is scandalous; for *Overberry* in his Characters says, *That he comes not near, that comes to be denied.**

SIR W. SAGE. Then I will entertain the Strangers, and keep you in your Chamber.

LADY. I shall so.

MIMICK. Madam, my Master having Strangers to morrow, pray let me add one dish to the Feast.

SIR W. SAGE. What Dish is that, a dress'd Lady?

MIMICK. No; for my skill in Physick doth plainly prove, that Ladies are unwholsome meat, they will give a Man a Surfeit; besides, they are not tastable, unless they be very tender and young; also they are very chargable in dressing, they require so many Ingrediences and garnishings to set them off, and so much sauce to make them relish well, as would undo a poor Man; besides, much art is required in the Dressing: So all considered, they are not worth the charge, labour and time, being but a faint, weak and sickly meat at the best, but I have thought of other meat, which will be tastable meat to a great Monarch.

SIR W. SAGE. What meat is that?

----

* *Overberry . . . Characters*] Sir Thomas Overbury, *Characters* (1614).

MIMICK. An Hodge-Podge.*

SIR W. SAGE. It seems it is for a *Dutch* Monarch; but let us know how you will make it?

MIMICK. First, I will take Widows dissembling Tears, Maids dissembling Modesty, Wives dissembling Chastity, Curtisans dissembling Virginity, Puritanical Sisters dissembling Piety, Autumnal Ladies dissembling Beauty; and mixing all these Ingrediences together, I will put them into a Mystical pot, and set it on a heartless fiery Meteor a stewing, and after it has stew'd some time, I'le put these Ingrediences to them, the Pride of Favourites, the Vanity of Courtiers, the Jugling of Statesmen, the Fears of Cowards, the mischiefs of Tumults,† the Extortion of Magistrates, the Covetousness of Usurers, the Retards‡ of Judges, the Quirks of Lawyers, the Opinionateness of Schollars, the Jealousie of Lovers, the Deceit of Tradesmen, the Brags of Soldiers, the Oaths of Gamesters, the Prodigality of young Heirs, the Diseases of Drunkards, the Surfeits of Gluttons, and the dishonour of Cuckolds; Likewise, I will put in a Fool's Brain, a Liers Tongue, a Traiterous Heart, and Thieves Hand; With which I'le stir all together, and after they have been well stew'd and stir'd together, I'le take this Hodg-podg and put it into a large dish of Infamy, and garnish it with the dotage§ of Age, the follies of Youth, the superstition of Idolators, and the expectations of Chymists, and then serve it up to *Pluto's*‖ Table.

LADY. For once I will try my Huswifry to Cook a dish of meat, which shall be a Bisk: First, I will take the Truth of Religion, the Piety of Saints, the Chastity of Nunns, the Purity of Virginity, the Constancy of true Love, the Unity of Friendship, the Innocency of Infants, the Wit of Poets, the Eloquence of Orators, the Learning of Scholars, the Valour of Soldiers, the Knowledg of Travellers, and Time's Experience; And put all these into a pot of Renown, and set it on a Cœlestial fire a stewing; after it has stew'd some time, I'le put in these Ingredients, Wholesome Temperance, strengthening Fortitude, comfortable Justice, and savory Prudence; also, I'll add the bowels of Compassion, the Heart of Honesty, the Brain of Wisdom, the Tongue of Truth, and the Hand of Generosity; and stir them well together, then I'le take them off, and put them into a dish of Happiness, and garnish it with the Plenty of Prosperity, the Ease of Rest, the Delight of Beauty, and the Tranquillity of

---

* Hodge-Podge] literally, a stew; figuratively, any ungainly mixture.
† Tumults] mobs.
‡ Retards] delays.
§ Misspelled as "dotgae" in the original.
‖ *Pluto's*] Roman god of the underworld.

Peace, and so serve it up to *Jove*'s* Table. Thus I am a Cook-maid for the gods; but you are a Cook-man for the Devil, and all the meat you Cook, is burnt.

MIMICK. I confess, Hell's fire is great and scorching, and Hell's Kitchin is very hot; but howsoever, my Master the Devil loves his meat thoroughly roasted, and tenderly stew'd; but your Master *Jove* loves all his meat cold and raw; for there is not any fire in Heaven, and that is the reason you chuse to be a Servant to the gods; because you would not burn your face, lest it should spoil your Complexion; for Ladies are more careful of their Faces then their Souls; besides, the cool and temperate air, and the cold diet of the gods, which breeds flegm, makes them patient; whereas, the Devil is dwelling in a Torrid Region, and eating dry roasted meat, which breeds Choller, makes him furious; in so much, as he tortures his Servants with grievous pains.

LADY. Why do you serve him then?

MIMICK. Because, he gives great wages; I serve him for necessity, but some serve him for worldly honour, and some for worldly wealth, and some for worldly power, and some for one thing, and some for another; for none serves him for love, neither do the Servants of the gods serve them for love but for some reward.

SIR W. SAGE. Let me perswade you to change your Service.

MIMICK. So I will, when I am old, and can serve the Devil no longer, then I will leave his Service, and serve the gods.

SIR W. SAGE. But the gods will not then accept of your Service.

MIMICK. But they will; for the gods refuse not any that offer their service; The truth is, the gods cannot get Servants enough to serve them, so as they are forced to take any that will but serve them; for the gods have but the Devils leavings and refusals, as those that are so old as to be past sin; or so sickly, as they cannot act sin; or those that are so young, as not to know sin; for most of the gods Servants are aged and weak persons, or young Children.

SIR W. SAGE. I perceive you will wear out sin, before you serve the gods.

MIMICK. No, sin shall wear out me, before I serve them.

LADY. You are a sinful Rogue.

MIMICK. All Mankind is so, more or less, even your Ladyship;† the gods bless you, and have mercy upon you.

LADY. Well, to punish you for your Sins, you shall eat no other meat but what your Poetical Fancy dresses.

---

* *Jove*'s] Roman king of the gods.
† Emended from "Lordship" in a seventeenth-century hand.

MIMICK. I shall be starved then.
Exeunt.

Scene 3

Enter Monsieur COURTLY, *and Monsieur* ADVISER.

MONSIEUR ADVISER. *Courtly!* 'tis strange to see you in this humour, as dying for the love of one Woman, when as I thought you had taken a surfeit of all Womenkind!

COURTLY. 'Tis true, I have Courted some Women, and many Women have Courted me; but I did never truly love any Woman but this Woman, which I cannot enjoy.

ADVISER. Have you no hopes to linger your life a little time longer?

COURTLY. Faith, I believe my life will continue, but my hopes are buried in despair.

ADVISER. If you had but the opportunity to Court this Lady, you are so madly in love with, at any time, I am confident you may gain her good will; for Women are various in their denials and consentings to their Lovers, as they are in their fashions and garments; for they will love and hate, and hate and love, one and the same, many several times; as now love, then hate, now hate, then love; for Ladies affections change like the Seasons, or the Weather, as sometimes hot, and sometimes cold, and sometimes luke-warm.

COURTLY. The affections of the Lady I love, are at all times cold, even to numness; for she is insensible towards me, and to all Lovers else, for any thing I can perceive.

ADVISER. Is she such a frozen Lady?

COURTLY. Yes faith; for I think she is composed of Ice, or a statue made of Snow.

ADVISER. If she be composed of Ice or Snow, I dare assure you, she may be melted.

COURTLY. How?

ADVISER. Why, be you in the Torrid Zone of Mode, in Speech, Behavior and Accoustrements, and let your Garments be so rich, as to shine in Gold and Silver, whose glistering rayes will cast a glorious splendor; then address yourself in Poetical flames, and being a hot Lover, you will thaw her into your arms, and melt her unto your desire: Thus a Western Lover, and a Northern Lady may meet in Conjunction together.

COURTLY. But cold Chastity has congealed and crystallined this Lady, in so much, as the hottest Lover with all his Poetical flames, and splenderous rayes of Youth, Beauty, Title, Wealth or Bravery, has not power to change or alter her worth and honour; for like a durable Diamond she is, and will remain.

ADVIS. Who is the Owner of this rich Jewel?

COURT. Sir *W. Sage,* who is a wise, valiant man, and will not part from her, nor suffer any Man to take her from him; for he wears her in his heart, and she is the delight of his Life, and the Crown of his Honour, in which he takes more Glory, pride and pleasure, then to be Crowned Emperor of the whole World.

ADVISER. He hath reason; for a Man may sooner conquer the World, then find such another Chast Woman as she is.

COURTLY. Well, since I cannot obtain my desire, I will travel.

ADVISER. That is the best for you to do, for so you may tire out Love.

COURTLY. Or Love tire out me.

ADVISER. Faith, you are tir'd out of Courtship, and if you tire out Love, you will do well; but before you can go to Travel, you must go to a dancing-meeting of Ladies and Gentlemen.

Exeunt. Enter LONGLIFE, *and* AGED.

AGED. Mr. *Longlife,* I am come to tell you, That your son *Mercury* hath stoln away my Daughter *Fancy,* and as I hear, they are gone to *Apollo*'s* Church to be Married.

LONGL. Mr. *Aged,* I am sorry for it, and wish he had stoln a Challenge, when he stole your Daughter.

AGED. And I wish my Daughter had Married an Ass, rather then Marry your Son.

LONGL. Well, if they be Married, as sure they are, if they have any Children we will endeavor to breed them Fools.

AGED. We will so.

Enter the Married Couple: They kneel down.

MERC. We desire your Blessing.

LONGL. Well, since you are Married, God bless you; but Son and Daughter in Law, I desire and command you in the name of a Father, that you will leave Versifying, Rhyming, Similizing, and the like, but study the Politicks, and that will abate your Wit.

AGED. They may study *Virgils Georgicks,*† for that treats of good Husbandry.

LONGL. Yes, Brother *Aged,* but it is in Verse, and whatsoever they get in Husbandry, they will lose by the Rhyme.

AGED. By the Mass you say true, Brother *Longlife.*

---

* *Apollo*'s] Roman sun god; also god of poets.

† *Virgils Georgicks*] Roman poet, author of the epic *Aeneid,* Virgil was the poet acknowledged as archetypal by most English people of the sixteenth and seventeenth centuries. His *Georgics* are poems about farming.

LONGL. Well Brother, although they have Married against our consent, yet we will celebrate their Marriage with Feasting, Mirth, and Musick.

MERC. Music Sir, is a part of Poetry, and belongs to the Muses.

LONGL. Yes, yes, but not such Musick as we will have, two or three Scraping Fidlers, that plays neither tune nor time.

Enter the Lady FANCY *as a Bride, and Sir* MERCURY POET *as a Bridegroom; and all the Ladies and Gentlemen that were Guests at the first Wedding.*

AGED. Brother *Longlife,* we are not for these active sports, our dancing-days are done.

LONGL. You say true, brother *Aged;* but in our younger years we were as agil as the best of them all.

A young lady takes out LONGLIFE *to dance.*

LADY. Sir, although you be old, you may walk a grave measure, as a Paven.*

LONGL. Say you so, my Girl; and i'faith I will try what my old legs will do; here brother *Aged* you shall hold my staff whil'st I dance.

AGED. Nay, b'r'lady, your staff brother *Longlife* will help to prop up your weakness; and since a young Lady hath chose you to dance with, I will chuse out a Lady to dance with me; but the Musicians must play slow, or we shall not keep time; wherefore, Musicians let not your Fiddles go faster then our Legs, nor your Tunes be younger then our years, but an old Paven.

The Old Men dance with two Young Ladies, they dance softly, but right, and keep time. The Young Men smile.

AGED. You young Men smile, but we could have danced as nimbly as you do now.

MERC. You will teach us a sober pace, Sir.

LONGL. No Son, Time must teach you that, to which we will leave you, and my Brother and I will rest our Legs whil'st you tire your Legs: come brother *Aged,* let us leave them to their Mirth, Musick, and Youth.

---

* Paven] pavanne; a grave and stately dance introduced into England from Spain in the sixteenth century.

The Convent of Pleasure

A Comedy

THREE GENTLEMEN	LADY HAPPY
MONSIEUR TAKE-PLEASURE	MADAME MEDIATOR
DICK, HIS MAN	LADY AMOROUS
MONSIEUR FACIL	LADY VERTUE
MONSIER ADVISER	THE LADIES OF THE CONVENT
THE PRINCE	SERVANT TO LADY HAPPY
MIMICK THE FOOL	

ACT I

Scene 1

Enter Three Gentlemen.

FIRST GENTLEMAN. *Tom,* Where have you been, you look so sadly of it?

2 GENT. I have been at the Funeral of the Lord *Fortunate,* who has left his Daughter, the Lady *Happy,* very rich, having no other Daughter but her.

1 GENT. If she be so rich, it will make us all Young Men, spend all our Wealth in fine Clothes, Coaches, and Lackies, to set out our Wooing hopes.

3 GENT. If all her Wooers be younger Brothers, as most of us Gallants are, we shall undo our selves upon bare hopes, without Probability: But is she handsome, *Tom?*

2 GENT. Yes, she is extream handsome, young, rich, and virtuous.

1 GENT. Faith, that is too much for one Woman to possess.

2 GENT. Not, if you were to have her.

1 GENT. No, not for me; but in my Opinion too much for any other Man.

Exeunt.

Scene 2

Enter the Lady HAPPY, *and one of her Attendants.*

SERVANT. Madam, you being young, handsome, rich, and virtuous, I hope you will not cast away those gifts of Nature, Fortune, and Heaven, upon a Person which cannot merit you?

L. HAPPY. Let me tell you, that Riches ought to be bestowed on such as are poor, and want means to maintain themselves; and Youth, on those that are old; Beauty, on those that are ill-favoured; and Virtue, on those that are vicious: So that if I should place my gifts rightly, I must Marry one that's poor, old, ill-favoured, and debauch'd.

SERV. Heaven forbid.

L. HAPPY. Nay, Heaven doth not only allow of it, but commands it; for we are commanded to give to those that want.

Enter Madam MEDIATOR *to the Lady* HAPPY.

MEDIAT. Surely, Madam, you do but talk, and intend not to go where you say.

L. HAPPY. Yes, truly, my Words and Intentions go even together.

MEDIAT. But surely you will not incloyster your self, as you say.

L. HAPPY. Why, what is there in the publick World that should invite me to live in it?

MEDIAT. More then if you should banish your self from it.

L. HAPPY. Put the case I should Marry the best of Men, if any best there be; yet would a Marry'd life have more crosses and sorrows then pleasure, freedom, or hapiness: nay Marriage to those that are virtuous is a greater restraint then a Monastery. Or, should I take delight in Admirers? they might gaze on my Beauty, and praise my Wit, and I receive nothing from their eyes, nor lips; for Words vanish as soon as spoken, and Sights are not substantial. Besides, I should lose more of my Reputation by their Visits, then gain by their Praises. Or, should I quit Reputation and turn Courtizan, there would be more lost in my Health, then gained by my Lovers, I should find more pain then Pleasure; besides, the troubles and frights I should be put to, with the Quarrels and Brouilleries* that Jealous Rivals make, would be a torment to me; and 'tis only for the sake of Men, when Women retire not: And since there is so much folly, vanity and falshood in Men, why should Women trouble and vex themselves for their sake; for retiredness bars the life from nothing else but Men.

---

* Brouilleries] disagreements; confusions.

MEDIAT. O yes, for those that incloister themselves, bar themselves from all other worldly Pleasures.

L. HAPPY. The more Fools they.

MEDIAT. Will you call those Fools that do it for the gods sake?

L. HAPPY. No Madam, it is not for the gods sake, but for opinion's sake; for, Can any Rational Creature think or believe, the gods take delight in the Creature's uneasie life? or, Did they command or give leave to Nature to make Senses for no use; or to cross, vex and pain them? for, What profit or pleasure can it be to the gods to have Men or Women wear coarse Linnen or rough Woollen, or to flea* their skin with Hair-cloth, or to eat or sawe thorow their flesh with Cords? or, What profit or pleasure can it be to the gods to have men eat more Fish then Flesh, or to fast? unless the gods did feed on such meat themselves; for then, for fear the gods should want it, it were fit for Men to abstein from it: The like for Garments, for fear the gods should want fine Clothes to adorn themselves, it were fit Men should not wear them: Or, what profit or pleasure can it be to the gods to have Men to lie uneasily on the hard ground, unless the gods and Nature were at variance, strife and wars; as if what is displeasing unto Nature, were pleasing to the gods, and to be enemies to her, were to be friends to them.

MEDIAT. But being done for the gods sake, it makes that which in Nature seems to be bad, in Divinity to be good.

L. HAPPY. It cannot be good, if it be neither pleasure, nor profit to the gods; neither do Men any thing for the gods but their own sake.

MEDIAT. But when the Mind is not imployed with Vanities, nor the Senses with Luxury;† the Mind is more free, to offer its Adorations, Prayers and Praises to the gods.

L. HAPPY. I believe, the gods are better pleased with Praises then Fasting; but when the Senses are dull'd with abstinency, the Body weakned with fasting, the Spirits tir'd with watching, the Life made uneasie with pain, the Soul can have but little will to worship: only the Imagination doth frighten it into active zeal, which devotion is rather forced then voluntary; so that their prayers rather flow out of their mouth, then spring from their heart, like rain-water that runs thorow Gutters, or like Water that's forced up a Hill by Artificial Pipes and Cisterns. But those that pray not unto the gods, or praise them more in prosperity then adversity, more in pleasures then pains, more

---

* flea] flay, scrape off.
† Luxury] riches, but with a strong sexual connotation.

in liberty then restraint, deserve neither the happiness of ease, peace, freedom, plenty and tranquillity in this World, nor the glory and blessedness of the next. And if the gods should take pleasure in nothing but in the torments of their Creatures, and would not prefer those prayers that are offer'd with ease and delight, I should believe, the gods were cruel: and, What Creature that had reason or rational understanding, would serve cruel Masters, when they might serve a kind Mistress, or would forsake the service of their kind Mistress, to serve cruel Masters? Wherefore, if the gods be cruel, I will serve Nature; but the gods are bountiful, and give all, that's good, and bid us freely please our selves in that which is best for us: and that is best, what is most temperately used, and longest may be enjoyed, for excess doth wast it self, and all it feeds upon.

MEDIAT. In my opinion your Doctrine, and your Intention do not agree together.

L. HAPPY. Why?

MEDIAT. You intend to live incloister'd and retired from the World.

L. HAPPY. 'Tis true, but not from pleasures; for, I intend to incloister my self from the World, to enjoy pleasure, and not to bury my self from it; but to incloister my self from the incumbred cares and vexations, troubles and perturbance of the World.

MEDIAT. But if you incloister your self, How will you enjoy the company of Men, whose conversation is thought the greatest Pleasure?

L. HAPPY. Men are the only troublers of Women; for they only cross and oppose their sweet delights, and peaceable life; they cause their pains, but not their pleasures. Wherefore those Women that are poor, and have not means to buy delights, and maintain pleasures, are only fit for Men; for having not means to please themselves, they must serve only to please others; but those Women, where Fortune, Nature, and the gods are joined to make them happy, were mad to live with Men, who make the Female sex their slaves; but I will not be so inslaved, but will live retired from their Company. Wherefore, in order thereto, I will take so many Noble Persons of my own Sex, as my Estate will plentifully maintain, such whose Births are greater then their Fortunes, and are resolv'd to live a single life, and vow Virginity: with these I mean to live incloister'd with all the delights and pleasures that are allowable and lawful; My Cloister shall not be a Cloister of restraint, but a place for freedom, not to vex the Senses but to please them.

For every Sense shall pleasure take,
And all our Lives shall merry make:
Our Minds in full delight shall joy,

Not vex'd with every idle Toy:
Each Season shall our Caterers be,
To search the Land, and Fish the Sea;
To gather Fruit and reap the Corn,
That's brought to us in Plenty's Horn;
With which we'l feast and please our tast,
But not luxurious make a wast.
Wee'l Cloth our selves with softest Silk,
And Linnen fine as white as milk.
Wee'l please our Sight with Pictures rare;
Our Nostrils with perfumed Air.
Our Ears with sweet melodious Sound,
Whose Substance can be no where found;
Our Tast with sweet delicious Meat,
And savory Sauces we will eat:
Variety each Sense shall feed,
And Change in them new Appetites breed.
Thus will in Pleasure's Convent *I*
Live with delight, and with it die.
Exeunt.

ACT II

Scene 1

Enter Monsieur TAKE-PLEASURE, *and his Man* DICK.

TAKEPL. *Dick,* Am I fine to day?

DICK. Yes, Sir, as fine as Feathers, Ribbons, Gold, and Silver can make you.

TAKEPL. Dost thou think I shall get the Lady *Happy?*

DICK. Not if it be her fortune to continue in that name.

TAKEPL. Why?

DICK. Because if she Marry your Worship she must change her Name; for the Wife takes the Name of her Husband, and quits her own.

TAKEPL. Faith, *Dick,* if I had her wealth I should be *Happy.*

DICK. It would be according as your Worship would use it; but, on my conscience, you would be more happy with the Ladie's Wealth, then the Lady would be with your Worship.

TAKEPL. Why should you think so?

DICK. Because Women never think themselves happy in Marriage.

TAKEPL. You are mistaken; for Women never think themselves happy until they be Married.

DICK. The truth is, Sir, that Women are always unhappy in their thoughts, both before and after Marriage; for, before Marriage they think themselves unhappy for want of a Husband; and after they are Married, they think themselves unhappy for having a Husband.

TAKEPL. Indeed Womens thoughts are restless.

Enter Monsieur FACIL, *and Monsieur* ADVISER, *to Monsieur* TAKE-PLEASURE; *all in their Wooing Accoustrements.**

TAKEPL. Gentlemen, I perceive you are all prepared to Woo.

FACIL. Yes faith, we are all prepared to be Wooers. But whom shall we get to present us to the Lady *Happy?*

ADVISER. We must set on bold faces, and present our selves.

TAKEPL. Faith, I would not give my hopes for an indifferent portion.

FACIL. Not I.

ADVISER. The truth is, We are all stuft with Hopes, as Cushions are with Feathers.

Enter Monsieur COURTLY.

COURT. O Gentlemen, Gentlemen, we are all utterly undone.

ADVISER. Why, what's the matter?

COURT. Why, the Lady *Happy* hath incloister'd her self, with twenty Ladies more.

ADVISER. The Devil she hath?

FACIL. The gods forbid.

COURT. Whether it was the devil or the gods that have perswaded her to it, I cannot tell; but gone in she is.

TAKEPL. I hope it is but a blast of Devotion, which will soon flame out.

Enter Madam MEDIATOR.

TAKEPL. O Madam *Mediator*, we are all undone, the Lady *Happy* is incloister'd.

MEDIAT. Yes, Gentlemen, the more is the pitty.

ADVISER. Is there no hopes?

MEDIAT. Faith, little.

FACIL. Let us fee† the Clergy to perswade her out, for the good of the Commonwealth.

---

* *Accoustrements*] clothing and accessories. In reference to female attire, Cavendish always spells this word "accoutrements."

† fee] pay money for service.

MEDIAT. Alas Gentlemen! they can do no good, for she is not a Votress to the gods but to Nature.

COURT. If she be a Votress to Nature, you are the only Person fit to be Lady Prioress; and so by your power and authority you may give us leave to visit your Nuns sometimes.

MEDIAT. Not but at a Grate,* unless in time of Building, or when they are sick; but howsoever, the Lady *Happy* is Lady-Prioress her self, and will admit none of the Masculine Sex, not so much as to a Grate, for she will suffer no grates about the Cloister; she has also Women-Physicians, Surgeons and Apothecaries, and she is the chief Confessor her self, and gives what Indulgences or Absolutions she pleaseth: Also, her House, where she hath made her Convent, is so big and convenient, and so strong, as it needs no addition or repair: Besides, she has so much compass of ground within her walls, as there is not only room and place enough for Gardens, Orchards, Walks, Groves, Bowers, Arbours, Ponds, Fountains, Springs, and the like; but also conveniency for much Provision, and hath Women for every Office and Employment: for though she hath not above twenty Ladies with her, yet she hath a numerous Company of Female Servants, so as there is no occasion for Men.

TAKEPL. If there be so many Women, there will be the more use for Men: But pray Madam *Mediator,* give me leave, rightly to understand you, by being more clearly informed: you say, The Lady *Happy* is become a Votress to Nature; and if she be a Votress to Nature, she must be a Mistress to Men.

MEDIAT. By your favour, Sir, she declares, That she hath avoided the company of Men, by retirement, meerly, because she would enjoy the variety of Pleasures, which are in Nature; of which, she says, Men are Obstructers; for, instead of increasing Pleasure, they produce Pain, and instead of giving Content, they increase Trouble; instead of making the Femal-Sex Happy, they make them Miserable; for which, she hath banished the Masculine Company for ever.

ADVISER. Her Heretical Opinions ought not to be suffer'd, nor her Doctrine allow'd; and she ought to be examined by a Masculine Synod, and punish'd with a severe Husband, or tortured with a deboist† Husband.

MEDIAT. The best way, Gentlemen, is to make your Complaints, and put up a Petition to the State, with your desires for a Redress.

---

* Grate] small barred opening in a convent wall.
† deboist] debauched.

COURT. Your Counsel is good.

FACIL. We will follow it, and go presently about it.

Exeunt.

Scene 2

Enter the Lady HAPPY, *with her Ladies; as also Madam* MEDIATOR.

L. HAPPY. Ladies, give me leave to desire your Confession, whether or no you repent your Retirement.

LADIES. Most excellent Lady, it were as probable a repentance could be in Heaven amongst Angels as amongst us.

L. HAPPY. Now Madam *Mediator,* let me ask you, Do you condemn my act of Retirement?

MEDIAT. I approve of it with admiration and wonder, that one that is so young should be so wise.

L. HAPPY. Now give me leave to inform you, how I have order'd this our *Convent of Pleasure;* first, I have such things as are for our Ease and Conveniency; next for Pleasure, and Delight; as I have change of Furniture, for my house; according to the four Seasons of the year, especially our Chambers: As in the Spring, our Chambers are hung with Silk-Damask, and all other things suitable to it; and a great Looking-Glass in each Chamber, that we may view our selves and take pleasure in our own Beauties, whilst they are fresh and young; also, I have in each Chamber a Cup-board of such plate, as is useful, and whatsoever is to be used is there ready to be imployed; also, I have all the Floor strew'd with sweet Flowers: In the Summer I have all our Chambers hung with Taffety, and all other things suitable to it, and a Cupboard of Purseline,* and of Plate, and all the Floore strew'd every day with green Rushes or Leaves, and Cisternes placed neer our Beds-heads, wherein Water may run out of small Pipes made for that purpose: To invite repose in the Autumn, all our Chambers are hung with Gilt Leather, or Franchipane;† also, Beds and all other things suitable; and the Rooms Matted with very fine Mats: In the Winter our Chambers must be hung with Tapestry, and our Beds of Velvet, lined with Sattin, and all things suitable to it, and all the Floor spread over with *Turkie* Carpets, and a Cup-board of Gilt Plate; and all the Wood for Firing to be Cypress and Juniper; and all the Lights to be Perfumed Wax; also, the Bedding and Pillows are ordered according to each Season; *viz.* to be stuft with Feathers in the Spring and Autumn, and with Down in

---

* Purseline] porcelain; chinaware.

† Franchipane] frangipani, perfume made from red jasmine.

the Winter, but in the Summer to be only Quilts, either of Silk, or fine Holland;* and our Sheets, Pillows, Table-Clothes and Towels, to be of pure fine Holland, and every day clean; also, the Rooms we eat in, and the Vessels we feed withal, I have according to each Season; and the Linnen we use to our Meat, to be pure fine Diaper, and Damask,† and to change it fresh every course of Meat: As for our Galeries, Stair-Cases, and Passages, they shall be hung with various Pictures; and, all along the Wall of our Gallery, as long as the Summer lasts, do stand, upon Pedestals, Flower-pots, with various Flowers; and in the Winter Orange-Trees: and my Gardens to be kept curiously,‡ and flourish, in every Season of all sorts of Flowers, sweet Herbs and Fruits, and kept so as not to have a Weed in it, and all the Groves, Wildernesses, Bowers and Arbours pruned, and kept free from dead Boughs Branches or Leaves; and all the Ponds, Rivolets, Fountains, and Springs, kept clear, pure and fresh: Also, we will have the choisest Meats every Season doth afford, and that every day our Meat, be drest several ways, and our drink cooler or hotter according to the several Seasons; and all our Drinks fresh and pleasing: Change of Garments are also provided, of the newest fashions for every Season, and rich Trimming; so as we may be accoutred properly, and according to our several pastimes: and our Shifts shall be of the finest and purest Linnen that can be bought or spun.

LADIES. None in this World can be happier.

L. HAPPY. Now Ladies, let us go to our several Pastimes, if you please.
Exeunt.

Scene 3

Enter Two Ladies.

L. AMOROUS. Madam, how do you, since you were Married?

L. VERTUE. Very well, I thank you.

L. AMOR. I am not so well as I wish I were.

Enter Madam MEDIATOR *to them.*

M. MEDIAT. Ladies, do you hear the News?

L. VERTUE. What News?

M. MEDIAT. Why there is a great Foreign Princess arrived, hearing of the famous *Convent of Pleasure,* to be one of Nature's Devotes.

L. AMOR. What manner of Lady is she?

---

* Holland] linen fabric made in the Netherlands.

† Diaper, and Damask] diaper is linen or cotton fabric; damask, richly woven patterned linen fabric from Damascus.

‡ curiously] very carefully.

M. MEDIAT. She is a Princely brave Woman truly, of a Masculine Presence.

L. VERTUE. But, Madam *Mediator*, Do they live in such Pleasure as you say? for they'l admit you, a Widow, although not us, by reason we are Wives.

M. MEDIAT. In so much Pleasure, as Nature never knew, before this *Convent* was: and for my part, I had rather be one in the *Convent of Pleasure,* then Emperess of the whole World; for every Lady there enjoyeth as much Pleasure as any absolute Monarch can do, without the Troubles and Cares, that wait on Royalty; besides, none can enjoy those Pleasures They have, unless they live such a retired or retreated life free from the Worlds vexations.

L. VERTUE. Well, I wish I might see and know, what Pleasures they enjoy.

M. MEDIAT. If you were there, you could not know all their Pleasure in a short time, for their Varieties will require a long time to know their several Changes; besides, their Pleasures and Delights vary with the Seasons; so that what with the several Seasons, and the Varieties of every Season, it will take up a whole life's time.

L. VERTUE. But I could judg of their Changes by their single Principles.

M. MEDIAT. But they have Variety of one and the same kind.

L. VERTUE. But I should see the way or manner of them.

M. MEDIAT. That you might.

Exeunt.

Scene 4

Enter Monsieur ADVISER, COURTLY, TAKE-PLEASURE, *and* FACIL.

MONSIEUR COURTLY. Is there no hopes to get those Ladies out of their *Convent?*

ADVISER. No faith, unless we could set the *Convent* on fire.

TAKEPL. For *Jupiter's** sake, let us do it, let's every one carry a Fire-brand to fire it.

COURT. Yes, and smoak them out, as they do a Swarm of Bees.

FACIL. Let's go presently about it.

ADVISER. Stay, there is a great Princess there.

TAKEPL. 'Tis true, but when that Princess is gone, we will surely do it.

ADVISER. Yes, and be punish'd for our Villany.

TAKEPL. It will not prove Villany, for we shall do Nature good service.

ADVISER. Why, so we do Nature good service, when we get a Wench with Child, but yet the Civil Laws do punish us for it.

COURT. They are not Civil Laws that punish Lovers.

ADVISER. But those are Civil Laws that punish Adulterers.

---

* *Jupiter's*] Jupiter was the Roman king of the gods and a famous rapist.

COURT. Those are Barbarous Laws that make Love Adultery.

ADVISER. No, Those are Barbarous that make Adultery Love.

FACIL. Well, leaving Love and Adultery, They are foolish Women that vex us with their Retirement.

ADVISER. Well, Gentlemen, although we rail at the Lady *Happy* for Retiring, yet if I had such an Estate as she, and would follow her Example; I make no doubt but you would all be content to encloister your selves with me upon the same conditions, as those Ladies incloister themselves with her.

TAKEPL. Not unless you had Women in your *Convent.*

ADVIS. Nay, faith, since Women can quit the pleasure of Men, we Men may well quit the trouble of Women.

COURT. But is there no place where we may peak into the *Convent?*

ADVISER. No, there are no Grates, but Brick and Stone-walls.

FACIL. Let us get out some of the Bricks or Stones.

ADVISER. Alas! the Walls are a Yard-thick.

FACIL. But nothings is difficult to Willing-minds.

ADVISER. My Mind is willing, but my Reason tells me, It is impossible; wherefore, I'le never go about it.

TAKEPL. Faith, let us resolve to put our selves in Womens apparel, and so by that means get into the *Convent.*

ADVISER. We shall be discover'd.

TAKEPL. Who will discover Us?

ADVISER. We shall discover our Selves.

TAKEPL. We are not such fools as to betray our Selves.

ADVISER. We cannot avoid it, for, our very Garb and Behaviour; besides, our Voices will discover us: for we are as untoward to make Courtsies in Petticoats, as Women are to make Legs in Breeches; and it will be as great a difficulty to raise our Voices to a Treble-sound, as for Women to press down their Voices to a Base; besides, We shall never frame our Eyes and Mouths to such coy, dissembling looks, and pretty simpering Mopes and Smiles, as they do.

COURT. But we will go as strong lusty Country-Wenches, that desire to serve them in Inferior Places, and Offices, as Cook-maids, Laundry-maids, Dairy-maids, and the like.

FACIL. I do verily believe, I could make an indifferent Cook-maid, but not a Laundry, nor a Dairy-maid; for I cannot milk Cows, nor starch Gorgets,* but I think I could make a pretty shift, to wash some of the Ladies Night-Linnen.

---

* Gorgets] neckpieces; fancy collars.

TAKEPL. But they imploy Women in all Places in their Gardens; and for Brewing, Baking and making all sorts of things; besides, some keep their Swine, and twenty such like Offices and Employments there are which we should be very proper for.

FACIL. O yes, for keeping of Swine belongs to Men; remember the *Prodigal Son.*[*]

ADVISER. Faith, for our Prodigality we might be all Swin-heards.

COURT. Also we shall be proper for Gardens, for we can dig, and set, and sow.

TAKEPL. And we are proper for Brewing.

ADVISER. We are more proper for Drinking, for I can drink good Beer, or Ale, when 'tis Brew'd; but I could not brew such Beer, or Ale, as any man could drink.

FACIL. Come, come, we shall make a shift one way or other: Besides, we shall be very willing to learn, and be very diligent in our Services, which will give good and great content; wherefore, let us go and put these designes into execution.

COURTLY. Content, content.

ADVISER. Nay, faith, let us not trouble our Selves for it, 'tis in vain.

Exeunt.

ACT III

Scene 1

Enter the PRINCESS, *and the Lady* HAPPY, *with the rest of the Ladies belonging to the Convent.*

LADY HAPPY. Madam, Your Highness has done me much Honour, to come from a Splendid Court to a retired *Convent.*

PRIN. Sweet Lady *Happy,* there are many, that have quit their Crowns and Power, for a Cloister of Restraint; then well may I quit a Court of troubles for a *Convent of Pleasure:* but the greatest pleasure I could receive, were, To have your Friendship.

L. HAPPY. I should be ungrateful, should I not be not only your Friend, but humble Servant.

PRIN. I desire you would be my Mistress, and I your Servant; and upon this agreement of Friendship I desire you will grant me one Request.

L. HAPPY. Any thing that is in my power to grant.

---

[*] the *Prodigal Son*] for the Prodigal Son as a swineherd, see Luke 15:15–16.

PRIN. Why then, I observing in your several Recreations, some of your Ladies do accoutre Themselves in Masculine-Habits, and act Lovers-parts; I desire you will give me leave to be sometimes so accoutred and act the part of your loving Servant.

L. HAPPY. I shall never desire to have any other loving Servant then your Self.

PRIN. Nor I any other loving Mistress then Your Self.

L. HAPPY. More innocent Lovers never can there be,
Then my most Princely Lover, that's a She.

PRIN. Nor never Convent did such pleasures give,
Where Lovers with their Mistresses may live.

Enter a Lady, asking whether they will see the Play.

LADY. May it please your Highness, the Play is ready to be Acted.

The Scene is opened, the PRINCESS *and* L. HAPPY *sit down, and the Play is Acted within the Scene; the* PRINCESS *and the* L. HAPPY *being Spectators. Enter one drest like a Man that speaks the Prologue.*

Noble Spectators, you shall see to night
A Play, which though't be dull, yet's short to sight;
For, since we cannot please your Ears with Wit,
We will not tyre your limbs, long here to sit.

Scene 2

Enter Two mean* Women.

FIRST WOMAN. O Neighbour well met, where have you been?

2 WOMAN. I have been with my Neighbour the Cobler's Wife to comfort her for the loss of her Husband, who is run away with Goody *Mettle* the Tinker's Wife.

1 WOMAN. I would to Heaven my Husband would run away with Goody *Shred* the Butcher's Wife, for he lies all day drinking in an Ale-house, like a drunken Rogue as he is, and when he comes home, he beats me all black and blew, when I and my Children are almost starved for want.

2 WOMAN. Truly Neighbour, so doth my Husband; and spends not only what he gets, but what I earn with the sweat of my brows, and whilst my Children cry for bread, and he drinks that away, that should feed my small Children, which are too young to work for themselves.

1 WOMAN. But I will go, and pull my Husband out of the Ale-house, or I'le break their Lattice-windows down.

---

* mean] lower-class.

2 WOMAN. Come, I'le go and help; for my Husband is there too: but we shall be both beaten by them.

1 WOMAN. I care not: for I will not suffer him to be drunk, and I and my Children starve; I had better be dead.

Exeunt.

Scene 3

Enter a Lady and her Maid.

LADY. Oh, I am sick.

MAID. You are breeding a Child, Madam.

LADY. I have not one minutes time of health.

Ex.

Scene 4

Enter Two Ladies.

FIRST LADY. Why weep you, Madam?

2 LADY. Have I not cause to weep when my Husband hath play'd all his Estate away at Dice and Cards, even to the Clothes on his back?

1 LADY. I have as much cause to weep then as you; for, though my Husband hath not lost his Estate at play, yet he hath spent it amongst his Whores; and is not content to keep Whores abroad, but in my house, under my roof, and they must rule as chief Mistresses.

2 LADY. But my Husband hath not only lost his own Estate, but also my Portion; and hath forced me with threats, to yield up my Jointure,* so that I must beg for my living, for any thing I know as yet.

1 LADY. If all Married Women were as unhappy as I, Marriage were a curse.

2 LADY. No doubt of it.

Exeunt.

Scene 5

Enter a Lady, as almost distracted, running about the Stage, and her Maid follows her.

LADY. Oh! my Child is dead, my Child is dead, what shall I do, what shall I do?

MAID. You must have patience, Madam.

LADY. Who can have patience to lose their only Child? who can! Oh I shall run mad, for I have no patience.

Runs off the Stage. Exit Maid after her.

---

* Jointure] the part of a husband's estate entailed for life on his wife or widow.

Scene 6

Enter a Citizen's Wife, as into a Tavern, where A BUSH *is hung out,* and meets some Gentlemen there.*

CITIZEN'S WIFE. Pray Gentlemen, is my Husband, Mr. *Negligent* here?

1 GENT. He was, but he is gone some quarter of an hour since.

CIT. WIFE. Could he go, Gentlemen?

2 GENT. Yes, with a Supporter.

CIT. WIFE. Out upon him! must he be supported? Upon my credit Gentlemen, he will undo himself and me too, with his drinking and carelesness, leaving his Shop and all his Commodities at six's and seven's; and his Prentices and Journey-men are as careless and idle as he; besides, they cozen† him of his Wares. But, was it a He or She-Supporter, my Husband was supported by?

1 GENT. A She-supporter; for it was one of the Maid-servants, which belong to this Tavern.

CIT. WIFE. Out upon him Knave, must he have a She-supporter, in the Devil's name? but I'le go and seek them both out with a Vengeance.

2 GENT. Pray, let us intreat your stay to drink a cup of Wine with us.

CIT. WIFE. I will take your kind Offer; for Wine may chance to abate Cholerick‡ vapours, and pacifie the Spleen.

1 GENT. That it will, for Wine and good Company are the only abaters of Vapours.

2 GENT. It doth not abate Vapours so much as cure Melancholy.§

CIT. WIFE. In truth, I find a cup of Wine doth comfort me sometimes.

1 GENT. It will cheer the Heart.

2 GENT. Yes, and enlighten the Understanding.

CIT. WIFE. Indeed, and my understanding requires enlightening.

Exeunt.

Scene 7

Enter a Lady big with Child, groaning as in labour, and a Company of Women with her.

---

* where a Bush is hung out] A branch hung outside a tavern was a signal that the tavern is open.

† cozen] cheat.

‡ Cholerick] angry, irritable.

§ Melancholy] depressed. *Melancholy, Cholerick, Sanguine* (stupidly cheerful), and *Phlegmatic* (morally and physically inert) are the terms used to describe personalities disordered by an excess of black bile, yellow bile, blood, and phlegm, respectively.

LADY. Oh my back, my back will break, Oh! Oh! Oh!

1 WOMAN. Is the Midwife sent for?

2 WOMAN. Yes, but she is with another Lady.

LADY. Oh my back! Oh! Oh! Oh! *Juno,** give me some ease.

Exeunt.

Scene 8

Enter two Ancient Ladies.

1 LADY. I have brought my Son into the World with great pains, bred him with tender care, much pains and great cost; and must he now be hang'd for killing a Man in a quarrel? when he should be a comfort and staff of my age, is he to be my ages affliction?

2 LADY. I confess it is a great affliction; but I have had as great; having had but two Daughters, and them fair ones, though I say it, and might have matched them well: but one of them was got with Child to my great disgrace; th' other run away with my Butler, not worth the droppings of his Taps.

1 LADY. Who would desire Children, since they come to such misfortunes?

Exeunt.

Scene 9

Enter one Woman meeting another.

1 WOMAN. Is the Midwife come, for my Lady is in a strong labour?

2 WOMAN. No, she cannot come, for she hath been with a Lady that hath been in strong labour these three days of a dead child, and 'tis thought she cannot be delivered.

Enter another Woman.

3 WOMAN. Come away, the Midwife is come.

1 WOMAN. Is the Lady deliver'd, she was withall?

3 WOMAN. Yes, of life; for she could not be delivered, and so she died.

2 WOMAN. Pray tell not our Lady so: for, the very fright of not being able to bring forth a Child will kill her.

Exeunt.

Scene 10

Enter a Gentleman who meets a fair Young Lady.

GENT. Madam, my Lord desires you to command whatsoever you please, and it shall be obey'd.

---

* Juno] Roman queen of the gods and also the goddess of childbirth.

LADY. I dare not command, but I humbly intreat, I may live quiet and free from his *Amours.*

GENT. He says he cannot live, and not love you.

LADY. But he may live, and not lie with me.

GENT. He cannot be happy, unless he enjoy you.

LADY. And I must be unhappy, if he should.

GENT. He commanded me to tell you that he will part from his Lady for your sake.

LADY. Heaven forbid, I should part Man and Wife.

GENT. Lady, he will be divorced for your sake.

LADY. Heaven forbid I should be the cause of a Divorce between a Noble Pair.

GENT. You had best consent; for, otherwise he will have you against your will.

LADY. I will send his Lordship an answer to morrow; pray him to give me so much time.

GENT. I shall, Lady.

Exit Gentleman. LADY *Sola.*

LADY. I must prevent my own ruin, and the sweet virtuous Ladies, by going into a Nunnery; wherefore, I'le put my self into one to night:
There will I live, and serve the Gods on high,
And leave this wicked World and Vanity.

Exeunt. One enters and speaks the EPILOGUE.
Marriage is a Curse we find,
Especially to Women kind:
From the Cobler's Wife we see,
To Ladies, they unhappie be.

L. HAPPY *to the* PRIN. Pray Servant, how do you like this Play?

PRIN. My sweet Mistress, I cannot in conscience approve of it; for though some few be unhappy in Marriage, yet there are many more that are so happy as they would not change their condition.

L. HAPPY. O Servant, I fear you will become an Apostate.*

PRIN. Not to you sweet Mistress.

Exeunt. Enter the Gentlemen.

1 GENT. There is no hopes of dissolving this *Convent of Pleasure.*

2 GENT. Faith, not as I can perceive.

3 GENT. We may be sure, this *Convent* will never be dissolved, by reason it is ennobled with the company of great Princesses, and glorified with a great

---

* Apostate] one who betrays his or her vows.

Fame; but the fear is, that all the rich Heirs will make *Convents*, and all the Young Beauties associate themselves in such *Convents*.

1 GENT. You speak reason; wherefore, let us endeavor to get Wives, before they are Incloister'd.

Exeunt.

ACT IV

Scene 1

Enter Lady HAPPY *drest as a Shepherdess; She walks very Melancholy, then speaks as to her self.*

My Name is *Happy*, and so was my Condition, before I saw this Princess; but now I am like to be the most unhappy Maid alive: But why may not I love a Woman with the same affection I could a Man?

No, no, Nature is Nature, and still will be

The same she was from all Eternity.

Enter the PRINCESS *in Masculine Shepherd's Clothes:*

PRIN. My dearest Mistress, do you shun my Company? is your Servant become an offence to your sight?

L. HAPPY. No, Servant! your Presence is more acceptable to me then the Presence of our Goddess Nature, for which she, I fear will punish me, for loving you more then I ought to love you.

PRIN. Can Lovers love too much?

L. HAPPY. Yes, if they love not well.

PRIN. Can any Love be more vertuous, innocent and harmless then ours?

L. HAPPY. I hope not.

PRIN. Then let us please our selves, as harmless Lovers use to do.

L. HAPPY. How can harmless Lovers please themselves?

PRIN. Why very well, as, to discourse, imbrace and kiss, so mingle souls together.

L. HAPPY. But innocent Lovers do not use to kiss.

PRIN. Not any act more frequent amongst us Women-kind; nay, it were a sin in friendship, should not we kiss: then let us not prove our selves Reprobates.

They imbrace and kiss, and hold each other in their Arms.

PRIN. These my Imbraces though of Femal kind,

May be as fervent as a Masculine mind.

The Scene is open'd and the PRINCESS *and* L. HAPPY *go in. A Pastoral within the Scene. The Scene is changed into a Green, or Plain, where Sheep are feeding, and a*

MAY-POLE* *in the middle. L.* HAPPY *as a Shepherdess, and the* PRINCESS *as a Shepherd are sitting there. Enter another Shepherd, and Wooes the Lady* HAPPY.

SHEPHERD. Fair Shepherdess do not my Suit deny,
>O grant my Suit, let me not for Love die:
>Pity my Flocks, Oh save their Shepherd's life;
>Grant you my Suit, be you their Shepherd's Wife.

L. HAPPY. How can I grant to every ones request?
>Each Shepherd's Suit lets me not be at rest;
>For which I wish, the Winds might blow them far,
>That no Love-Suit might enter to my Ear.

Enter Madam MEDIATOR *in a Shepherdess dress, and another Shepherd.*

SHEP. Good Dame unto your Daughter speak for me.
>Perswade her I your Son in Law may be:
>I'le serve your Swine, your Cows bring home to Milk;
>Attend your Sheep, whose Wool's as soft as Silk;
>I'le plow your Grounds, Corn I'le in Winter sow,
>Then reap your Harvest, and your Grass I'le mow;
>Gather your Fruits in Autumn from the Tree.
>All this and more I'le do, if y'speak for me.

SHEPHERDESS. My Daughter vows a single life,
>And swears, she n're will be a Wife;
>But live a Maid, and Flocks will keep,
>And her chief Company shall be Sheep.

The PRINCESS *as a Shepherd, speaks to the Lady* HAPPY.

PRIN. My Shepherdess, your Wit flies high,
>Up to the Skie,
>And views the Gates of Heaven,
>Which are the Planets Seven;†
>Sees how fixt Stars are plac'd,
>And how the Meteors wast;
>What makes the Snow so white,
>And how the Sun makes light;
>What makes the biting Cold
>On every thing take hold;
>And Hail a mixt degree,

---

* May-Pole] a phallic fertility symbol; remnant of pagan fertility rituals.

† Planets Seven] in early astronomy, in order of their distance from Earth: the Moon, Mercury, Venus, the Sun, Mars, Jupiter, and Saturn.

'Twixt Snow and Ice you see
From whence the Winds do blow;
What Thunder is, you know,
And what makes Lightning flow
Like liquid streams, you show
From Skie you come to th' Earth,
And view each Creature's birth;
Sink to the Center deep,
Where all dead bodies sleep;
And there observe to know,
What makes the Minerals grow;
How Vegetables sprout,
And how the Plants come out;
Take notice of all Seed,
And what the Earth doth breed;
Then view the Springs below,
And mark how Waters flow;
What makes the Tides to rise
Up proudly to the Skies,
And shrinking back descend,
As fearing to offend.
Also your Wit doth view
The Vapour and the Dew,
In Summer's heat, that Wet
Doth seem like the Earth's Sweat;
In Winter-time, that Dew
Like paint's white to the view,
Cold makes that thick, white, dry;
As Cerusse* it doth lie
On th' Earth's black face, so fair
As painted Ladies are;
But, when a heat is felt,
That Frosty paint doth melt.
    Thus Heav'n and Earth you view,
And see what's Old, what's New;
How Bodies Transmigrate,
Lives are Predestinate.

---

* Cerusse] white lead paint often used as a cosmetic.

Thus doth your Wit reveal
What Nature would conceal.

L. HAPPY. My Shepherd,
All those that live do know it,
That you are born a Poet,
Your Wit doth search Mankind,
In Body and in Mind;
The Appetites you measure,
And weigh each several Pleasure,
Do figure every Passion,
And every Humor's fashion;
See how the Fancie's wrought,
And what makes every Thought;
Fadom* Conceptions low,
From whence Opinions flow;
Observe the Memorie's length,
And Understanding's strength
Your Wit doth Reason find,
The Centre of the Mind,
Wherein the Rational Soul
Doth govern and controul,
There doth she sit in State,
Predestinate by Fate,
And by the Gods Decree,
That Sovereign She should be.

    And thus your Wit can tell,
How Souls in Bodies dwell;
As that the Mind dwells in the Brain,
And in the Mind the Soul doth raign,
And in the Soul the life doth last,
For with the Body it doth not wast;
Nor shall Wit like the Body die,
But live in the World's Memory.

PRIN. May I live in your favour, and be possest with your Love and Person, is the height of my ambitions.

L. HAPPY. I can neither deny you my Love nor Person.

PRIN. In amorous Pastoral Verse we did not Woo.

* Fadom] fathom.

As other Pastoral Lovers use to doo.

L. HA. Which doth express, we shall more constant be,
And in a Married life better agree.

PRIN. We shall agree, for we true Love inherit,
Join as one Body and Soul, or Heav'nly Spirit.

Here come Rural Sports, as Country Dances about the May-Pole: that Pair which Dances best is Crowned King and Queen of the Shepherds that year; which happens to be the PRINCESS, *and the Lady* HAPPY.

L. HAPPY *to the* PRINC. Let me tell you, Servant, that our Custome is to dance about this May-Pole, and that Pair which dances best is Crown'd King and Queen of all Shepherds and Shepherdesses this year: Which Sport if it please you we will begin.

PRIN. Nothing, Sweetest Mistress, that pleases you, can displease me.

They Dance; after the Dancing the PRINCESS *and Lady* HAPPY *are Crowned with a Garland of Flowers: a Shepherd speaks.*

*Written by my Lord Duke**

You've won the prize; and justly; so we all
Acknowledg it with joy, and offer here
Our Hatchments† up, our Sheep-hooks as your due,
And Scrips of Corduant,‡ and Oaten Pipe;§
So all our Pastoral Ornaments we lay
Here at your Feet, with Homage to obay
All your Commands, and all these things we bring
In honour of our dancing Queen and King;
For Dancing heretofore has got more Riches
Then we can find in all our Shepherds Breeches;
Witness rich Holmby:‖ long then may you live,
And for your Dancing what we have we give.

---

  * Newcastle is credited with his contributions on printed strips pasted into the text of both *Playes* (1662) and *Plays, Never Before Printed* (1668). Here, since no terminus is given, it seems that he is the author of the final two scenes and the epilogue.

  † Hatchments] heraldic emblems, as on a family crest.

  ‡ Scrips of Corduant] bags of cordovan leather.

  § Oaten Pipe] shepherd's musical instrument made of oat stems.

  ‖ rich Holmby] Sir Christopher Hatton, chamberlain and favorite of Queen Elizabeth known for his graceful dancing, used largesse from the queen to build a grand house on his family estate at Holmby, now known as Holdenby. Later King Charles was imprisoned by Parliament in this house.

A Wassel is carried about and Syllibubs.* Another Shepherd speaks, or Sings this that follows.

Written by my Lord Duke

> The Jolly Wassel now do bring,
> With Apples drown'd in stronger Ale,
> And fresher Syllibubs, and sing;
> Then each to tell their Love-sick Tale;
> So home by Couples, and thus draw
> Our selves by holy Hymen's Law.†

The Scene Vanishes. Enter the PRINCESS *Sola, and walks a turn or two in a Musing posture, then views her Self, and speaks.*

PRIN. What have I on a Petticoat, Oh *Mars!* thou God of War, pardon my sloth; but yet remember thou art a Lover, and so am I; but you will say, my Kingdom wants me, not only to rule, and govern it, but to defend it: But what is a Kingdom in comparison to a Beautiful Mistress? Base thoughts flie off, for I will not go; did not only a Kingdom, but the World want me.

Exeunt. Enter the Lady HAPPY *Sola, and Melancholy, and after a short Musing speaks.*

L. HAPPY. O Nature, O you gods above,
> Suffer me not to fall in Love;
> O strike me dead here in this place
> Rather then fall into disgrace.

Enter Madam MEDIATOR.

M. MEDIAT. What, Lady *Happy,* solitary alone! and Musing like a disconsolate Lover!

L. HAPPY. No, I was Meditating of Holy things.

M. MEDIAT. Holy things! what Holy things?

L. HAPPY. Why, such Holy things as the Gods are.

M. MEDIAT. By my truth, whether your Contemplation be of Gods or of Men, you are become lean and pale since I was in the *Convent* last.

Enter the PRINCESS.

PRINC. Come my sweet Mistress, shall we go to our Sports and Recreations?

M. MEDIAT. Beshrew me, your Highness hath sported too much I fear.

---

* *Wassel . . . Syllibubs*] wassail was spiced wine used for toasting, especially at Christmas; syllabub, a holiday punch made of milk and wine.

† Hymen's Law] marriage; Hymen was the Roman god of marriage.

PRINC. Why, Madam *Mediator,* say you so?

M. MEDIAT. Because the Lady *Happy* looks not well, she is become pale and lean.

PRINC. Madam *Mediator,* your eyes are become dim with Time; for my sweet Mistress appears with greater splendor then the God of Light.

M. MEDIAT. For all you are a great Princess, give me leave to tell you,
I am not so old, nor yet so blind,
But that I see you are too kind.

PRINC. Well, Madam *Mediator,* when we return from our Recreations, I will ask your pardon, for saying, your eyes are dim, conditionally you will ask my pardon for saying, my Mistress looks not well.

Exeunt. The SCENE *is opened, and there is presented a Rock as in the Sea; whereupon sits the Princess and the Lady* HAPPY; *the* PRINCESS *as the Sea-God* NEPTUNE, *the Lady* HAPPY *as a Sea-Goddess: the rest of the Ladies sit somewhat lower, drest like Water-Nymphs; the* PRINCESS *begins to speak a Speech in Verse, and after her the Lady* HAPPY *makes her Speech.*

I Am the King of all the Seas,
All Watry Creatures do me please,
Obey my Power and Command,
And bring me Presents from the Land;
The Waters open their Flood-gates,
Where Ships do pass, sent by the Fates;*
Which Fates do yearly, as *May*-Dew,
Send me a Tribute from *Peru,*
From other Nations besides,
Brought by their Servants, Winds and Tides,
Ships fraught and Men to me they bring;
My Watery Kingdom lays them in.
Thus from the Earth a Tribute I
Receive, which shews my power thereby:
Besides, my Kingdom's richer far
Then all the Earth and every Star.

L. HAPPY. I feed the Sun, which gives them light,
And makes them shine in darkest night,
Moist vapour from my brest I give,
Which he sucks forth, and makes him live,

---

* the Fates] a trio of goddesses held responsible for good or ill fortune.

Or else his Fire would soon go out,
Grow dark, or burn the World throughout.
PRINC. What Earthly Creature's like to me,
That hath such Power and Majestie?
My Palaces are Rocks of Stone,
And built by Nature's hand alone,
No base, dissembling, coz'ning Art
Do I imploy in any part,
In all my Kingdom large and wide,
Nature directs and doth provide
Me all Provisions which I need,
And Cooks my Meat on which I feed.
L. HAPPY. My Cabinets are Oyster-shells,
In which I keep my Orient-Pearls,
To open them I use the Tide,
As Keys to Locks, which opens wide,
The Oyster-shells then out I take;
Those, Orient-Pearls and Crowns do make;
And modest Coral I do wear,
Which blushes when it touches air.
On Silver-Waves I sit and sing,
And then the Fish lie listening:
Then sitting on a Rocky stone,
I comb my Hair with Fishes bone;
The whil'st Apollo,* with his Beams,
Doth dry my Hair from wat'ry streams.
His light doth glaze the Water's face,
Make the large Sea my Looking-Glass;
So when I swim on Waters high,
I see my self as I glide by:
But when the Sun begins to burn,
I back into my Waters turn,
And dive unto the bottom low:
Then on my head the Waters flow,
In Curled waves and Circles round;
And thus with Waters am I Crown'd.

* Apollo] Greek and Roman god of the sun; also god of poetry.

PRINC. Besides, within the Waters deep,
    In hollow Rocks my Court I keep;
    Of Amber-greece* my Bed is made,
    Whereon my softer Limbs are laid,
    There take I Rest; and whil'st I sleep,
    The Sea doth guard, and safe me keep
    From danger; and, when I awake,
    A Present of a Ship doth make.
    No Prince on Earth hath more resort,
    Nor keeps more Servants in his Court;
    Of Mare-maids you're waited on,
    And Mare-men do attend upon
    My Person; some are Councellors,
    Which order all my great Affairs;
    Within my wat'ry Kingdom wide,
    They help to rule, and so to guide
    The Common-wealth; and are by me
    Prefer'd unto an high degree.
    Some Judges are, and Magistrates,
    Decide each Cause, and end Debates;
    Others, Commanders in the War;
    And some to Governments prefer;
    Others are *Neptun*'s Priests which pray
    And preach when is a Holy-day.
    And thus with Method order I,
    And govern all with Majesty;
    I am sole Monarch of the Sea,
    And all therein belongs to me.
A Sea-Nymph Sings this following SONG.
    1. We Watery Nymphs Rejoyce and Sing
    About God Neptune *our Sea's King;*
    In Sea-green Habits, for to move
    His God-head, for to fall in love.

    2. That with his Trident he doth stay
    Rough foaming Billows which obay:
    And when in Triumph he doth stride
    His manag'd Dolphin for to ride.

---

* Amber-greece] ambergris, a rare substance from sperm whales used in making perfume.

3. *All his Sea-people to his wish,*
   From Whale *to* Herring *subject Fish,*
   With Acclamations do attend him,
   And pray's more Riches still to send him.
Exeunt. The SCENE *Vanishes.*

ACT V

Scene 1

Enter the PRINCESS *and the Lady* HAPPY; *The* PRINCESS *is in a Man's Apparel as going to Dance; they Whisper sometime; then the Lady* HAPPY *takes a Ribbon from her arm, and gives it to the* PRINCESS, *who gives her another instead of that, and kisses her hand. They go in and come presently out again with all the Company to Dance, the Musick plays; And after they have Danced a little while, in comes Madam* MEDIATOR *wringing her hands, and spreading her arms; and full of Passion cries out.*

M. MEDIAT. O Ladies, Ladies! you're all betrayed, undone, undone; for there is a man disguised in the *Convent,* search and you'l find it.

They all skip from each other, as afraid of each other, only the PRINCESS *and the Lady* HAPPY *stand still together.*

PRINC. You may make the search, Madam *Mediator;* but you will quit me, I am sure.

M. MEDIAT. By my faith but I will not, for you are most to be suspected.

PRINC. But you say, the Man is disguised like a Woman, and I am accoustred like a Man.

M. MEDIAT. Fidle, fadle, that is nothing to the purpose.

Enter an Embassador to the PRINCE; *the Embassador kneels, the* PRINCE *bids him rise.*

PRINC. What came you here for?

EMBASS. May it please your Highness, the Lords of your Council sent me to inform your Highness, that your Subjects are so discontented at your Absence, that if your Highness do not return into your Kingdom soon, they'l enter this Kingdom by reason they hear you are here; and some report as if your Highness were restrained as Prisoner.

PRINC. So I am, but not by the State, but by this Fair Lady, who must be your Soveraigness.

The Embassador kneels and kisses her hand.

PRINC. But since I am discover'd, go from me to the Councellors of this State, and inform them of my being here, as also the reason, and that I ask their leave I may marry this Lady; otherwise, tell them I will have her by force of Arms.

Exit Embassador.

M. MEDIAT. O the Lord! I hope you will not bring an Army, to take away all the Women; will you?

PRINC. No, Madam *Mediator,* we will leave you behind us.

Exeunt.

Scene 2

Enter Madam MEDIATOR *lamenting and crying with a Handkerchief in her hand.*

Written by my Lord Duke.

O Gentlemen, that I never had been born, we're all undone and lost!

ADVIS. Why, what's the matter?

M. MEDIAT. Matter? nay, I doubt, there's too much Matter.

ADVIS. How?

M. MEDIAT. How, never such a Mistake; why we have taken a Man for a Woman.

ADVIS. Why, a Man is for a Woman.

M. MEDIAT. Fidle fadle, I know that as well as you can tell me; but there was a young Man drest in Woman's Apparel, and enter'd our *Convent,* and the Gods know what he hath done: He is mighty handsome, and that's a great Temptation to Virtue; but I hope all is well: But this wicked World will lay aspersion upon any thing or nothing; and therefore I doubt, all my sweet young Birds are undone, the Gods comfort them.

COURTLY. But could you never discover it? nor have no hint he was a Man?

M. MEDIAT. No truly, only once I saw him kiss the Lady *Happy;* and you know Womens Kisses are unnatural, and me-thought they kissed with more alacrity then Women use, a kind of Titillation, and more Vigorous.

ADVIS. Why, did you not then examine it?

M. MEDIAT. Why, they would have said, I was but an old jealous fool, and laught at me; but Experience is a great matter; If the Gods had not been merciful to me, he might have faln upon me.

COURTLY. Why, what if he had?

M. MEDIAT. Nay, if he had I care not: for I defie the Flesh as much as I renounce the Devil and the pomp of this wicked World; but if I could but have sav'd my young sweet Virgins, I would willingly have sacrificed my body for them; for we are not born for our selves but for others.

ADVIS. 'Tis piously said, truly, lovingly and kindly.

M. MEDIAT. Nay, I have read the Practice of Piety;* but further they say, He is a Foreign Prince; and they say, They're very hot.

COURTLY. Why, you are a Madam *Mediator,* you must mediate and make a friendship.

M. MEDIAT. What do you talk of Mediation, I doubt they are too good Friends; Well, this will be news for Court, Town and Country, in private Letters, in the Gazette, and in abominable Ballets† before it be long, and jeered to death by the pretending Wits; but, good Gentlemen, keep this as a Secret, and let not me be the Author, for you will hear abundantly of it before it be long.

ADVIS. But, Madam *Mediator,* this is no Secret, it is known all the Town over, and the State is preparing to entertain the Prince.

M. MEDIAT. Lord! to see how ill news will fly so soon abroad?

COURTLY. Ill news indeed for us Wooers.

ADVIS. We only wooed in Imagination but not in Reality.

M. MEDIAT. But you all had hopes.

ADVIS. We had so; but she only has the fruition: for it is said, the Prince and she agreed to Marry; and the State is so willing, as they account it an honour, and hope shall reap much advantage by the Match.

M. MEDIAT. Yes, yes; but there is an old and true Saying, *There's much between the Cup and the Lip.*

Exeunt.

Scene 3

Enter the PRINCE *as Bridegroom, and the Lady* HAPPY *as Bride, hand in hand under a Canopy born over their heads by Men; the Magistrates march before, then the Hoboys;‡ and then the Bridal Guests, as coming from the Church, where they were Married. All the Company bids them joy, they thank them.*

M. MEDIAT. Although your Highness will not stay to feast with your Guests, pray Dance before you go.

PRINC. We will both Dance and Feast before we go; come Madam let us Dance, to please Madam *Mediator.*

The PRINCE *and* PRINCESS *Dance.*

---

* the Practice of Piety] *The Practice of Piety: directing a Christian how to walk that he may please God,* by Lewes Baily (d. 1631), a tract so popular that it had been reprinted at least 59 times by 1734 and translated into both Welsh (1675) and Algonquin (1665).

† Ballets] ballads; popular, often satiric songs about current events.

‡ Hoboys] oboes.

PRINC. Now, Noble Friends, Dance you; and the *Princess*, and I, will rest our selves.

After they have Danced, the Lady HAPPY, *as now* PRINCESS, *speaks to the Lady* VERTUE.

L. HAPPY *speaks to* L. VERTUE. Lady *Vertue*, I perceive you keep *Mimick* still.

L. HAPPY *to the* PRINCE. Sir, this is the *Mimick* I told you of.

L. HAPPY *to* MIMICK. *Mimick*, will you leave your Lady and go with me?

MIMICK. I am a Married Man, and have Married my Ladies Maid *Nan*, and she will keep me at home do what I can; but you've now a *Mimick* of your own, for the *Prince* has imitated a Woman.

L. HAPPY. What you Rogue, do you call me a Fool?

MIMICK. Not I, please your Highness, unless all Women be Fools.

PRINC. Is your Wife a Fool?

MIMICK. Man and Wife, 'tis said, makes but one Fool.

He kneels to the PRINCE.

MIMICK. I have an humble Petition to your Highness.

PRINC. Rise; What Petition is that?

MIMICK. That your Highness would be pleased to divide the *Convent* in two equal parts; one for Fools, and th' other for Married Men, as mad Men.

PRINC. I'le divide it for Virgins and Widows.

MIMICK. That will prove a *Convent of Pleasure* indeed; but they will never agree, especially if there be some disguised Prince amongst them; but you had better bestow it on old decrepit and bed-rid Matrons, and then it may be call'd the *Convent of Charity*, if it cannot possibly be named the *Convent of Chastity*.

PRINC. Well, to shew my Charity, and to keep your Wife's Chastity, I'le bestow my bounty in a Present, on the Condition you speak the *Epilogue*. Come, Noble Friends, let us feast before we part.

Exeunt. MIMIC *Solus.*

MIMICK. An *Epilogue* says he, the devil an *Epilogue* have I: let me study.

He questions and answers Himself.

I have it, I have it; No faith, I have it not; I lie, I have it, I say, I have it not; Fie *Mimick*, will you lie? Yes, *Mimick*, I will lie, if it be my pleasure: But I say, it is gone; What is gone? The *Epilogue*; When had you it? I never had it; then you did not lose it; that is all one, but I must speak it, although I never had it; How can you speak it, and never had it? I marry, that's the question; but words are nothing, and then an *Epilogue* is nothing, and so I may speak nothing; Then nothing be my Speech.

HE SPEAKS THE EPILOGUE

Noble Spectators by this Candle-light,
I know not what to say, but bid, Good Night:
I dare not beg Applause, our Poetess then
Will be enrag'd, and kill me with her Pen;
For she is careless, and is void of fear;
If you dislike her Play she doth not care.
But I shall weep, my inward Grief shall show
Through Floods of Tears, that Through my Eyes will flow.
And so poor Mimick *he for sorrow die.*
And then through pity you may chance to cry:
But if you please, you may a Cordial give,
Made up with Praise, and so he long may live.

Finis

Appendixes

The appendixes include the extensive front matter preceding the plays them-selves in *Playes,* 1662, the single long letter to the readers at the end of that volume, the single letter to the readers with which Cavendish prefaces *Plays Never Before Printed,* 1668, and errata for *Loves Adventures* and *Bell in Campo* appearing at the end of some copies of *Playes,* 1662.

Cavendish's letter to her husband in appendix A throws interesting light on their relationship. Although she insists with wifely modesty on his superiority as a playwright, it is obvious that his example and approval are foundational to her courage to write and publish. Both in the epistle dedicating *Playes* to the marquis and in the first letter to the readers she declares that her next (and last) literary project will be to write his biography, though in fact she produced several volumes between the first collection of plays and the *Life.*

The numerous, often lengthy epistles to the readers offer a fascinating pic-ture of the author's milieu and her frequent resistance to it. The second epistle affords a contemporary analysis of the condition of the London theaters as they struggle to reopen and regain their popularity in the early years of the Restora-tion, while the third shows Cavendish arguing, against the neoclassical impulse of the time, that art should be as diverse and unpredictable as life. In the fourth she argues that "the nobler sort" should act in plays because unlike the profes-sional player who only parrots the playwright's words, they will absorb the writer's moral teachings as they gain poise and confidence by performing. The fifth epistle is puzzling in its treatment of "gender" (see Jeffrey Masten, "Mistres corrivall: Margaret Cavendish's Dramatic Production," in Masten, *Textual In-tercourse,* 156–64). In the sixth Cavendish satirizes female long-windedness on the subject of male verbosity, and in the seventh she seems to claim that female heroism is not just fantasy but truly possible. In the eighth epistle she claims that the plays are her own original work, a claim she makes in her rhymed preface and at some point in most of her other publications as well. In the ninth epistle she again acknowledges the encouragement and support of her husband, who himself praises her originality in his commendatory poem. The tenth epistle returns to a theme begun in the Epistle Dedicatory: Cavendish's fear that her plays, if produced without her control, will be badly acted. The single epistle appended to the 1662 collection (appendix C) is an essay explaining to the readers both why she writes and why she writes so much. Finally, it is interesting to compare the one fierce statement that introduces the 1668 collection (appendix D) with the anxious iterations of the 1662 prefaces and epistles. The worst has apparently happened, but Margaret Cavendish is a writer still.

Dedicatory Poems and Author's Epistles Preceding the Texts in *Playes*, 1662

The Dedication

To those that do delight in Scenes and wit,
I dedicate my Book, for those I writ;
Next to my own Delight, for I did take
Much pleasure and delight these Playes to make;
For all the time my Playes a making were,
My brain the Stage, my thoughts were acting there.

The Epistle Dedicatory

MY LORD,

My resolution was, that {*blot out* that} when I had done writing, to have dedicated all my works in gross to your Lordship; and I did verily believe that this would have been my last work: but I find it will not, unless I dye before I have writ my other intended piece. And as for this Book of Playes, I believe I should never have writ them, nor have had the capacity nor Ingenuity to have writ Playes, had not you read to me some Playes which your Lordship had writ, and lye by for a good time to be Acted, wherein your Wit did Create a desire in my Mind to write Playes also, although my Playes are very unlike those you have writ, for your Lordships Playes have as it were a natural life, and a quick spirit in them, whereas mine are like dull dead statues, which is the reason I send them forth to be printed, rather than keep them concealed in hopes to have them first Acted; and this advantage I have, that is, I am out of the fear of having them hissed off from the Stage, for they are not like to come thereon; but were they such as might deserve applause, yet if Envy did make a faction against them, they would have had a publick Condemnation; and though I am not such a Coward, as to be affraid of the hissing Serpents, or stinged Tongues of Envy, yet it would have made me a little Melancholy to have my harmless and innocent Playes go weeping from the Stage, and whipt by malicious and hard hearted censurers; but the truth is, I am careless, for so I have your applause I desire no more, for your Lordships approvement is a sufficient satisfaction to me.

My Lord,
Your Lordships honest Wife,
and faithfull Servant,
M.N.

To the Readers

NOBLE READERS,

I Must ask pardon for that I said I should not trouble you with more of my works than this Book of Playes, but since I have considered with my self, there is one work more, which is very fit for me to do, although I shall not be able to do it so well as the subject will deserve, being the Life of my Noble Lord; but that work will require some time in the gathering together some several passages; for although I mean not to write of all the particulars of these times, yet forasmuch as is concerning that subject I shall write of, it will be requirable; but it is a work that will move so slowly, as perchance I shall not live to finish it; but howsoever, I will imploy my time about it, and it will be a satisfaction to my life that I indeavor it.

M.N.

To the Readers

NOBLE READERS,

The reason why I put out my Playes in print, before they are Acted, is, first, that I know not when they will be Acted, by reason they are in English, and *England* doth not permit {admit} I will not say of Wit, yet not of Plays; and if they should, yet by reason all those that have been bred and brought up to Act, are dead, or dispersed, and it would be an Act of some time, not only to breed and teach some Youths to Act, but it will require some time to prove whether they be good Actors or no; for if they are not bred to it whilst they be young, they will never be good Actors when they are grown up to be men; for although some one by chance may have naturally, a facility to Action, and a Volubility of Speech, and a good memory to learn, and get the Parts by heart, or wrote,* yet it is very unlikely, or indeed impossible, to get a whole Company of good Actors†

---

* wrote] rote.
† This read "Astors" in the original.

without being taught and brought up thereto; the other reason is, that most of my Playes would seem tedious upon the Stage, by reason they are somewhat long, although most are divided into first and second Parts; for having much variety in them, I could not possibly make them shorter, and being long, it might tire the Spectators, who are forced, or bound by the rules of Civility to sit out a Play, if they be not sick; for to go away before a Play is ended, is a kind of an affront, both to the Poet and the Players; yet, I believe none of my Playes are so long as *Ben. Johnson's* Fox, or Alchymist, which in truth, are somewhat too long;* but for Readers, the length of the Playes can be no trouble, nor inconveniency, because they may read as short or as long a time as they please, without any disrespect to the Writer; but some of my Playes are short enough; but the printing of my Playes spoils them for ever to be Acted; for what men are acquainted with, is despised, at lest neglected; for the newness of Playes, most commonly, takes the Spectators, more than the Wit, Scenes, or Plot, so that my Playes would seem lame or tired in action, and dull to hearing on the Stage, for which reason, I shall never desire they should be Acted; but if they delight or please the Readers, I shall have as much satisfaction as if I had the hands of applause from the Spectators.

M.N.

To the Readers

NOBLE READERS,

Although I expect my Playes will be found fault with, by reason I have not drawn the several persons presented in a Circular line, or to a Triangular point, making all the Actors to meet at the latter end upon the Stage in a flock together; likewise, that I have not made my Comedies of one dayes actions or passages; yet I have adventured to publish them to the World: But to plead in my Playes behalf, first, I do not perceive any reason why that the several persons presented should be all of an acquaintance, or that there is a necessity to have them of one Fraternity, or to have a relation to each other, or linck'd in alliance as one Family, when as Playes are to present the general Follies, Vanities, Vices, Humours, Dispositions, Passions, Affections, Fashions, Customs, Manners, and practices of the whole World of Mankind, as in several persons; also particular Follies, Vanities, Vices, Humours, Passions, Affections, Fashions,

---

* Ben Jonson (1572–1637), a dramatist, poet, critic, was the most influential man of English letters until John Dryden (1631–1700). The five acts of Ben Jonson's *Volpone* ("Fox") cover 74 folio pages of 12-point type, exactly the same as the ten acts that make up parts 1 and 2 of *Loves Adventures*, Cavendish's longest play. The *Alchemist* is 72 pages long; the ten acts of *Bell in Campo*, 54.

Customs, Fortunes, and the like, in particular persons; also the Sympathy and Antipathy of Dispositions, Humours, Passions, Customs, and Fashions of several persons; also the particular Virtues and Graces in several persons, and several Virtues and Graces in particular persons, and all these Varieties to be drawn at the latter end into one piece, as into one Company, which in my opinion shews neither Usual, Probable, nor Natural. For since the world is wide and populated, and their various actions dispersed, and spread about by each particular, and Playes are to present them severally, I perceive no reason they should force them together in the last Act, as in one Community, bringing them in as I may say by Head and Shoulders, making the persons of each Humour, good Fortunes, Misfortunes, Nations and Ages, to have relations to each other; but in this I have not followed the steps of precedent Poets, for in my opinion, I think it is as well, if not better, if a Play ends but with two persons, or one person upon the Stage; besides, I would have my Playes to be like the Natural course of all things in the World, as some dye sooner, some live longer, and some are newly born, when some are newly dead, and not all to continue to the last day of Judgment; so my Scenes, some last longer than othersome, and some are ended when others are begun; likewise some of my Scenes have no acquaintance or relation to the rest of the Scenes, although in one and the same Play, which is the reason many of my Playes will not end as other Playes do, especially Comedies, for in Tragi-Comedies I think Poets do not alwayes make all lye bleeding together; but I think for the most part they do; but the want of this swarm in the last Act and Scene, may make my Playes seem dull and vacant, but I love ease so well, as I hate constraint even in my works; for I had rather have a dull easy life, than be forced to active gayeties, so I had rather my Playes should end dully than unnecessarily be forced into one Company, but some of my Playes are gathered into one sheaf or bundel in the latter end. Likewise my Playes may be Condemned, because they follow not the Antient Custome, as the learned sayes, which is, that all Comedies should be so ordered and composed; as nothing should be presented therein, but what may be naturally, or usually practiced or Acted in the World in the compass of one day; truly in my opinion those Comedies would be very flat and dull, and neither profitable nor pleasant, that should only present the actions of one day; for though *Ben. Johnson* as I have heard was of that opinion, that a Comedy cannot be good, nor is a natural or true Comedy, if it should present more than one dayes action, yet his Comedies that he hath published, could never be the actions of one day; for could any rational person think that the whole Play of the Fox could be the action of one day? or can any rational person think that the Alchymist could be the action of one day? as that so many several Cozenings* could be Acted in one day, by Captain *Face* and *Doll Common;* and could the Alchymist make any believe they could make gold in one day? could they burn so many Coals, and draw the purses of so many, or so often from one person, in one day? and the like is in all his Playes, not any of them presents the actions of one day, although it were a day at the Poles, but of many dayes, nay I may say some years. But to my reason, I do not perceive a necessity that Comedies should be so closely packt or thrust up together; for if Comedies are either to delight, or to profit, or to both, they must follow no other rule or example, but to put them into Scenes and Acts, and to order their several discources in a Comedy, so as Physicians do their Cordials, wherein they mix many several Ingrediences together into one Electuary, as sharp, bitter, salt, and sweet, and mix them so, as they are both pleasing to the Tast, and comfortable to the Stomach; so Poets should order the several Humours, Passions, Customs, Manners, Fashions, and practice of Mankind, as to intermix them so, as to be both delightfull to the Mind and Senses, and profitable to the Life; also Poets should do as Physicians or Apothecaries, which put not only several sorts, but several kinds of Drugs into one Medicine, as Minerals and Vegetables together, which are very different; also they will mix several Druggs and Simples out of several Climates and Countries gathered out from all the parts of the World, and upon occasion they will mix new and old Simples together, although of one and the same sort and kind; so Poets both in their Comedies and Tragedies, must, or at leastwise may, represent several Nations, Governments, People, Customs, Fashions, Manners, Natures, Fortunes, Accidents, Actions, in one Play; as also several times of Ages to one person if occasion requires, as from Children to Manhood in one Play; for Poets are to describe in Playes the several Ages, Times, Actions, Fortunes, Accidents and Humours in Nature, and the several Customs, Manners, Fashions, and Speeches of men: thus Playes are to present the natural dispositions and practices of Mankind; also they are to point at Vanity, laugh at Follies, disgrace Baseness, and persecute Vice; likewise they are to extol Virtue, and to honour Merit, and to praise the Graces, all which makes a Poet Divine, their works edifying to the Mind or Soul, profitable to the Life, delightfull to the Senses, and recreative to Time; but Poets are like Preachers, some are more learned than others, and some are better Orators than others, yet from the worst there may be some good gained by them, and I do not despair, although but a Poetress, but that my works may be some wayes or other

---

* Cozenings] confidence tricks.

serviceable to my Readers, which if they be, my time in writing them is not lost, nor my Muse unprofitable.

M.N.

To the Readers

NOBLE READERS,

I Cannot chuse but mention an erronious opinion got into this our Modern time and men, which is, that it should be thought a crime or debasement for the nobler sort to Act Playes, especially on Publick Theatres, although the *Romans* were of another opinion, for not only the noble youth did Act in publick, but some of the Emperours themselves; though I do not commend it in the Emperours; who should spend their times in realities, and not in feigning; yet certainly it was commendable in the noblest youths, who did practice what ought to be followed or shunn'd: for certainly there is no place, wayes or means, so edifying to Youth as publick Theatres, not only to be Spectators but Actors; for it learns them gracefull behaviours and demeanors, it puts Spirit and Life into them, it teaches them Wit, and makes their Speech both voluble and tunable, besides, it gives them Confidence, all which ought every man to have, that is of quality. But some will say if it would work such effects, why are not mercenary Players benefited so thereby? I answer, that they only Act for the lucre of Gain, and not for the grace of Behaviour, the sweetness of Speech, nor the increasing of Wit, so as they only Act as Parrots speak, by wrote, and not as Learning gives to Education; for they making not a benefit of the wit, but only by the wit receive it; not neither into their consideration, understanding, nor delight, for they make it a work of labour, and not of delight, or pleasure, or honour; for they receive it into the memory, and no farther than for to deliver it out, as Servants or Factors to sell, and not keep it as purchasors to their own use; that is the reason that as soon as the Play is done, their wit and becoming graces are at an end, whereas the nobler sort, that Act not for mercenary Profit, but for Honour, and becoming, would not only strive to Act well upon the Stage, but to practise their actions when off from the Stage, besides, it would keep the youths from misimploying time with their foolish extravagancies, deboist* luxuries, and base Vices, all which Idleness and vacant time produceth; and in my opinion, a publick Theatre were a shorter way of education than their tedious and expensive Travels, or their dull and solitary Studies; for Poets teach them more in one Play, both of the Nature of the World and Mankind, by

---

* deboist] debauched.

which they learn not only to know other men, but their own selves, than they can learn in any School, or in any Country or Kingdome in a year; but to conclude, a Poet is the best Tutor; and a Theatre is the best School that is for youth to be educated by or in.

M.N.

To the Readers

NOBLE READERS,

I Know there are many Scholastical and Pedantical persons that will condemn my writings, because I do not keep strictly to the Masculine and Feminine Genders, as they call them; as for example, a Lock and a Key, the one is the Masculine Gender, the other the Feminine Gender, so Love is the Masculine Gender, Hate the Feminine Gender, and the Furies are shees, and the Graces are shees, the Virtues are shees, and the seven deadly Sins are shees, which I am sorry for; but I know no reason but that I may as well make them Hees for my use, as others did Shees, or Shees as others did Hees. But some will say, if I did do so, there would be no forms or rules of Speech to be understood by; I answer, that we may as well understand the meaning or sense of a Speaker or Writer by the names of Love or Hate, as by the names of he or she, and better: for the division of Masculine and Feminine Genders doth confound a Scholar more and takes up more time to learn them, than they have time to spend; besides, where one doth rightly understand the difference a hundred, nay a thousand do not, and yet they are understood, and to be understood is the end of all Speakers and Writers; so that if my writings be understood, I desire no more; and as for the nicities of Rules, Forms, and Terms, I renounce, and profess, that if I did understand and know them strictly, as I do not, I would not follow them: and if any dislike my writings for want of those Rules, Forms, and Terms, let them not read them; for I had rather my writings should be unread than be read by such Pedantical Scholastical* persons.

M.N.

To the Readers

NOBLE READERS,

'Tis likely you will condemn my Playes as being dull and flat, by reason they have not the high seasoning of Poetical Salt; but Suger is more commonly used

---

* Misspelled "Sholastical" in the original.

amongst our Sex than Salt. But I fear my Wit is tasteless, which I am sorry for; for though a Satyrical Speaker is discommendable, being for the most part abusive; for Bitter reproofs only are fit for rigid Pedants, Censuring and backbiting fit for pot Companions, and sharp replies is a wit for mean persons, being in a degree of scolding; a Ralery Wit, for Buffons and Jesters which abuse under the Veil of Mirth, Familiarity, and Freedome; whereas a generous discoursitive Wit, although it be free, yet it is sweet and pleasing: thus as I said Satyrical Speakers are discommendable, yet Satyrical Writers are highly to be praised, as most profitable, because those reprove only the generality, as the general Vices, Follies, and errors of Mankind, pointing at no particular; and the sharpest Writers are most commonly the sweetest Speakers. But I have observed one general Folly amongst many which is, that it is expected by most Readers that the Writers should speak as they write, which would be very ridiculous; as for example, a lyrick poet should speak nothing but Sonnets, a Comedian or Tragedian Poet should speak nothing but set Speeches, or blanck Verse, or such Speeches which are only proper to present such and such humours, which in ordinary discourse would be improper; and though *Virgil* whose greatest praise is Language, yet I do verily believe he did not speak in his ordinary Conversation in such a stile, forms and Speeches, nor in such high, fine, and choice Latin, nor in such high and lofty expressions, nor apt similitudes, nor the sence of his discourse wrapt in such Metaphors, as in his writings; nay Eloquent Speakers or Orators do not always speak Orations, but upon an occasion, and at set times, but their ordinary Conversation is with ordinary discourses; for I do verily believe, the greatest and most Eloquents Orators that ever were in the World, in their ordinary Conversations, converst and spoke but as other men. Besides, in Common and ordinary Conversations, the most Wittiest, Learnedst and Eloquentest Men, are forced to speak according to the Wit, Learning, Language, and Capacities of those they are in Company and Conversation with, unless they will speak all themselves, which will be no Conversation; for in Conversation every particular person must have his turn and time of speaking as well as hearing; yet such is the folly of the world, as to despise the Authors of Witty, Learned and Eloquent Writings, if their Conversations be as other mens, and yet would laugh at them, or account them mad, if they should speak otherwise, as out of this ordinary way; but the greatest talkers are not the best writers, which is the cause women cannot be good Writers; for we for fear of being thought Fools, make our selves Fools, in striving to express some Wit, whereas if we had but that power over our selves to keep silence, we perchance might be thought Wits, although we were Fools, but to keep silence is impossible for us to do, so long as we have Speech we shall talk although to no purpose, for nothing but Death can force us to silence, for we often talk in our Sleep; but to speak without partiality, I do not perceive that men are free from this imperfection, nor from condemning us, although they are guilty of the same fault; but we have this advantage of men, which is, that we know this imperfection in our selves, although we do not indeavor to mend it; but men are so Partial to themselves, as not to perceive this imperfection in themselves, and so they cannot mend it; but in this, will not or cannot is as one; but this discourse hath brought me to this, that if I have spoke at any time to any person or persons impertinently, improperly, untimely, or tediously, I ask their pardon: but lest I should be impertinently tedious in this Epistle, and so commit a fault in asking pardon, I leave my Readers to what may be more pleasing to them.

M.N.

To the Readers

NOBLE READERS,

I make no question but my Playes will be censured, and those Censurors severe, but I hope not malicious; but they will perchance say that my Playes are too serious, by reason there is no ridiculous Jest in them, nor wanton Love, nor Impossibilities; also 'tis likely they will say that there are no plots, nor designs, nor subtil Contrivances, and the like; I answer that the chief Plots of my Playes were to imploy my idle time, the designs to please and entertain my Readers, and the contrivance was to join edifying Profit and Delight together, that my Readers may neither lose their time, nor grow weary in the reading; but if they find my Playes neither Edifying, nor Delightfull, I shall be sorry; but if they find either, I shall be pleased, and if they find both, I shall much rejoyce, that my time hath been imployed to some good use.

M.N.

To the Readers

WORTHY READERS,

I have heard that such Poets that write Playes, seldome or never join or sow the several Scenes together; they are two several Professions, at least not usual for rare Poets to take that pains; like as great Taylors, the Master only cuts out and shapes, and his Journy-men and Apprentices join and sow them together; but I like as a poor Taylor was forced to do all my self, as to cut out, shape, join, and sow each several Scene together, without any help or direction; wherefore I fear they are not so well done but that there will be many faults found; but howsoever, I did my best indeavour, and took great pains in the ordering and joining thereof, for which I hope my Learned Readers will pardon the errors therein, and excuse me the worker thereof.

M.N.

To the Readers

NOBLE READERS,

My Lord was pleased to illustrate my Playes with some Scenes of his own Wit, to which I have set his name, that my Readers may know which are his, as not to couzen them, in thinking they are mine; also Songs, to which my Lords name is set; for I being no Lyrick Poet, my Lord supplied that defect of my Brain with the superfluity of his own Brain; thus our Wits join as in Matrimony, my Lords the Masculine, mine the Feminine Wit, which is no small glory to me, that we are Married, Souls, Bodies, and Brains, which is a treble marriage, united in one Love, which I hope is not in the power of Death to dissolve; for Souls may love, and Wit may live, though Bodies dye.

M.N.

I Must trouble my Noble Readers to write of one thing more, which is concerning the Reading of Playes; for Playes must be read to the nature of those several humours, or passions, as are exprest by Writing: for they must not read a Scene as they would read a Chapter; for Scenes must be read as if they were spoke or Acted. Indeed Comedies should be read a Mimick way, and the sound of their Voice must be according to the sense of the Scene; and as for Tragedies, or Tragick Scenes, they must not be read in a pueling* whining Voice, but a sad serious Voice, as deploring or complaining: but the truth is there are as few good Readers as good Writers; indeed an ill Reader is, as great a disadvantage to wit as wit can have, unless it be ill Acted, for then it 'tis doubly disgraced, both in the Voice and Action, whereas in Reading only the voice is imployed; but when as a Play is well and skillfully read, the very sound of

---

* pueling] puling, whining.

the Voice that enters through the Ears, doth present the Actions to the Eyes of the Fancy as lively as if it were really Acted; but howsoever Writings must take their Chance, and I leave my Playes to Chance and Fortune, as well as to Censure and Reading.

M.N.

To The Lady Marchioness of Newcastle *upon her Playes*

Terence and *Plautus** Wits we now do scorn,
Their Comick Socks worn out, in pieces torn,
Only their rags of Wit remain as toyes
For Pedants to admire, to teach School Boyes;
It is not time hath wasted all their Fame,
But your High Phancies, and your nobler flame,
Which burnt theirs up, in their own ashes lies,
Nor Phoenix like e'r out of those will rise;
Old Tragick Buskins† now are thrown away,
When we read your each Passion in each Play,
No stupid block or stony heart forbears
To drown their Cheeks in Seas of salter Tears;
Such power you have in Tragick, Comick stile,
When for to fetch a tear or make a smile,
Still at your pleasure all our passions ly
Obedient to your pen, to laugh or cry;
So even with the thread of Natures fashion,
As you play on her heart-strings still of passion;
So we are all your Subjects in each Play,
Unwilling willingly still to obey;
Or have a thought but what you make or draw
Us by the power of your wits great law;
Thus Emperess in Soveraign power yours sits
Over the wise, and tames Poetick wits.

W. Newcastle.

---

* *Terence* and *Plautus*] Terence (c. 195–159 B.C.) and Plautus (c. 254–184 B.C.) were the best-known classical Roman writers of comedy.

† Buskins] high laced boots associated with ancient Greek drama.

A General Prologue to all my Playes

Noble Spectators, do not think to see
Such Playes, that's like *Ben. Johnsons* Alchymie,
Nor Fox, nor Silent Woman: for those Playes*
Did Crown the Author with exceeding praise;
They were his Master-pieces, and were wrought
By Wits Invention, and his labouring thought,
And his Experience brought Materials store,
His reading several Authors brought much more:
What length of time he took those Plays to write;
I cannot guess, not knowing his Wits flight;
But I have heard, *Ben. Johnsons* Playes came forth,
To the Worlds view, as things of a great worth;
Like Forein Emperors, which do appear
Unto the Subjects, not 'bove once a year;
So did *Ben. Johnsons* Playes so rarely pass,
As one might think they long a writing was.
But my poor Playes, like to a common rout,
Gathers in throngs, and heedlessly runs out,
Like witless Fools, or like to Girls and Boyes,
Goe out to shew new Clothes, or such like toyes:
This shews my Playes have not such store of wit,
Nor subtil plots, they were so quickly writ,
So quickly writ, that I did almost cry
For want of work, my time for to imploy:
Sometime for want of work, I'm forc'd to play,
And idlely to cast my time away:
Like as poor Labourers, all they desire,
Is, to have so much work, it might them tire:
Such difference betwixt each several brain,
Some labour hard, and offer life to gain;
Some lazie lye, and pampred are with ease,
And some industrious are, the World to please:
Some are so quick, their thoughts do move so fast,
They never stay to mold, or to forecast:

* See also the third epistle, above. Cavendish's attention to Ben Jonson is indicative of his fame and literary power, which continued long after his death.

Some take great pains to get, and yet are poor,
And some will steal, for to increase their store:
Some brains know not what Subjects for to chuse,
And with considering, they their wit do lose:
Some only in designs do spend their time,
And some without designs do only rhime;
And some do take more pains a Plot to lay,
Than other some to plot, and write a Play.
As for *Ben. Johnsons* brain, it was so strong,
He could conceive, or judge, what's right, what's wrong:
His Language plain, significant and free,
And in the English Tongue, the Masterie:
Yet Gentle *Shakespear** had a fluent Wit,
Although less Learning, yet full well he writ;
For all his Playes were writ by Natures light,
Which gives his Readers, and Spectators sight.
But Noble Readers, do not think my Playes,
Are such as have been writ in former daies;
As *Johnson, Shakespear, Beamont, Fletcher*† writ;
Mine want their Learning, Reading, Language, Wit:
The Latin phrases I could never tell,
But *Johnson* could, which made him write so well.
Greek, Latin Poets, I could never read,
Nor their Historians, but our English *Speed;*‡
I could not steal their Wit, nor Plots out take;
All my Playes Plots, my own poor brain did make:
From *Plutarchs*§ story I ne'r took a Plot,
Nor from Romances, nor from *Don Quixot,*‖
As others have, for to assist their wit,

---

* *Shakespear*] *William Shakespeare (1564–1616) was second in reputation to Ben Jonson in Cavendish's time.

† *Beamont, Fletcher*] Francis Beaumont (1585–1616) and John Fletcher (1579–1625) collaborated to write comedies and tragedies in the early seventeenth century.

‡ our English *Speed*] probably John Speed (1552–1629), cartographer and author of *The History of Great Britain* (1611).

§ *Plutarchs*] Plutarch (A.D. 46–c. 119) was a Greek biographer and historian whose works influenced and provided source material for many sixteenth- and seventeenth-century English writers.

‖ *Don Quixot*] *Don Quixote de la Mancha,* a popular Spanish novel by Miguel de Cervantes (1547–1616).

But I upon my own Foundation writ;
Like those that have a little patch of Land,
Even so much whereon a house may stand:
The Owner builds a house, though of no shew
A Cottage warm and clean, though thatch'd and low;
Vitruvius* Art and Skill he doth not take,
For to design, and so his house to make;
Nor Carpenters, nor Masons doth not hire,
But builds a house himself, whole and intire:
Materials none from forein parts are brought;
Nor hath he Stone and Timber with art wrought;
But some sound Tree, which on his ground did grow,
Which he cuts down with many a labouring blow;
And with his hatchet, and his saw, he cuts
His Tree in many parts, those parts he puts
In several places, beams, posts, planchers layes,
And thus a house with his own stock doth raise:
He steals nor borrows not of any Neighbour,
But lives contentedly of his own labour;
And by his labour, he may thrive, and live
To be an old rich man, and then may leave
His Wealth, to build a Monument of Fame,
Which may for ever keep alive his name.
Just so, I hope, the works that I have writ,
Which are the buildings of my natural wit;
My own Inheritance, as Natures child,
But the Worlds Vanities would me beguild:
But I have thriftly been, houswiv'd my time,
And built both Cottages of Prose and Rhime,
All the materials in my head did grow,
All is my own, and nothing do I owe:
But all that I desire when as I dye,
My memory in my own Works may lye:

---

* Vitruvius] an engineer in charge of Augustus Caesar's artillery, author of De architectura, a ten-book treatise on the theory and practice of architecture long read for its direct applicability to the craft. His rhetoric, however, is clumsy and untrained (Moses Hadas, A History of Latin Literature [New York: Columbia Univ. Press, 1952], 235–36).

And when as others build them Marble Tombs,
To inurn their dust, and fretted vaulted Rooms,
I care not where my dust, or bones remain,
So my Works live, the labour of my brain.
I covet not a stately, cut, carv'd Tomb,*
But that my works, in Fames house may have room:
Thus I my poor built Cottage am content,
When that I dye, may be my Monument.

* In fact, Margaret Cavendish's earthly remains rest beneath a "stately, cut, carv'd Tomb" in Westminster Abbey, not in the Poets' Corner, but beside her husband among soldiers and statesmen. Her epitaph, written by the duke, praises her as a wise and witty writer of many books but emphasizes her excellence as a wife.

Appendix B

An Introduction, 1662

Enter 3. Gentlemen.

1. GENTLEMAN. Come *Tom* will you goe to a play?

2. GENTLEMAN. No.

1. GENTLEMAN. Why?

2. GENTLEMAN. Because there is so many words, and so little wit, as the words tire me more than the wit delights me; and most commonly there is but one good part or humour, and all the rest are forced in for to enter-line that part, or humour; Likewise not above one or two good Actors, the rest are as ill Actors as the parts they Act, besides their best and principle part or humour is so tedious, that I hate at last what I liked at first, for many times a part is very good to the third Act, but continued to the fifth is stark naught.

1. GENTLEMAN. The truth is, that in some Playes the Poets runs so long in one humour, as he runs himself out of breath.

3. GENTLEMAN. Not only the Poet but the humour he writes of seems to be as broken-winded.

1. GENTLEMAN. I have heard of a broken-winded Horse, but never heard of a broken-winded Poet, nor of a broken-winded Play before.

3. GENTLEMAN. I wonder why Poets will bind themselves, so as to make every humour they write or present, to run quite through their Play.

2. GENTLEMAN. Bind say you? they rather give themselves line and liberty, nay they are so far from binding, as for the most part they stretch the Line of a humour into pieces.

3. GENTLEMAN. Let me tell you, that if any man should write a Play wherein he should present an humour in one Act, and should not continue it to the end: although it must be stretched, as you say, to make it hold out, he would be condemned, and not only accounted an ill Poet, but no Poet, for it would be accounted as ill as wanting a Rhime in a Copie of Verses, or a word too short,

or too much in number, for which a Poet is condemned, and for a word that is not spell'd right, he is damned forever.

1. GENTLEMAN. Nay, he is only damned if he doth not write strictly to the Orthographie.

3. GENTLEMAN. Scholars only damne Writers and Poets for Orthographie, but for the others, they are damned by the generality: that is, not only all readers, but all that are but hearers of the works.

1. GENTLEMAN. The generality for the most part is not foolishly strict, or rigid as particulars are.

3. GENTLEMAN. Yes faith, they are led by one Bell-weather like a company of silly Sheep.

1. GENTLEMAN. Well, if I were to write a Play, I would write the length of a humour according to the strength of the humour and breadth of my wit. Let them judge me and condemn as they would; for though some of the past, and present ages be erroniously or malitiously foolish in such cases; yet the future Ages may be more wise, and better natur'd as to applaud what the others have condemned. But prithy *Tom* let us goe.

2. GENTLEMAN. No, I will not goe for the reasons before mentioned, which is, they tire me with their empty words, dull speeches, long parts, tedious Acts, ill Actors; and the truth is, theres not enough variety in an old play to please me.

1. GENTLEMAN. There is variety of that which is bad, as you have divided it, but it seems you love youth and variety in playes, as you doe in Mistresses.

3. GENTLEMAN. Playes delights Amorous men as much as a Mistris doth.

1. GENTLEMAN. Nay, faith more, for a man and his Mistris is soon out of breath in their discourse, and then they know not what to say, and when they are at a *Non-pluss,* they would be glad to be quit of each other, yet are ashamed to part so soon, and are weary to stay with each other long, when a Play entertains them with Love, and requires not their answers, nor forceth their braines, nor pumps their wits, for a Play doth rather fill them than empty them.

2. GENTLEMAN. Faith most Playes doth rather fill the spectators with wind, than with substance, with noise, than with newes;

1. GENTLEMAN. This Play that I would have you go to, is a new Play.

2. GENTLEMAN. But is there newes in the Play, that is (is there new wit, fancyes, or new Scenes) and not taken out of old storyes, or old Playes newly translated.

1. GENTLEMAN. I know not that, but this Play was writ by a Lady, who on my

Conscience hath neither Language, nor Learning, but what is native and naturall.

2. GENTLEMAN. A woman write a Play! Out upon it, out upon it, for it cannot be good, besides you say she is a Lady, which is the likelyer to make the Play worse, a woman and a Lady to writ a Play; fye, fye.

3. GENTLEMAN. Why may not a Lady write a good Play?

2. GENTLEMAN. No, for a womans wit is too weak and too conceited to write a Play.

1. GENTLEMAN. But if a woman hath wit, or can write a good Play, what will you say then.

2. GENTLEMAN. Why, I will say no body will believe it, for if it be good, they will think she did not write it, or at least say she did not, besides the very being a woman condemnes it, were it never so excellent and rare, for men will not allow women to have wit, or we men to have reason, for if we allow them wit, we shall lose our prehemency.

1. GENTLEMAN. If you will not goe *Tom*, farewell; for I will go see this Play, let it be good, or bad.

2. GENTLEMAN. Nay stay, I will go with thee, for I am contented to cast away so much time for the sake of the sex. Although I have no faith of the Authresses wit.

3. GENTLEMAN. Many a reprobate hath been converted and brought to repentance by hearing a good Sermon, and who knowes but that you may be converted from your erroneous opinion; by seeing this Play, and brought to confesse that a Lady may have wit.

Appendix C

Epistle Appended to *Playes*, 1662

To the Readers

NOBLE READERS,

I Said in the beginning of this Book of Playes, in one of my Epistles, that I should not trouble you with any more of my works, unless one, which was a History of the Life of my Noble Lord; but since this Book of Playes was not only writ, but pack'd up, ready to send into *England* to be printed, I by chance have entred into another Work, like those that travel and know not where to go, wander about, and at last light upon a path-way that leads them to some Village; so I wanting some Informations from those that could truly, and would faithfully inform me of such actions and passages as were to be inscribed in my History, so as I could not go so readily on with that work, I was forced to sit idle, as having no work to do, which troubled me much, not knowing what to write of: for though I am lazie, and unactive to any other Imployments, and had rather sit still, and do nothing, than have my thoughts obstructed, or disturbed from their usual Contemplations, with noise, or company, or any other Action or Imployment, but writing; for writings is as pencilling thoughts, and I take as much delight as Painters, which draw men, and other creatures; So I, to draw my fancies opinions and conceptions upon white Paper, with Pen and Ink, words being the figures of thoughts, and letters of words, but writing is but the figuring of the figure, and Writers are but Copyers: But after some idle time, at last I fell upon a vein of writing Letters, and so fast did the vein run at first, as in one Fortnight I wrote above threescore Letters, but I find it begins to flag, like one that hath been let much bloud formerly, it may gush, or stream full out at the opening of a vein, but cannot bleed long, they will faint for want of bloud, or spirit, having let out much bloud formerly; so is it my writing; for though I desire to make them up a hundred, yet I believe I shall not go much further,[*]

[*] This becomes *CCXI Sociable Letters* (1664).

finding my spirits of Fancy grow weak, and dull, and the vein of Wit empty, having lately writ 21 Playes, with 12 Epistles; and one Introduction, besides Prologues, and Epilogues. My Readers may say this is an Inventory, or a bill of Fare; no, it is to let them understand my Wit is drawn dry: for though Histories of Truth need not the flourish of Wit, and no fancy ought to be inscrib'd therein; yet all such Writers, which are rather to get Fame by Feigning, than to divulge Truth by Explaining, should be attended with Wit, and drest with Fancy. But these Letters I mention, I thought to joyn them to this Book of Playes, believing there would not be so many of them, as to be in Folio by themselves, but fearing I should surfeit my Readers with too great a Volume, I have altered that intention, and will rather chuse to present them one Book at a time, like those that entertain with one dish of meat, to whet their Appetites, than to present more to cloy their Gusto. But it may be some will say there is enough of my Playes, to surfeit, as being not delicious, and choyce food for the mind, as pleasant and profitable reading: My advice is, that they may taste, and feed of one Play, and if they find it unpleasant, or hard of digestion, let them feed of no more, but let them feed of other Poetical Dishes, drest by other Poetical Cooks, that may better please them; for as French Cooks are accounted the best for corporal meats, so the Greeks and Latins for poetical Meats, but I am neither a Greek nor a Latin Cook; I cannot dress, or cook after the Fashions or Phancies; I never was bound Apprentice to Learning, I am as ignorant of their Arts and Meats, as of their Persons and Nations; I am like a plain, cleanly English Cook-maid, that dresses Meat rather wholsomely than luxuriously, a roast Capon without lard, a shoulder of Mutton with a sawce of Capers and Olives, a piece of boyld Beef and Turnips, and for desert, a plain Apple-tart, or a Pear-pye; 'Tis true, on Feastival daies I have dressed Olioes,* and Bisks, but neither after the French, Italian, nor Spanish way, but a compound of my own dressing, that might please home-bred Persons, although not Great, or Forein Travellers, as great Scholars, or learned Men; neither have I Cookery to please queasie Appetites: I have only this to say for my self, I am more industrious than expensive, more cleanly than curious; and if you do not like, nor approve of my service, I will not expect much praise for my Wages: You may turn me away, which is, to put my Works out of your Studies. I only desire I may not depart with your displeasures, but as an honest, poor Servant, that rather wanted Art and Skill in my Works, than Will, or Indeavour to make, or dresse them to every Palate. *And so Farewell.*

---

*   Olioes] stews.

Author's Epistle Preceding *Plays,*
Never Before Printed, 1668

To the Readers

It is most certain, That those that perform Publick Actions, expose themselves to Publick Censures; and so do Writers, live they never so privately and retir'd, as soon as they commit their Works to the Press. Which should perswade wise Persons to be very cautious what they publish; especially in a malicious, and envious Age. I do not say, that this is so; but if it be, I can truly say, that I am sorry of it, meerly for the Age's sake, and not in relation to my Self, or my Books; which I write and disperse abroad, only for my own pleasure, and not to please others: being very indifferent, whether any body reads them or not; or being read, how they are esteem'd. For none but poor and mean spirits will think themselves concern'd in spightful Censures.

Having observ'd, that the most Worthy and most Meritorious Persons have the most envious Detractors, it would be a presumptuous opinion in me to imagine my self in danger to have any: but however, their malice cannot hinder me from Writing, wherein consists my chiefest delight and greatest pastime; nor from Printing what I write, since I regard not so much the present as future Ages, for which I intend all my Books.

When I call this new one, *Plays,* I do not believe to have given it a very proper Title: for it would be too great a fondness to my Works to think such Plays as these suitable to ancient Rules, in which I pretend no skill; or agreeable to the modern Humor, to which I dare aknowledg my aversion: But having pleased my Fancy in writing many Dialogues upon several Subjects, and having afterwards order'd them into *Acts* and *Scenes,* I will venture, in spight of the Criticks, to call them *Plays;* and if you like them so, well and good; if not, there is no harm done: And so Farewell.

Appendix E
Errata

The printer's errors listed below appear at the end of some but not all of the copies of *Playes*, 1662. In some copies, though not the Newberry's, all or most of these corrections have been made in the text in a seventeenth-century hand. I include in a modernized transcription only the corrections that apply to the 1662 works in this edition, *Loves Adventures* and *Bell in Campo*, with page references to this text in brackets below. In the edited text I have left the original errors and added these changes in curly brackets following them.

Loves Adventures

Page 5, scene 1 [24], last line, for "sent" read "send."

Scene 2, line 1 [24], to "servant" prefix "your."

Page 8, line 26 [28], for "solus" read "sola."

Page 9, line 1 [28], for "as" read "at"; line 19 [29], for "offers to go forth" read "offers not to go forth."

Page 12, line 17 [32], for "virtue" read "virtuous."

Page 19, line 6 [40], for "corn" read "scorn." [In fact, "scorn" is printed correctly in the copytext.]

Page 22, line 26 [44], add "divorce."

Page 23, line 9 [44], for "not" read "that."

Page 30, line 4 [53], for "desire" read "disswade."

Page 31, scene 22, line 1 [55], add at the end of the line "ever I."

Page 32, scene 25 [56], at the end add "maturity of time; yet what it doth afford, although but bracks or mosse; if you command, I shall present them to you."

Page 38, scene 32, line 10 [62], for "her" read "he."

The Second Part of *Loves Adventures*

Page 51, scene 13, line 16 [77], to "shot" add "fire."
Page 58, scene 18, line 5 [85], blot out "noth."
Page 60, scene 20, line 13 [87], for "kinds" read "kindness."
Page 62, line 22 [89], for "shame" read "shun."
Page 73, line 4 [101], for "verify" read "rarify."

The First Part of *Bell in Campo*

Page 587, line 6 [117], for "ingenious" read "Engines."
Page 592, line 8 [123], for "tripping" read "pitching."

The Second Part of *Bell in Campo*

Page 633, scene 21, line 5 [169], blot out "Nell Careless."

Appendix A

In the Epistle Dedicatory line 1 [253], blot out "that."
In the 2nd Epistle to the reader line 3 [254], for "permit" read "admit."

Selected Bibliography

Works by Margaret Cavendish

The Description of a New World, called the Blazing World. London, 1668. In *The Blazing World and Other Writings,* ed. Kate Lilley. London: Penguin, 1994. Ann Arbor: University Microfilms International. Catalog no. 1509:10.

De Vita et Rebus Gestis Nobilisseme Illustrissimique Principis, Guilielmi Ducis Novocastrensis, commentarii. Trans. Walter Charleton. London, 1668. Ann Arbor: University Microfilms International. Catalog no. 430:10.

Grounds of Natural Philosophy. London, 1668. Ann Arbor: University Microfilms International. Catalog no. 468:11.

The Life of the Thrice Noble, High, and Puissant Prince William Cavendishe, Duke, Marquess, and Earl of Newcastle. . . . 1667. Reprint, London, 1675. Ann Arbor: University Microfilms International. Catalog nos. 1467:5 and 611:9.

The Life of William Cavendish, Duke of Newcastle, to which is added the true relation of my birth, breeding and life, by Margaret, Duchess of Newcastle. Ed. C. H. Firth. 1886. Reprint, London: G. Routledge, 1906.

The Lives of William Cavendish, Duke of Newcastle, and of his wife, Margaret Duchess of Newcastle. Ed. M. A. Lower. London, 1872.

Margaret Cavendish: Sociable Letters. Ed. James Fitzmaurice. New York: Garland, 1997.

Natures Pictures Drawn by Fancy from the Life. Includes *A True Relation of My Birth, Breeding, and Life.* 1656. Reprint, London, 1671. Ann Arbor: University Microfilms International. Catalog nos. 1575:38 and 611:10.

Observations Upon Experimental Philosophy, To which is added, the Description of a New Blazing World. London, 1666. 2d ed. London, 1668. The second edition (1668) omits *Blazing World.* Ann Arbor: University Microfilms International. Catalog nos. 1532:17 and 1020:9.

Orations of Divers Sorts. London, 1662. Ann Arbor: University Microfilms International. Catalog no. 1364:12.

Philosophical and Physical Opinions. 1655. Reprint, London, 1663. Ann Arbor: University Microfilms International. Catalog nos. 1489:37 and 611:11.

Philosophical Fancies. London, 1653.

Philosophical Letters. London, 1664. Ann Arbor: University Microfilms International. Catalog no. 542:10.

Playes. London, 1662. Ann Arbor: University Microfilms International. 502:11.

Plays, Never Before Printed. London, 1668. Ann Arbor: University Microfilms International. Catalog no. 674:2.

Poems and Fancies. 1653. Facs. reprint, New York: Scolar Press, 1972. Ann Arbor: University Microfilms International. Catalog no. 503:1.

These Selected Poems of Margaret Cavendish, Duchess of Newcastle. Ed. Sir Egerton Brydges. Kent: Lee Priory Press, 1813.

A True Relation of the Birth, Breeding, and Life of Margaret Cavendish, Duchess of Newcastle by Herself. Ed. Egerton Brydges. Kent, 1814.

CCXI Sociable Letters. 1664. Facs. reprint, New York: Scolar Press, 1969. Ann Arbor: University Microfilms International. Catalog no. 1553:10.

The World's Olio. 1655. Reprints, London, 1664, 1671. Ann Arbor: University Microfilms International. Catalog nos. 503:2 and 612:2.

Further Reading

Bacon, Francis. *The New Atlantis*. 1626–27. Reprint, Kila, Mont.: Kessinger, n.d.

Battigelli, Anna. "Between the Glass and the Hand: The Eye in Margaret Cavendish's *Blazing World*." *1650–1850: Ideas, Aesthetics, and Inquiries in the Early Modern Era* 2 (1996): 25–38.

——. *A Strange Enchantment: Margaret Cavendish and the Exiles of the Mind*. Lexington: Univ. Press of Kentucky, 1998.

Blaydes, Sophia. "Nature Is a Woman: The Duches of Newcastle and Seventeenth Century Philosophy." In *Man, God, and Nature in the Enlightenment*, ed. Donald C. Mell Jr. et al., 51–64. East Lansing, Mich.: Colleagues, 1988.

Bowerbank, Sylvia. "The Spider's Delight: Margaret Cavendish and the 'Female' Imagination." *English Literary Renaissance* 14, no. 3 (1984): 392–408.

Brown, Sylvia. "Margaret Cavendish: Strategies Rhetorical and Philosophical against the Charges of Wantoness: Or, Her Excuses for Writing So Much." *Critical Matrix* 6, no. 1 (1991): 20–45.

Cavendish, William, ed. *Letters and Poems in honour of the Incomparable Princess, Margaret, Dutchess of Newcastle*. London, 1676.

Cavendish, William, and Margaret Lucas. *The Phanseys of William Cavendish . . . Addressed to Margaret Lucas and Her Letters in Reply*. Ed. Douglas Grant. London: Nonesuch, 1956.

Dash, Irene. "Single-Sex Retreats in Two Early Modern Dramas: *Love's Labor's Lost* and *The Convent of Pleasure*." *Shakespeare Quarterly* 47 (1996): 387–95.

Evelyn, Mary. "Letter to Mr. Bohun." In *Diary and Correspondence of John Evelyn*, ed. William Bray, 8. 2d ed. Vol. 4. London, 1857.

Fitzmaurice, James. "Fancy and the Family: Self-Characterizations of Margaret Cavendish." *Huntington Library Quarterly* 53, no. 3 (1990): 198–209.

Fitzmaurice, James, Josephine A. Roberts, Carol L. Barash, Eugene R. Cunnar, and
Nancy A. Gutiérrez, eds. *Major Writers of the Seventeenth Century*. New York: Oxford
Univ. Press, 1997.

Fowler, Ellayne. "Margaret Cavendish and the Ideal Commonwealth." *Utopian Studies* 7,
no. 1 (1996): 38–48.

Gallagher, Catherine. "Embracing the Absolute: The Politics of the Female Subject in
Seventeenth Century England." *Genders* 1 (spring 1988): 24–29.

Grant, Douglas. *Margaret the First*. Toronto: Univ. of Toronto Press, 1957.

Hintz, Carrie. "'But One Opinion': Fear of Dissent in Cavendish's *New Blazing World*."
Utopian Studies 7, no. 1 (1996): 25–37.

Jones, Kathleen. *A Glorious Fame*. London: Bloomsbury, 1988.

Kahn, Victoria. "Margaret Cavendish and the Romance of Contract." *Renaissance Quarterly* 50 (1997): 526–66.

Kegl, Rosemary. "'The World I Have Made': Margaret Cavendish, Feminism, and the
Blazing World." In *Feminist Readings of Early Modern Culture: Emerging Subjects*, ed.
Valerie Traub et al., 119–41. Cambridge: Cambridge Univ. Press, 1996.

Keller, Eve. "Producing Petty Gods: Margaret Cavendish's Critique of Experimental
Science." *English Literary History* 64, no. 2 (1997): 447–71.

Khanna, Lee Cullen. "The Subject of Utopia: Margaret Cavendish and Her Blazing-
World." In *Utopian and Science Fiction by Women: Worlds of Difference*, ed. Jame L.
Donawerth and Carol A. Kolmerton, 15–34. Syracuse: Syracuse Univ. Press, 1994.

Kramer, Annette. "'Thus by the Musick of a Ladyes Tongue': Margaret Cavendish's
Dramatic Innovations in Women's Education." *Women's History Review* 2, no. 1
(1993): 57–80.

Leslie, Marina. "Gender, Genre, and the Utopian Body in Margaret Cavendish's *Blazing
World*." *Utopian Studies* 7, no. 1 (1996): 6–24.

Lewalski, Barbara. *Writing Women in Jacobean England*. Cambridge: Harvard Univ.
Press, 1992.

Masten, Jeffrey. *Textual Intercourse: Collaboration, Authorship, and Sexualities in Renaissance Drama*. Cambridge: Cambridge Univ. Press, 1997.

Mendelson, Sara Heller. *The Mental World of Stuart Women: Three Studies*. Amherst:
Univ. of Massachusetts Press, 1987.

Osborne, Dorothy. *The Letters of Dorothy Osborne to William Temple*. Ed. G. C. Moore
Smith. Oxford: Clarendon, 1928.

Payne, Linda R. "Dramatic Dreamscape: Women's Dreams and Utopian Vision in the
Works of Margaret Cavendish, Duchess of Newcastle." In *Curtain Calls: British and
American Women and the Theater, 1660–1820*, ed. Mary Anne Schofield and Cecelia
Macheski, 18–33. Athens: Ohio Univ. Press, 1991.

Pearson, Jacqueline. *The Prostituted Muse: Images of Women and Women Dramatists,
1642–1737*. New York: St. Martin's, 1988.

Pepys, Samuel. *Diary.* Ed. E. B. Wheatley. London: G. Bell, 1924.

Perry, Henry Ten Eyck. *The First Duchess of Newcastle and Her Husband as Figures in Literary History.* Cambridge: Harvard Univ. Press, 1918.

Phillips, Patricia. *The Scientific Lady: A Social History of Women's Scientific Interests, 1520–1918.* New York: St. Martin's, 1990.

Rose, Mary Beth. "Gender, Genre, and History: Seventeenth Century English Women and the Art of Autobiography." In *Women in the Middle Ages and the Renaissance,* 245–78. Syracuse: Syracuse Univ. Press, 1986.

Sarasohn, Lisa T. "A Science Turned Upside Down: Feminism and the Natural Philosophy of Margaret Cavendish." *Huntington Library Quarterly* 47, no. 4 (1984): 289–307.

Schiebinger, Linda. *The Mind Has No Sex? Women in the Origins of Modern Science.* Cambridge: Harvard Univ. Press, 1989.

Sherman, Sandra. "Trembling Texts: Margaret Cavendish and the Dialectic of Authorship." *English Literary Renaissance* 24, no. 1 (1994): 184–210.

Stevenson, Jay. "The Mechanist-Vitalist Soul of Margaret Cavendish." *Studies in English Literature, 1500–1900* 36, no. 3 (1996): 427–43.

Straznicky, Marta. "Reading the Stage: Margaret Cavendish and Commonwealth Closet Drama." *Criticism* 37 (1995): 355–90.

Suzuki, Mihoko. "Margaret Cavendish and the Female Satirist." *Studies in English Literature, 1500–1900* 37, no. 3 (1997): 483–500.

Tomlinson, Sophie. "My Brain the Stage: Margaret Cavendish and the Fantasy of Female Performance." In *Women, Texts, and Histories: 1575–1760,* ed. Claire Brant and Diane Purkiss, 134–63. New York: Routledge, 1992.

Trubowitz, Rachel. "The Reenchantment of Utopia and the Female Monarchical Self: Margaret Cavendish's *Blazing World.*" *Tulsa Studies in Women's Literature* 11, no. 2 (1992): 229–46.

Wilputte, Earla A. "Margaret Cavendish's Imaginary Voyage to the Blazing World: Mapping a Feminist Discourse." In *Transatlantic Crossings: Eighteenth Century Explorations,* ed. Donald W. Nichol, 109–17. St. John's: Memorial Univ. of Newfoundland, 1995.

Wiseman, Susan. "Gender and Status in Dramatic Discourse: Margaret Cavendish, Duchess of Newcastle." In *Women, Writing, History, 1640–1740,* ed. Isobel Grundy and Susan Wiseman, 159–77. Athens: Univ. of Georgia Press, 1992.

Woolf, Virginia. "The Duchess of Newcastle." In *On Women and Writing,* selected and introduced by Michèle Barrett, 79–88. London: Women's Press, 1992.

——. *A Room of One's Own.* 1929. Reprint, New York: Harcourt Brace Jovanovich, 1989.

Library of Congress Cataloging-in-Publication Data

Newcastle, Margaret Cavendish, Duchess of, 1624?–1674.
   The convent of pleasure and other plays / Margaret Cavendish,
Duchess of Newcastle ; edited by Anne Shaver.
        p.   cm.
   Includes bibliographical references (p.   ).
   ISBN 0-8018-6099-7. — ISBN 0-8018-6100-4 (pbk. :   )
   1. Women—Drama.   I. Shaver, Anne, 1940–   . II. Title.
PR3605.N2A6   1999
822′.4—dc21   98-48352
                                                                  CIP